THE DRAWING HABIT

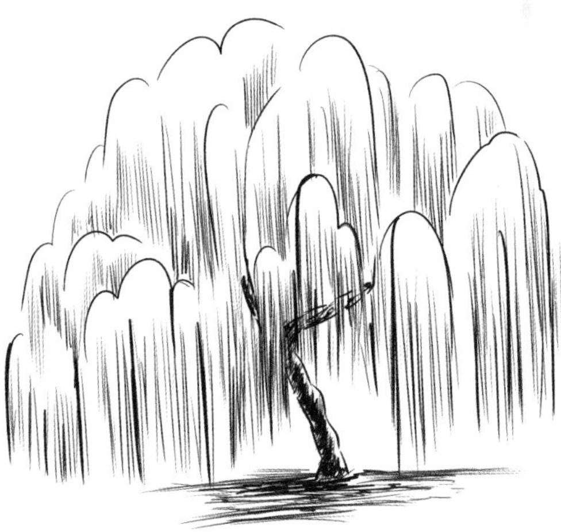

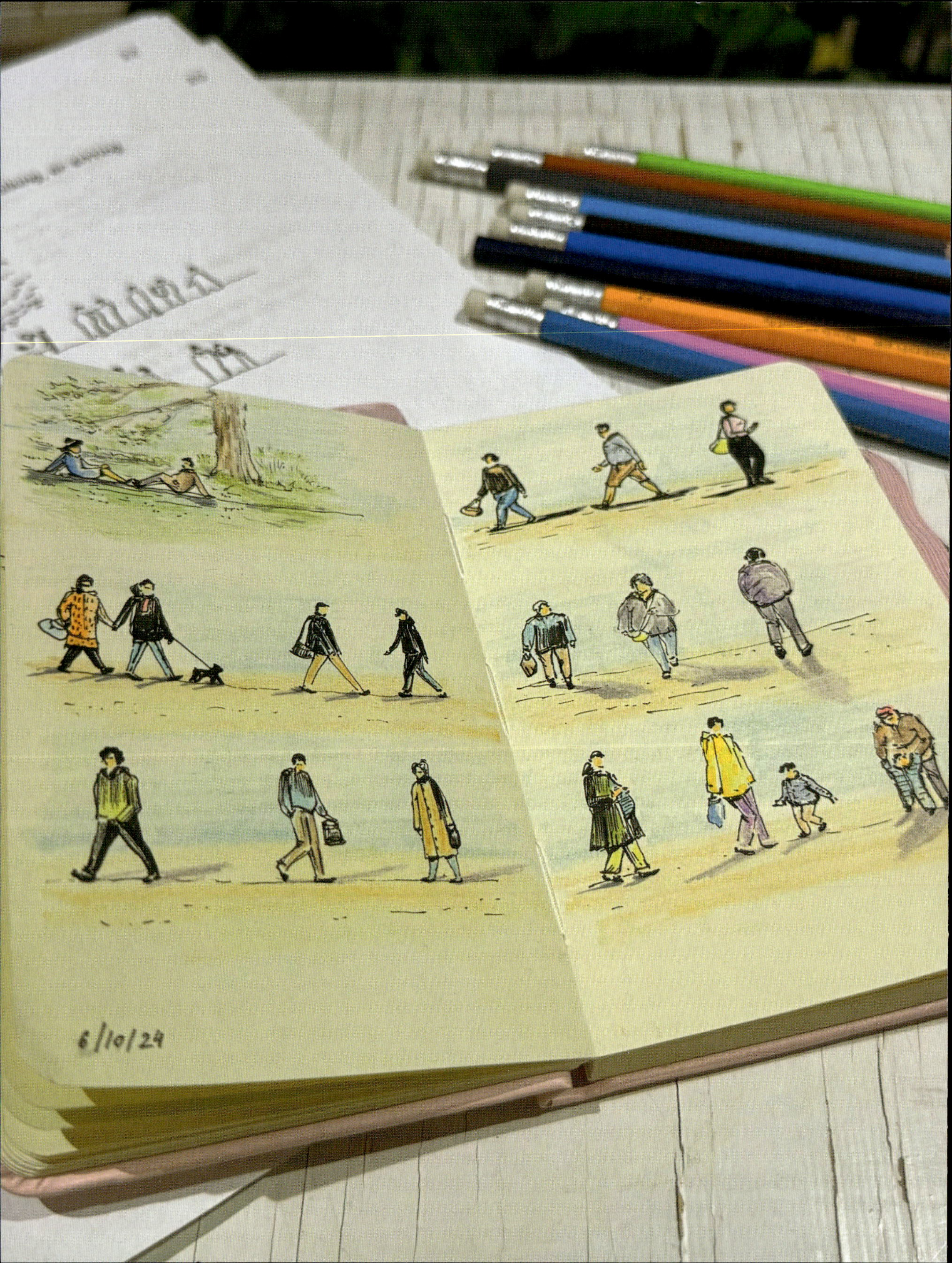
6/10/24

THE DRAWING HABIT

A STEP-BY-STEP GUIDE TO
Improving Your Drawing Skills and Cultivating a Lifelong Practice of Creativity

DARIA BOGDANOVA

QUARRY

To everyone who tried my practice materials and encouraged me to continue. Without them this book wouldn't be possible.

Quarto.com

First Published in 2026 by Quarry Books,
an imprint of The Quarto Group,
100 Cummings Center, Suite 265-D, Beverly, MA 01915, USA.
T (978) 282-9590 F (978) 283-2742

EEA Representation, WTS Tax d.o.o.,
Žanova ulica 3, 4000 Kranj, Slovenia.
www.wts-tax.si

10 9 8 7 6 5 4

ISBN: 978-0-7603-9728-2

Digital edition published in 2026
eISBN: 978-0-7603-9729-9

Library of Congress Cataloging-in-Publication Data

Names: Bogdanova, Daria author
Title: The drawing habit : a step-by-step guide to improving your drawing skills and cultivating a lifelong practice of creativity - includes downloadable practice sheets! / Daria Bogdanova.
Description: Beverly, MA : Quarry Books, 2026. | Includes index.
Identifiers: LCCN 2025023375 (print) | LCCN 2025023376 (ebook) | ISBN 9780760397282 paperback | ISBN 9780760397299 ebook
Subjects: LCSH: Drawing--Technique
Classification: LCC NC730 .B547 2026 (print) | LCC NC730 (ebook) | DDC 741.2--dc23/eng/20250619
LC record available at https://lccn.loc.gov/2025023375
LC ebook record available at https://lccn.loc.gov/2025023376

Design and Page Layout: Kate Frances Design

Printed in Huizhou City, Guangdong, China TT062026

ACKNOWLEDGMENTS

I would like to extend my heartfelt gratitude to my teacher, Sanni Virjula, whose encouragement to explore hand drawing for landscape design sparked a journey that led me to practice and share drawing techniques with others.

A special thank-you to my editor, Michelle Bredeson, whose belief in this project and unwavering support kept me going through moments of doubt. Your help and feedback were invaluable throughout the entire process.

Of course, I am deeply grateful to the whole Quarto team, whose hard work made this book possible! You are amazing. I have so many Quarto books on my shelf, and I'm honored to be part of such a talented group.

I am also truly thankful for all my followers on social media. Your support, kind words of encouragement, and especially your requests for more instructions have fueled my passion to share my practice and process. This book is as much a result of your enthusiasm as it is of my own experience.

And last but certainly not least, I want to thank my family. I love you very much.

—Daria

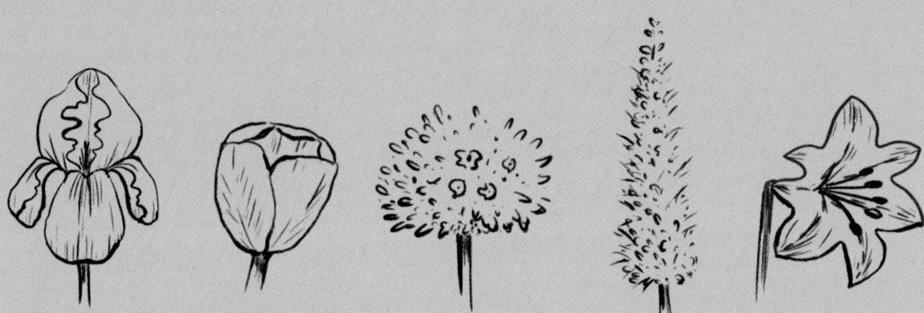

CONTENTS

Introduction: Why You Need a Drawing Habit | 8

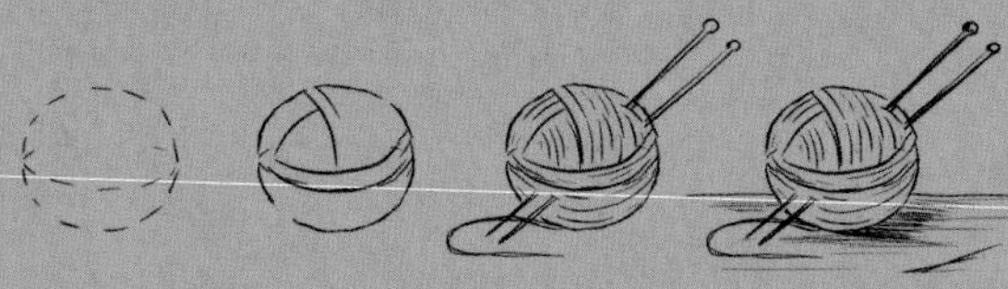

1

HOW TO DEVELOP A DRAWING HABIT | 11

Getting Started | 12
The Power of Daily Practice | 13
Focus on the Process, Not Results | 16
Keep It Simple, Very Simple | 17
All You Need Is a Pen and Paper | 18
Give Yourself Feedback (and a Pat on the Back) | 20
How to Use This Book for Practice | 21

2

START WITH THE BASICS | 25

Begin with Lines | 26
Basic Line Types | 28
Repetition and Even Spacing | 34
Why Is Hand-Eye Coordination Important? | 35
Palmer Handwriting Method | 36
Symmetry | 37
Hatching | 39
3D Basics: Drawing Geometric Shapes | 40
Step by Step: Everyday Objects | 41

3

DRAWING PLANTS AND FLOWERS | 47

Tips for Drawing Plants and Flowers | 48
Step by Step: Houseplants | 50
Step by Step: Spring Flowers | 58
Step by Step: Garden Plants | 61
Flowers and Grasses Composition | 66

4

DRAWING TREES AND SHRUBS | 69

Tree Silhouettes | 70
Sketching Aerial Views of Trees | 72
Creating Texture and Shading in Trees | 74
Drawing a Tree Trunk | 77
Step by Step: Trees | 78
Drawing Different Tree Leaves | 85
Step by Step: Group of Trees | 86

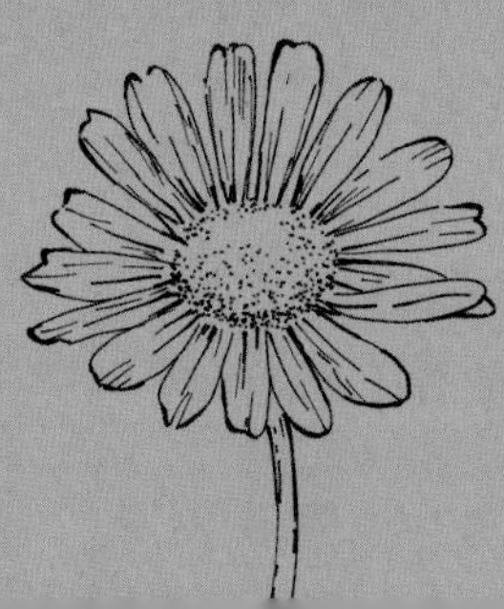

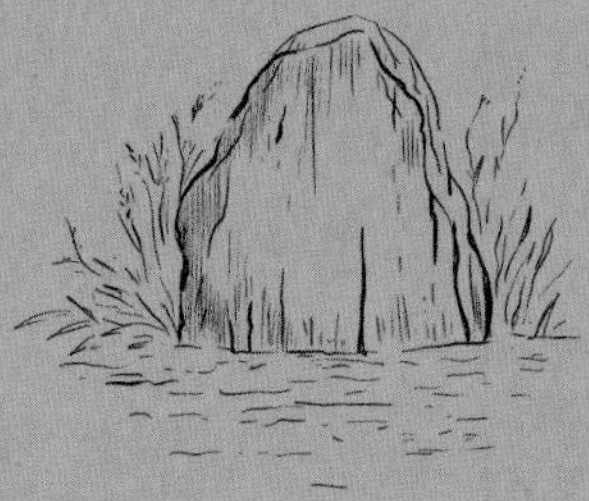

5

DRAWING WATER AND ROCKS | 89

Step by Step: Waterfall | 90

Step by Step: Small Pond | 92

Step by Step: Rocks and Stones | 93

Step by Step: Mountain and Water | 95

Step by Step: Ocean Scene | 96

6

DRAWING LANDSCAPE AND ARCHITECTURE | 99

Step by Step: House and Trees | 100

Step by Step: Stone Farmhouse | 102

Step by Step: Barn in Perspective | 104

Step by Step: Front Door | 106

Architecture and Proportions | 108

Drawing Windows | 109

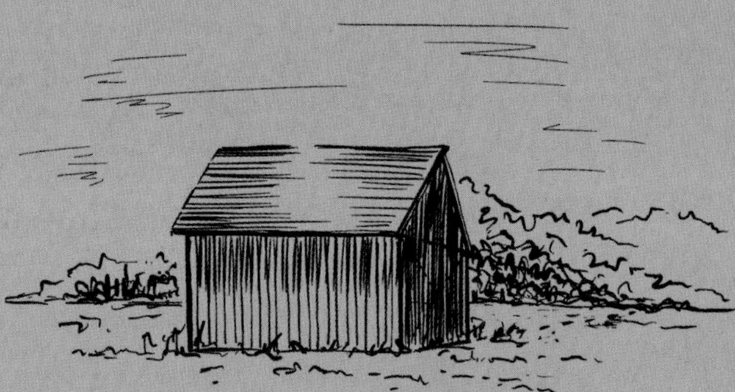

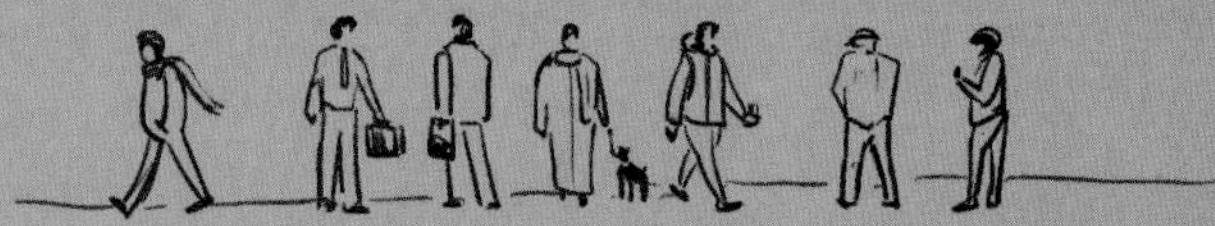

7

DRAWING PEOPLE | 113

Common Human Proportions | 114

Step by Step: Basic Figure | 116

Step by Step: Simplified Figure | 118

Tips for Drawing Tiny People | 120

Adding Color to Your Figures | 122

CONCLUSION | 123

HOW TO USE THE PRACTICE SHEETS | 124

ABOUT THE AUTHOR | 126

INDEX | 127

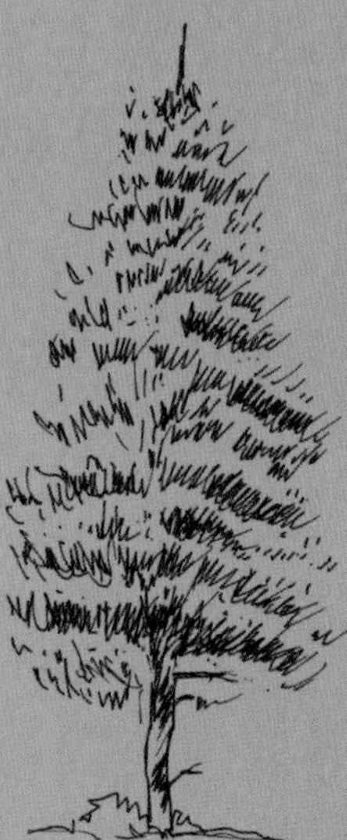

INTRODUCTION: WHY YOU NEED A DRAWING HABIT

Hi! I'm really glad you're here with me in this book. I hope the information I'm going to share with you helps you improve your drawing skills just as much as it has helped me—and continues to help me grow.

Drawing is an exciting and creative process. Whether you're drawing as a hobby, a profession, or both, the most important thing is to keep drawing. Consistency is the key to unlocking your full potential.

When you draw regularly, you begin to discover and sharpen talents you didn't know you had. Drawing involves many interconnected skills. For example, practicing something as simple as a straight line can also help you improve spatial awareness, concentration, hand-eye coordination, and design principles. Once you see the benefits of consistent practice, you won't want to stop. The longer you stick with it, the better you get, and that progress keeps you motivated to continue.

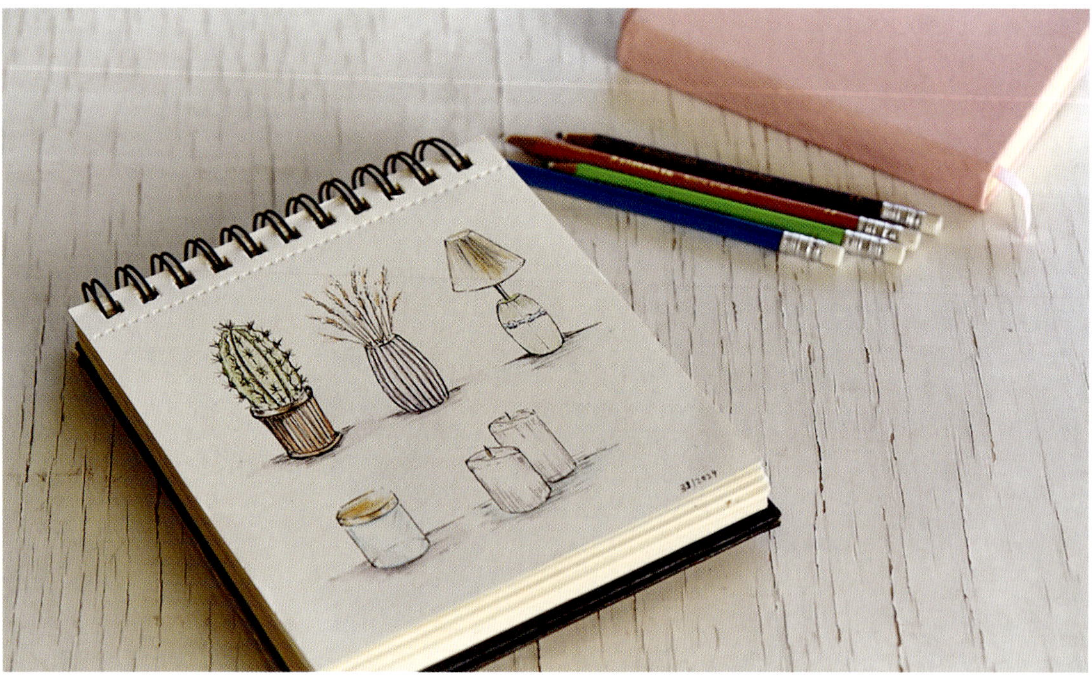

According to Oxford Languages, a habit is "a settled or regular tendency or practice, especially one that is hard to give up." The goal of this book is to help you build a drawing habit—a habit that will keep you drawing and improving so you'll never give up.

I learned just how powerful consistency is a couple of years ago when I decided to try something simple. After many failed attempts to start drawing, I made a commitment: draw every day for twenty-five minutes for a month. I chose to copy landscape design illustrations, since that was the focus of my studies at the time. All I had was a sketchbook, a textbook with illustrations to copy, and a pen. I focused on drawing as quickly and as well as I could, and mistakes didn't matter. I treated the whole process as an experiment, not a challenge. In an experiment, any result is valuable—you just observe what works and what doesn't—whereas a challenge might feel difficult, and that wasn't my intention.

As the days went by, I discovered something powerful: The more I drew, the easier it became to start. I stopped overthinking the process and just did it. I developed a "just-do-it" mindset, and soon enough, I wasn't hesitating to start or finish my drawing. I was hooked. The more I practiced, the more I enjoyed it—and before I knew it, I was eager to draw every day.

Thirty days later, the experiment was complete, and I didn't want to stop! I could see my drawing skills had improved. I didn't become an artist in just thirty days, but I definitely got **better**. That experience was so encouraging that I decided to keep practicing and learn more about drawing. I also started an Instagram account and began sharing my progress and my process. In just a few months, I saw noticeable improvement in my skills and had successfully built a new habit. If this strategy worked for me, I truly believe it can work for you too.

The goal of this book is to help you build the right mindset and give you practical exercises to start and keep a drawing habit. It's a journey full of discoveries, so take your time and enjoy each step!

Daria

DRAWING IS A JOURNEY FULL OF DISCOVERIES, SO TAKE YOUR TIME AND ENJOY EACH STEP!

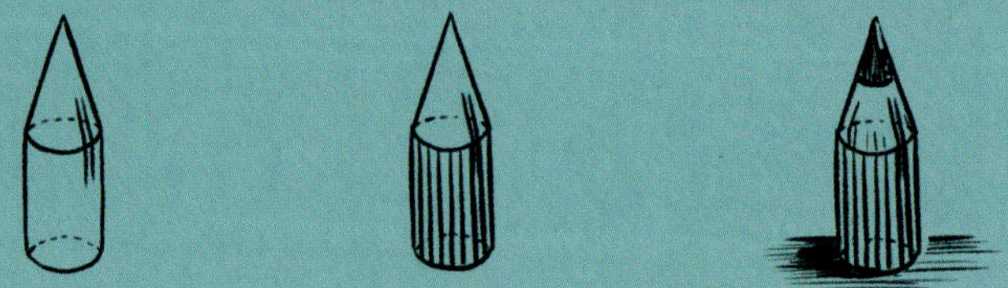

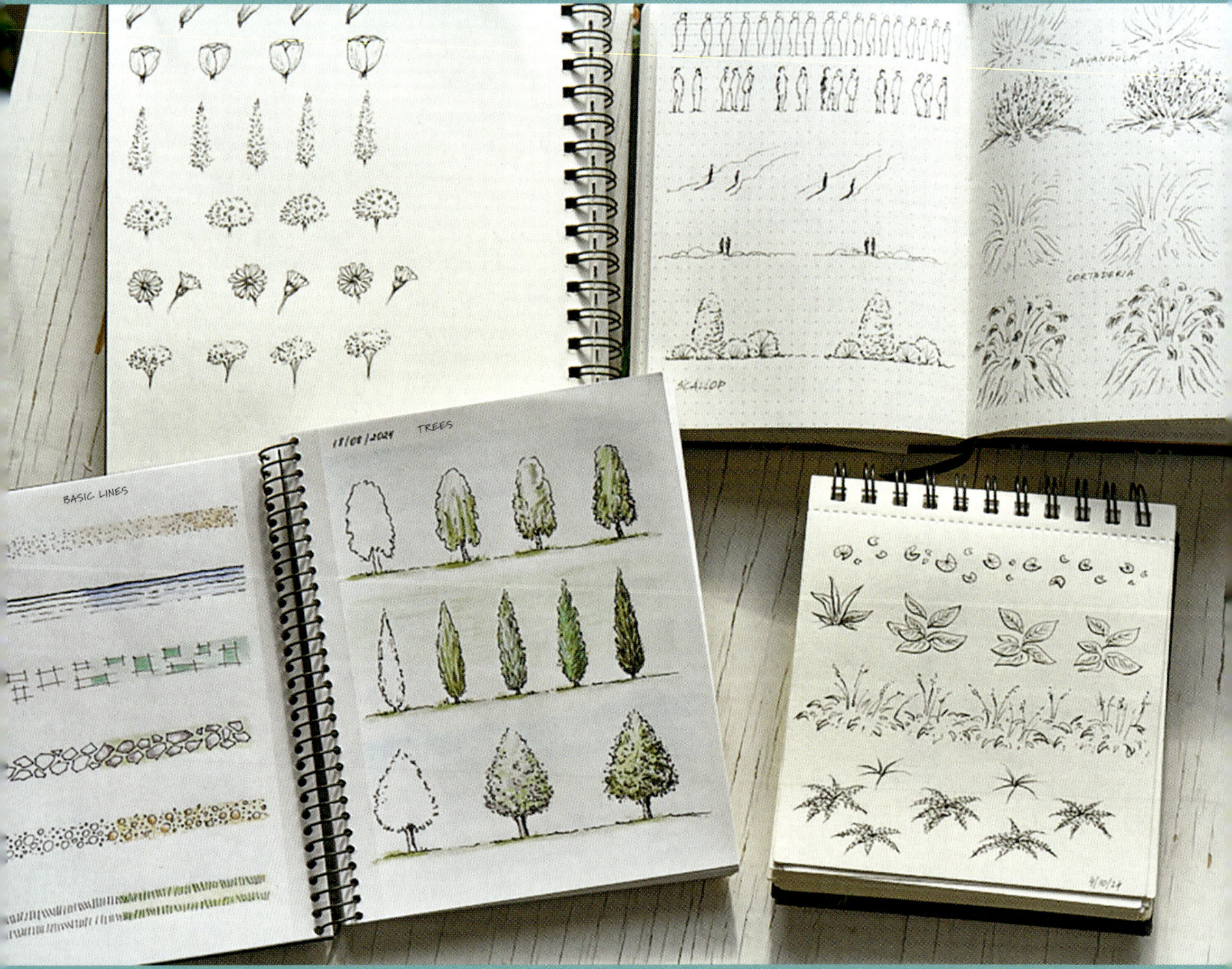
LAVANDULA
CORTADERIA
SCALLOP
BASIC LINES
18/08/2024
TREES

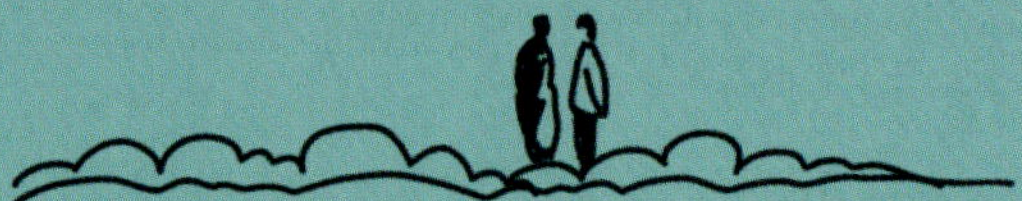

1

HOW TO DEVELOP A DRAWING HABIT

In this chapter, we'll talk about how to make drawing a regular part of your life. You'll learn why it's so important to focus on the process, not the results, and how setting simple, realistic goals can make all the difference. I'll walk you through the tools and materials you'll need and share tips for creating the right mindset to enjoy your drawing journey. By the end, you'll know exactly how to use this book to help you build and stick with your drawing habit.

GETTING STARTED

To improve at drawing, we need to develop muscle memory and hand-eye coordination—and both require consistent practice.

Why do athletes and dancers repeat the same movements over and over? Because once their movements become automatic, they can focus on more complex aspects of their performance and make quick decisions without thinking. The fluidity we admire comes from years of practice and repetition, making the difficult seem effortless.

This principle applies to drawing as well. When you no longer have to think about the basics, your mind is free to focus on more advanced tasks. Practice isn't just about repetition; it's about learning, refining, and improving step by step. Over time, as you practice, you start to see patterns and similarities between objects, textures, and shapes. For example, once you learn to draw a tree, you'll notice other plants have similar structures, making them easier to draw.

Think of handwriting—it's essentially a form of drawing. The first written symbols were pictures used to convey meaning. Whether your handwriting is neat or messy, you learned it through repetition. Eventually, writing becomes automatic. Drawing works the same way. Once you learn basic lines—like the alphabet—you can apply them to draw many different things. And just as with handwriting, everyone develops their own unique style, even when practicing the same exercises.

When I was learning, I had many questions: What should I practice? How often should I draw? What tools do I really need as a beginner? How can I keep it fun and avoid getting discouraged? And most importantly, how do I keep going?

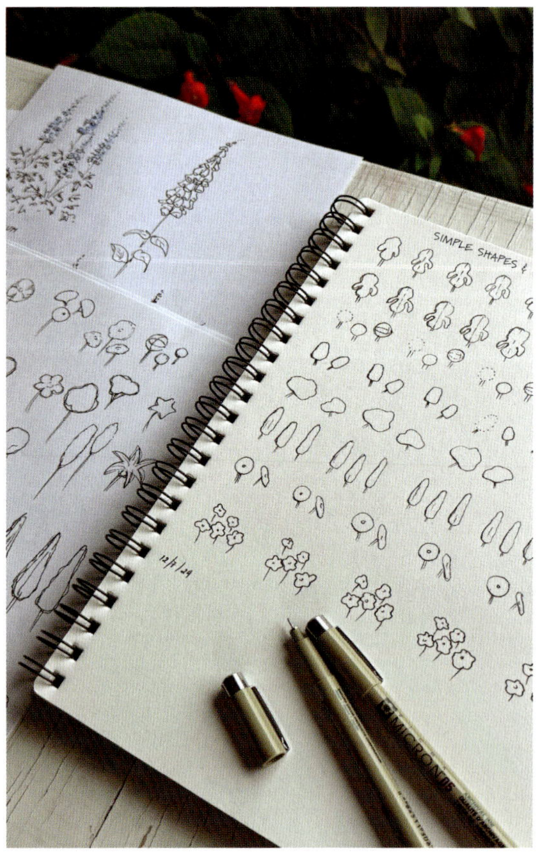

THE POWER OF DAILY PRACTICE

Starting a drawing habit is about discovering what works best for you. Everyone has different needs and interests, so view developing your drawing habit as a personal exploration of what helps you stay motivated and improve your skills.

Here are some principles and suggestions you can choose from and adjust to fit your needs.

KNOW THE RULES, AND THEN FEEL FREE TO CREATE YOUR OWN!

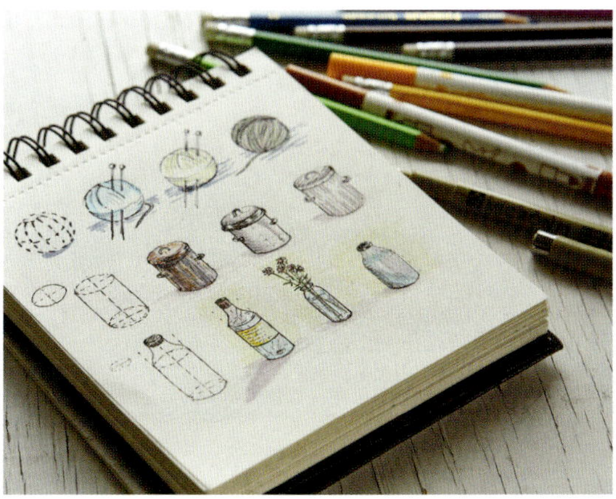

Find Time for Your Practice

To build a habit, it's important to find time for regular practice and aim for consistency. Figure out how much time you can commit each day—whether it's five, fifteen, twenty-five, forty-five, or sixty minutes. Start with a manageable amount of time that comfortably fits into your schedule.

Think about when you can practice: Is it in the morning when everything is calm? In the evening when you have energy? On your commute or during your lunch break? The beauty of drawing practice is that you can do it anywhere.

Once you find the time that works for you, stick with it. Build a habit and keep the promises you make to yourself. Each kept promise will boost your confidence and give you a sense of achievement, which fuels your motivation to keep going. This consistency will help you stay on track and make it easier to avoid skipping practice.

Mindful Practice

To tap into the meditative effect of drawing and experience a sense of peace, try to avoid multitasking and distractions that overload your thoughts. Focus solely on your drawing. For instance, don't actively listen to a podcast or watch a movie at the same time.

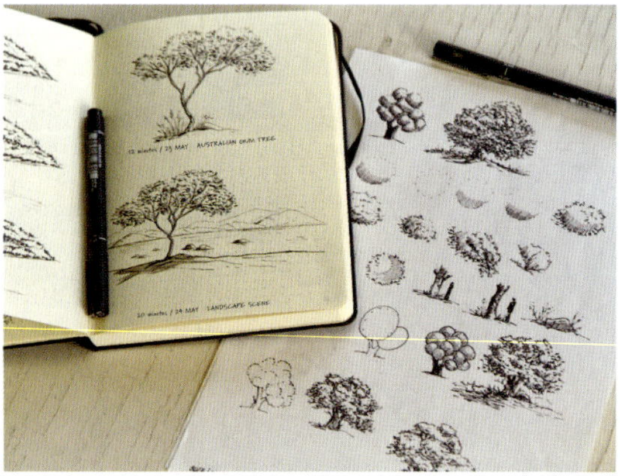

CONSISTENCY BEATS INTENSITY IF INTENSITY IS NOT CONSISTENT.

Relax both your mind and body as you draw, paying close attention to the lines you're creating. If you find certain music helps you focus, that's okay—just notice if it helps you concentrate or distracts you. The key is to see if it supports getting into the flow of drawing. Also, remember that sometimes you can fully concentrate while practicing outdoors, where the environment itself can help you stay present.

Why You Need to Set Goals

Starting a drawing habit is all about finding what works for you and making it a part of your everyday life. A habit is something that feels natural and rewarding, and you might even miss it when you don't do it. Drawing, for me, has become that kind of habit. I try to draw a little bit every day, and it always makes me feel good.

It's important to set clear goals. Having specific goals gives you focus and helps you figure out what you want to achieve with your drawing practice. For example, you could aim to fill a page in your sketchbook, complete one exercise, or dedicate a certain amount of time to drawing each day. These smaller, measurable goals are the keys to staying on track.

Every time you complete a goal, it's like a little victory that boosts your confidence and keeps you motivated. It takes away the stress of wondering where you're going because you have a clear path. This steady progress not only builds your skills but also helps you feel more secure in your practice. By focusing on the journey and celebrating each step, you can develop a drawing habit that transforms your skills and brings joy to your creative life.

Scan this QR code to download the 30-Day Habit Tracker, which will help you be more consistent in your practice and see results faster.

30 DAYS OF SKETCHING

To build a habit, practice sketching for _____ minutes every day for 30 days. Keep track of your progress, note the date, and write down what you've practiced.

Day 1 ☐ Practice:	Day 2 ☐ Practice:	Day 3 ☐ Practice:	Day 4 ☐ Practice:	Day 5 ☐ Practice:
Day 6 ☐ Practice:	Day 7 ☐ Practice:	Day 8 ☐ Practice:	Day 9 ☐ Practice:	Day 10 ☐ Practice:
Day 11 ☐ Practice:	Day 12 ☐ Practice:	Day 13 ☐ Practice:	Day 14 ☐ Practice:	Day 15 ☐ Practice:
Day 16 ☐ Practice:	Day 17 ☐ Practice:	Day 18 ☐ Practice:	Day 19 ☐ Practice:	Day 20 ☐ Practice:
Day 21 ☐ Practice:	Day 22 ☐ Practice:	Day 23 ☐ Practice:	Day 24 ☐ Practice:	Day 25 ☐ Practice:
Day 26 ☐ Practice:	Day 27 ☐ Practice:	Day 28 ☐ Practice:	Day 29 ☐ Practice:	Day 30 ☐ Practice:

FOCUS ON THE PROCESS, NOT RESULTS

Let's talk about results and the process. Which one is more important?

Paul Gardner once said, "Painting is never finished, it only stops at the interesting places." This means that the result in drawing is temporary—everything can be changed, continued, or redrawn.

When you're just starting out, it's natural to focus on the process, especially since you don't expect to be great right away. At this stage, it's crucial to develop consistent practice rituals and create a routine you enjoy. Building a drawing habit is key.

The more you draw, the more ambitious you may become. The learning curve is full of ups and downs. If you rush or get frustrated when things don't turn out as you hoped, you might start to doubt whether you have what it takes to be good at drawing. But remember, there's so much to discover and learn—and it all happens in the process. Trust the process.

To overcome my own fear of failure and self-doubt, I minimize the importance of the result. I remind myself, "I'm just practicing," and there's no need to worry about the final outcome. I continue to repeat the exercise until it feels easy, and then I move on to a new one. That's how my confidence grows.

So, have fun with these exercises and focus on the process. The results will come—and they might surprise you!

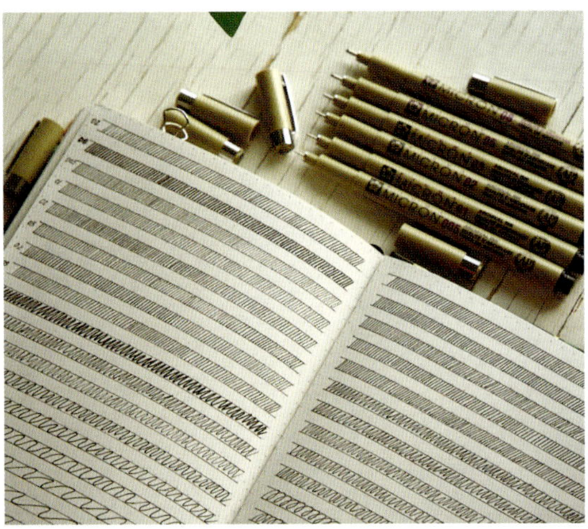

I REMIND MYSELF, "I'M JUST PRACTICING," AND THERE'S NO NEED TO WORRY ABOUT THE FINAL OUTCOME.

KEEP IT SIMPLE, VERY SIMPLE

I once watched an interview with the prolific writer Anne Rice, who showed her writing table right next to her bed. She literally rolls out of bed, sits at her table, and starts writing.

The easier and more accessible it is for you to start your drawing session, the better. This simplicity will help you stay committed to your practice.

Keep everything you need for your practice in one place and keep it close.

Have one sketchbook, one source of exercises—whether it's a practice book or materials you've downloaded and printed—and one pen. With everything ready and within reach, you can jump straight into your drawing session without delay. There's no need to watch a tutorial, search for references, or go through multiple books.

You don't need an extensive collection of art supplies either.

You can explore those things later, once you've developed your drawing habit and feel a greater need for learning and experimenting with new techniques. Right now, your goal is to focus on your drawing session without wasting time on extra preparation or decision-making.

Eliminate the time spent deciding on art tools and references for inspiration. Start drawing right away. Remember, you're not trying to create finished art; you're building basic skills and developing a habit.

There are many things to discover along the way, but tackle them one step at a time. This approach will help you stay focused and avoid feeling overwhelmed. Over time, this mindset can become an integral part of your drawing habit.

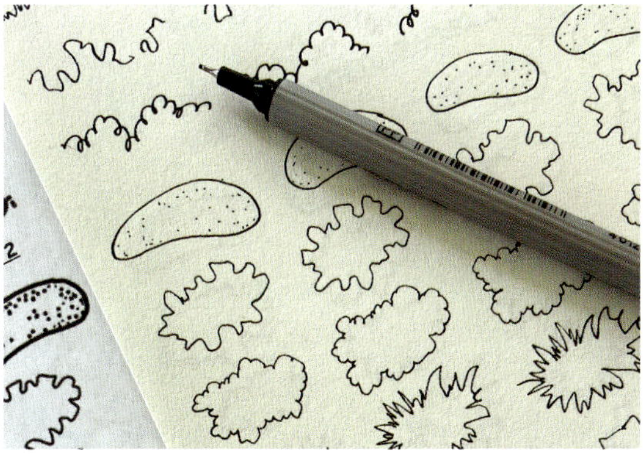

THE EASIER AND MORE ACCESSIBLE IT IS FOR YOU TO START YOUR DRAWING SESSION, THE BETTER.

ALL YOU NEED IS A PEN AND PAPER

When you start a new activity, like drawing, it's very tempting to rush out and buy lots of new materials. While I love art supplies as much as the next person, I really only use a few items in my drawing practice: a sketchbook or two and a few pens. I recommend you start simply too. Not only will you save money, but also you will be able to focus more on the process of drawing and not get distracted by too many options.

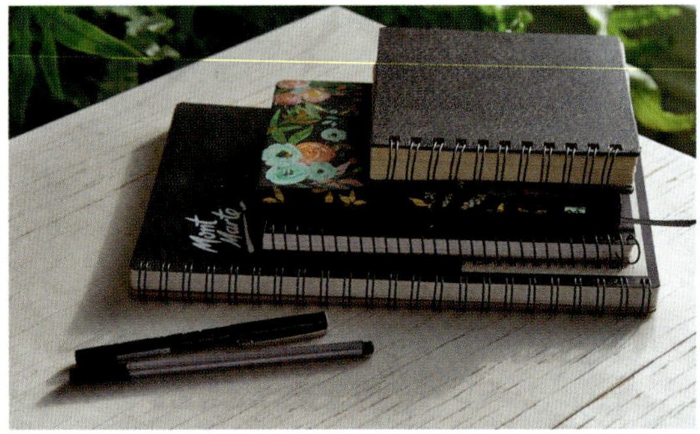

I like to use different size sketchbooks.

Sketchbooks

When I'm doing my drawing exercises, I like to work in a sketchbook, because I can keep all my drawings together and see my progress. For the purposes of this book, you don't need to use expensive, high-quality paper. The goal here is to draw a *lot*, so you don't want to spend a lot of money on paper. I suggest using a sketchbook you won't be afraid to use. If it's too nice, you might worry that you'll mess it up.

I usually have a few different sketchbooks in progress. I have a couple I keep at home as well as a smaller one I carry with me so I can practice when I have a moment. I sometimes dedicate a sketchbook to a particular subject, such as drawing plants or practicing basic marks and shapes.

You can also use inexpensive paper, such as copy paper, if you're hesitant to work in a sketchbook or you find it easier to use loose sheets with the downloadable practice sheets that come with this book (see page 23).

The most important thing is to use paper that will help get you drawing soon and **often!**

Fineliner Pens

When choosing a pen for practice, you can use any pen or pencil you prefer. However, I highly recommend trying a fineliner.

With a fineliner, you concentrate on the lines, learning to control them and develop your hand-eye coordination, which is foundational for drawing anything you want.

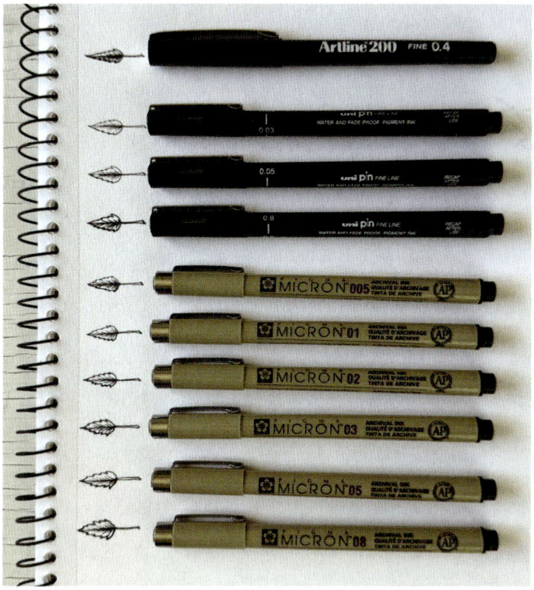

I encourage you to experiment with different brands and thicknesses of fineliners.

Fineliners make precise and consistent lines without smudging. They come in various tip sizes and even colors, allowing for versatility in line thickness and creativity in artwork. You can scan or take a photo of your drawing and further work on it digitally or with tracing paper. This makes fineliners a popular choice for designers and artists.

One of the most important features when learning to draw with fineliners is that they cannot be easily erased. This allows you to **learn from your mistakes and constantly improve.** While it may be intimidating at first, once you understand how it works, it transforms your drawing habit and gives you confidence not to fear mistakes and trust the process.

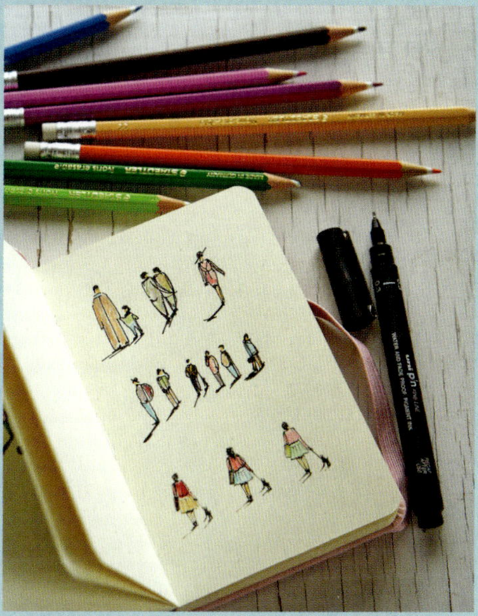

If you want to add color to your drawings, colored pencils are a great choice.

Colored Pencils

Most of my work is in black and white, but occasionally I like to add a little color to my drawings. Colored pencils are a great medium for that. They come in a range of colors and different price points. Again, use what you have or consider purchasing an inexpensive set if you would like to experiment with adding color to your drawings.

GIVE YOURSELF FEEDBACK (AND A PAT ON THE BACK)

When you're learning something new, feedback is essential. Often, after finishing a drawing, I share it with my parents. They're not art critics, but they can honestly tell me what they like or don't like. It's helpful to have someone you trust—whether online or offline—who can offer honest opinions and encouragement. But ultimately, the most important feedback comes from you.

I believe in constructive criticism, so I always try to view my drawings objectively, focusing on what works and what can be improved. As mentioned earlier, the process is more important than the result. Even my worst attempts are valuable—perhaps even the most valuable—because they show me how far I've come. Without those "failures," I wouldn't be able to track my progress or understand what I need to work on.

REMEMBER, YOU'RE DOING GREAT AS LONG AS YOU KEEP GOING!

There's a saying, "Beauty is in the eye of the beholder," meaning our perception of art can change over time as our skills and understanding evolve. However, the appreciation for the effort and process you put into your work remains constant.

So, keep going. Encourage yourself to continue, and give yourself honest feedback to guide your improvement. Be kind to yourself when things don't work out right away—remember, you're doing great as long as you keep going!

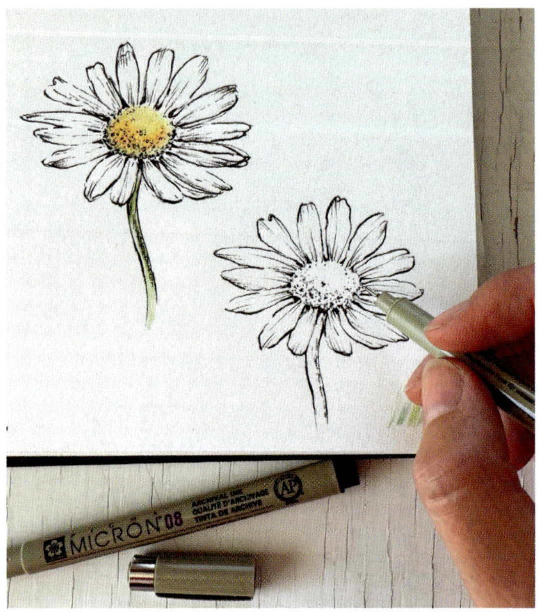

HOW TO USE THIS BOOK FOR PRACTICE

This book contains exercises to make your practice sessions easy, enjoyable, and efficient. Each chapter is designed to cover a specific topic, such as basic lines and shapes, trees, or people, for example.

If you're a beginner, practice each exercise multiple times to build a solid foundation. If you're more experienced, these exercises can serve as warm-ups or a way to refine your skills.

Read my explanations for each exercise. They include observations from my own practice sessions and learning materials I've studied, which you can use as examples of the thinking process you can develop as you practice.

Remember: No skill is mastered overnight, and progress might feel slow at times. Don't get discouraged! Every mark you make, whether it's "perfect" or not, is part of your growth.

During your practice, you'll absorb key art principles, drawing techniques, and art elements—the why, the how, and the what of drawing. You might be wondering, "What are art principles?" These are concepts like contrast, proportions, symmetry, unity, balance, repetition, and variety.

TIP

Write down the date and time spent on each exercise. Trust me, it will be interesting to look back and see how much progress you've made.

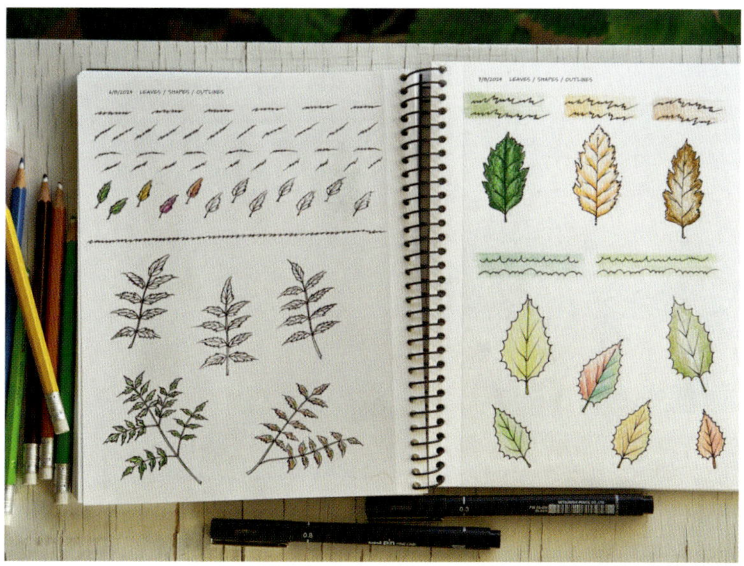

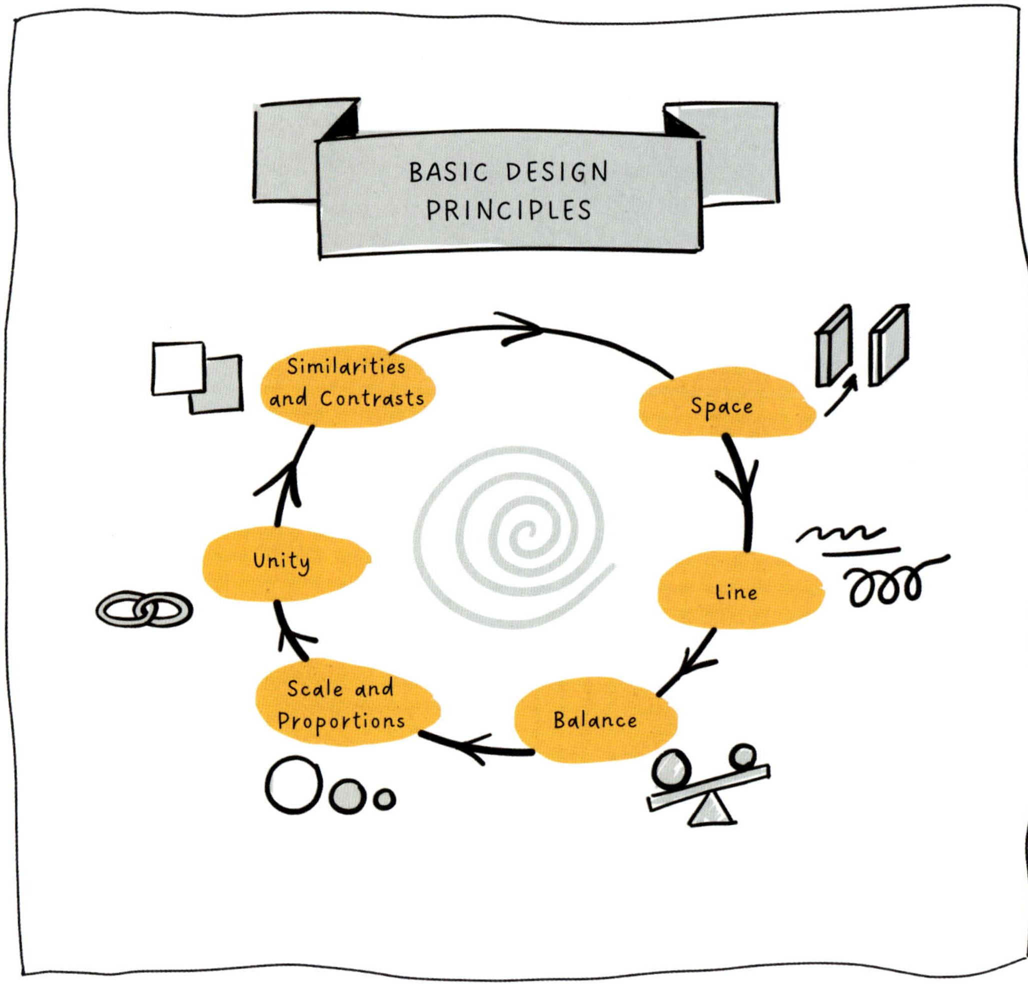

They help determine whether art and design are successful, depending on how well they are applied. You'll start noticing these principles all around you, and the key is learning to recognize them and use them in your own work.

As you digest this new knowledge, you'll gradually begin to apply it unconsciously in your drawings, making your work more effective without even thinking about it.

Don't rush your learning process. Take the time to truly understand each concept and make it your own. The more you embrace each exercise, the stronger your foundation will become.

Some exercises are step by step. If something feels challenging, focus on repeating the first step until it becomes easy, then move on to the second step, and so on. Eventually, you'll be able to complete the entire drawing with ease. "Easiness" is one of the key indicators I use to gauge my progress and whether I'm improving.

One of the main goals of practicing is learning to draw better from memory and imagination by building muscle memory. Go through all the exercises, and then revisit them from time to time. The improvement might not be immediately obvious—it takes time to develop, but it will gradually become second nature. It's always exciting to notice your progress when you find that certain exercises feel much easier than before.

Remember: Don't overwork yourself. As I mentioned earlier, it takes time to learn and digest new knowledge. Some concepts may take days or even weeks to fully grasp, and that's perfectly normal.

And did you know whenever you challenge yourself with something new, it's great for your brain? While it is challenging, new neurons are being formed, which is fantastic exercise for your brain. Once you've mastered a concept, this neuron-building process slows down, and you need to challenge yourself again to keep it active. So, the practice cycle looks like this—learn something new, repeat, master, then move on to something else. The key is to challenge yourself just enough. Trying too hard isn't recommended—it's like trying to run a marathon before you're ready!

Practice Sheets

I've created downloadable practice sheets to help you review and practice many of the exercises in the book. See page 124 for helpful tips on using the practice sheets.

Scan this code to download the practice sheets.

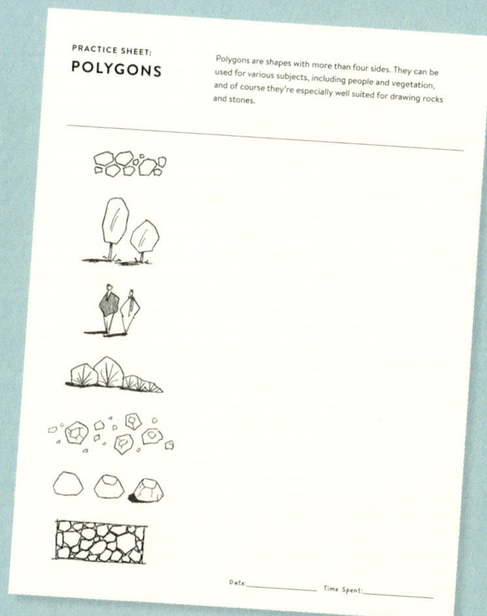
PRACTICE SHEET:
POLYGONS

Polygons are shapes with more than four sides. They can be used for various subjects, including people and vegetation, and of course they're especially well suited for drawing rocks and stones.

Date:________ Time Spent:________

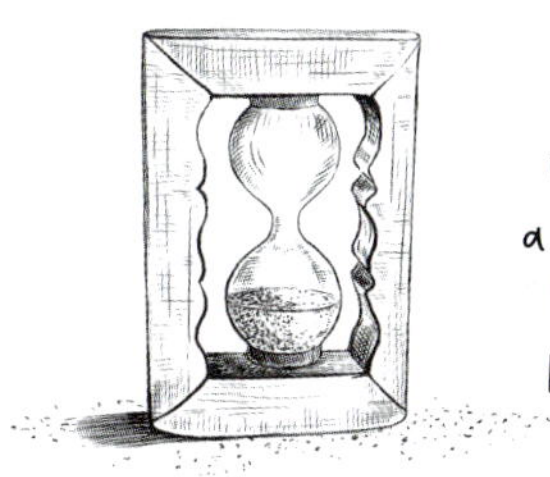

Use a timer—a timer is a powerful tool that can help you focus on the process, and it reminds you when to stop.

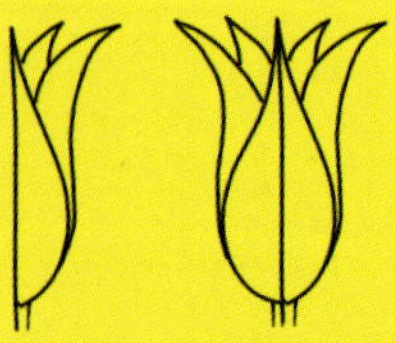
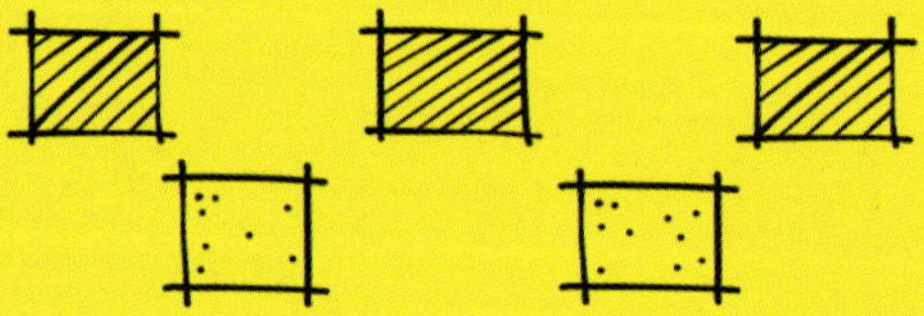
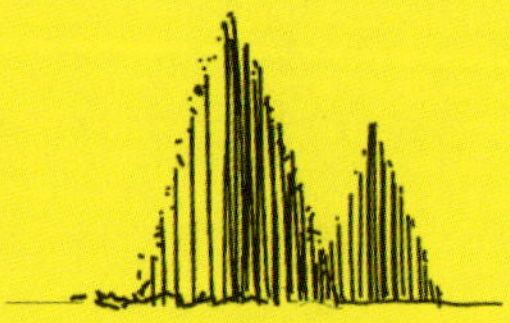
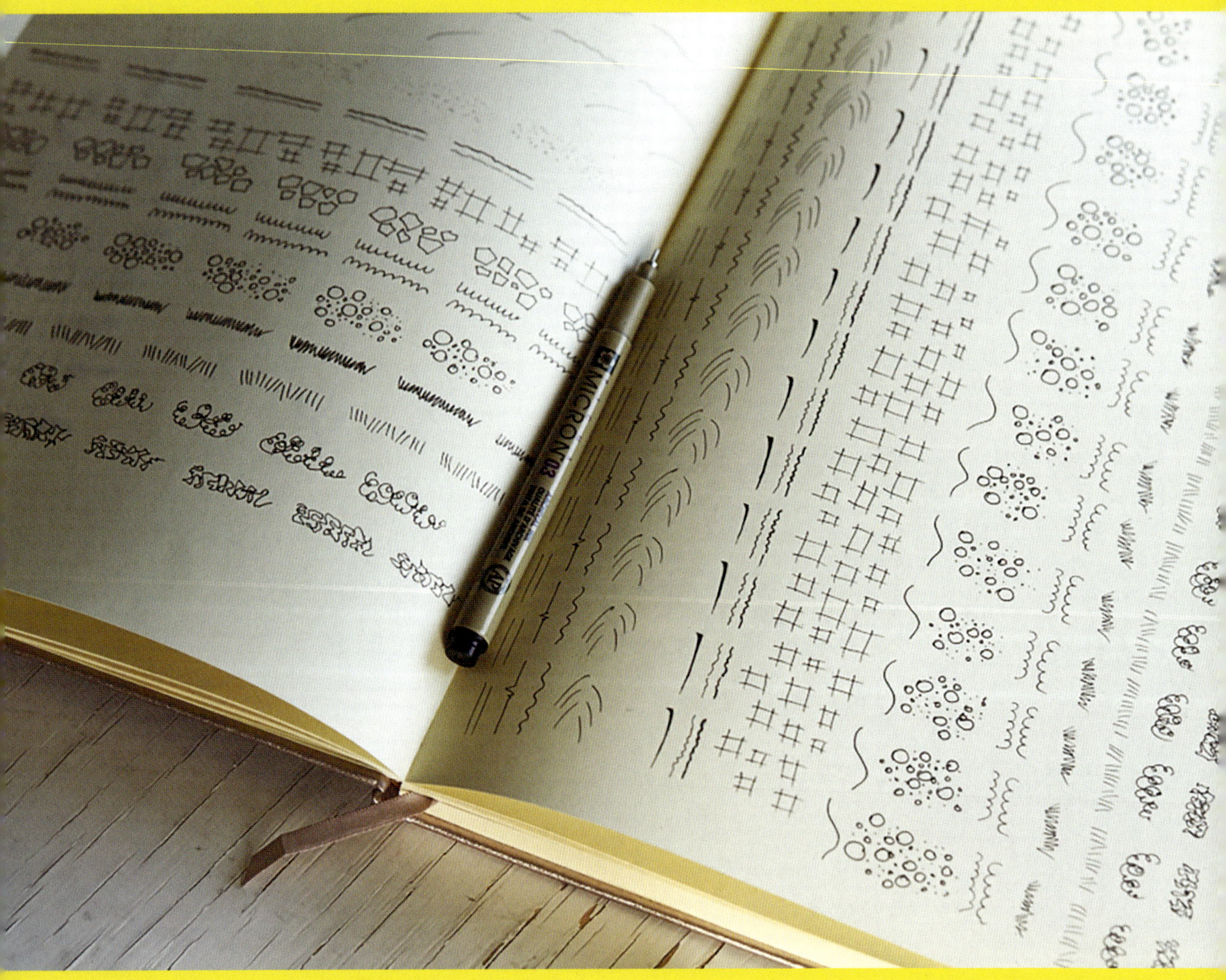
MICRON 03
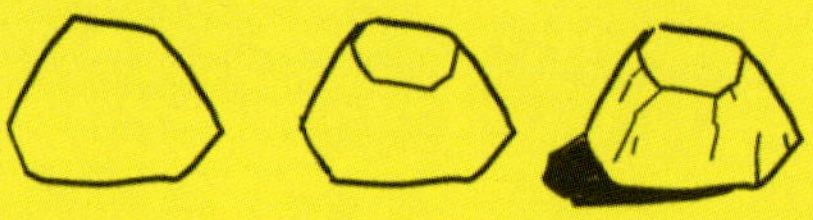
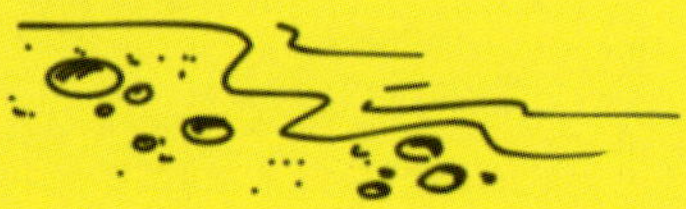

2

START WITH THE BASICS

In this chapter, we explore the essential skills that form the foundation of drawing. Whether you're just starting or looking to refine your technique, mastering the basics is key. You'll learn how line types, shapes, and hand-eye coordination contribute to your drawing abilities. We'll also draw three-dimensional shapes and sketch everyday objects from them—two important practices that will enhance your understanding of space and form, keeping your creativity flowing and your skills sharp.

BEGIN WITH LINES

Lines are the foundation of all drawing and design. They're the first step in creating anything, and understanding how to use them is essential. One of the first things I started practicing regularly was basic lines. They might seem simple, but they're incredibly powerful. The more you practice them, the more you start to see them everywhere—in illustrations, designs, all kinds of artwork, nature . . . It's like a light bulb moment. You begin to recognize how each piece is built, line by line.

As you start to notice how artists use lines in their work, you'll see how versatile lines really are. You can change their direction, thickness, and size to create different effects. Eventually, you'll develop your own unique way of drawing lines, which is the beginning of your personal style.

I recommend practicing these basic exercises by copying them carefully. This is actually quite relaxing. The more you repeat the exercises, the easier it becomes to enter a flow state, where the lines just seem to appear easily from your pen. You might even find yourself getting into a meditative rhythm. It's such an enjoyable practice, and adding some music can help you find your rhythm and make it even more fun.

Tips for Better Linework

Drawing lines is similar to handwriting, so it's helpful to hold your pen the same way you would when writing. This familiar grip makes it easier to get comfortable with drawing. Just be sure to **keep your hand relaxed**, avoiding any tension that might make your hand tired.

To create smoother and more controlled lines, rest your hand on the table to stabilize it. This helps maintain a steady motion and ensures your lines are more fluid.

Another tip is to experiment with a fineliner. Try holding the pen **at different angles** to see how the line thickness changes. You can also apply **varying pressure** to the pen, which will give you even more control over your lines.

EACH DRAWING IS BUILT LINE BY LINE.

Practicing Drawing Straight Lines

Follow these guidelines to improve your line drawing skills:

Relax Your Arm

- Ensure your arm is relaxed and free from tension.
- Avoid gripping the pen too tightly, as this can restrict movement.

Use Minimal Pressure

- Use minimal pressure on the pen to allow for smoother movement.
- Lighten your grip on the pen to prevent strain on your hand and wrist.

Move Your Whole Arm

- Instead of relying solely on your wrist, engage your whole arm in the drawing motion.
- Keep your wrist relatively stationary, and pivot from your shoulder for larger movements.
- This technique helps create straighter lines by reducing the likelihood of unintended arcs or wobbles.

Draw with Consistent Speed

- Maintain a consistent speed while drawing to achieve smoother lines.
- Experiment with different speeds to find what works best for you.
- Practice moving your arm steadily and smoothly to produce straight, uniform lines.

By practicing regularly, you can improve your ability to draw straight lines with greater precision and control.

Drawing Lines with a "Nervous Hand"

This exercise helps if you struggle with drawing longer lines. Start by placing two dots and connecting them. Draw slowly, allowing a slight wiggle so the lines look loose and sketchy. The key is to focus on keeping similar spacing, consistent angles, and equal distances.

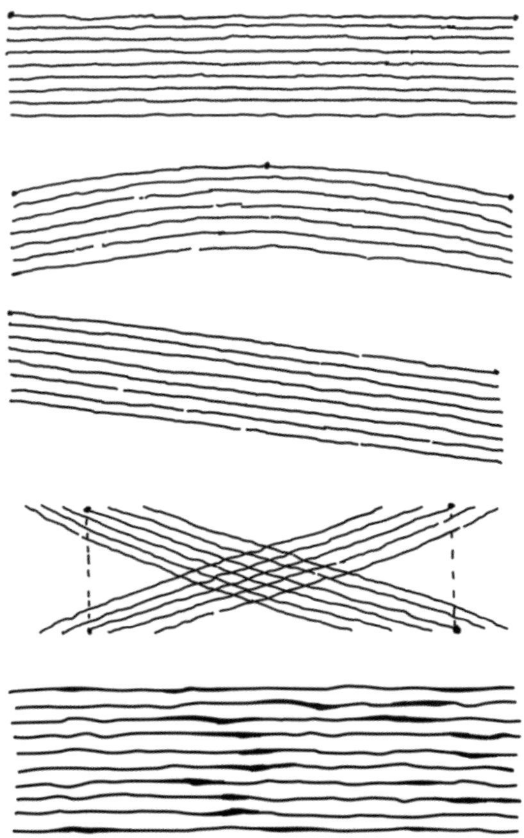

BASIC LINE TYPES

With these basic line types, you can draw different vegetation, materials and textures, human figures, water elements, rocks, and so on. Practice these lines often to gain confidence in sketching. We'll look at a few of the line types in more depth.

Straight line

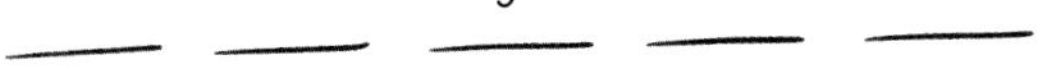

Heartbeat line

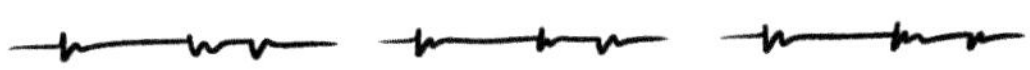

Feathered line

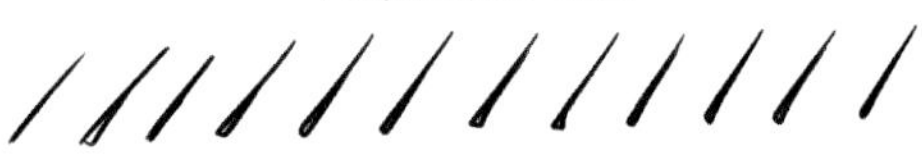

Flow line

Wavy line

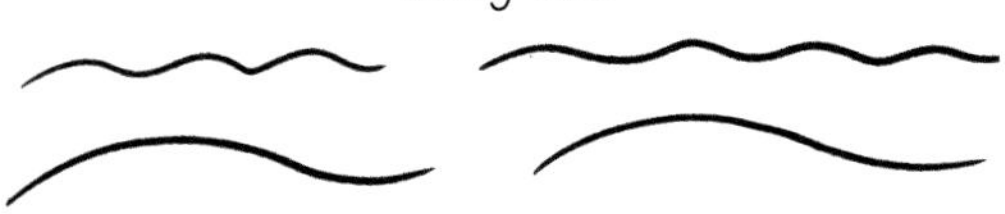

Curved line

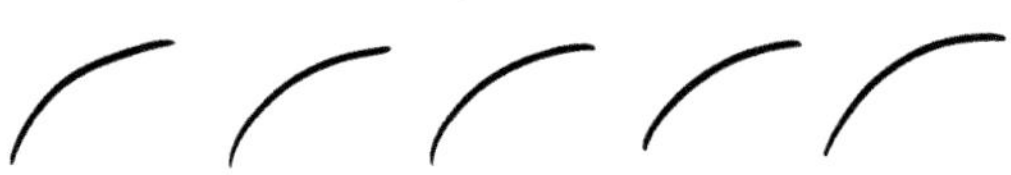

Dotted line

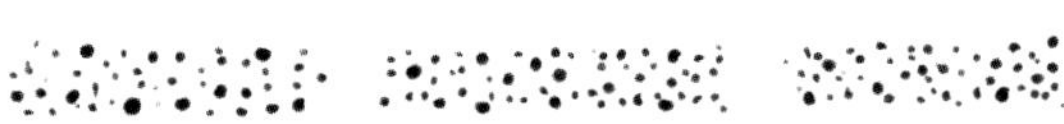

Trail line

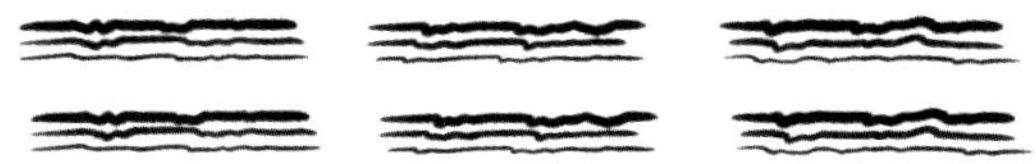

Polygons

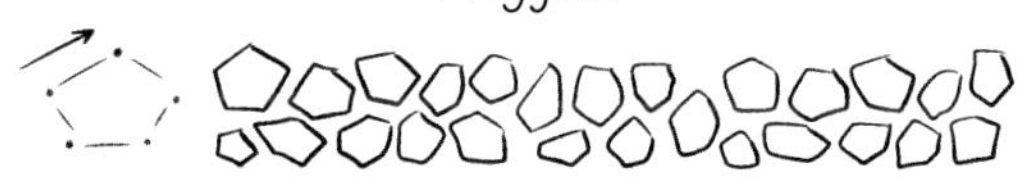

Short rows

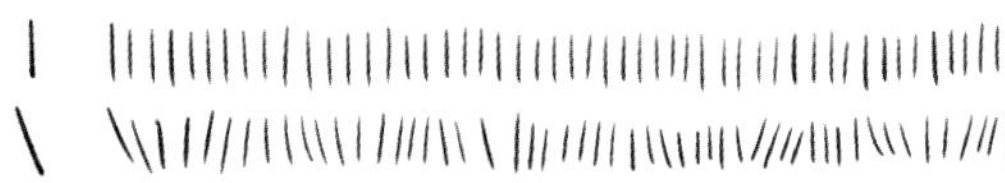

Zigzag line

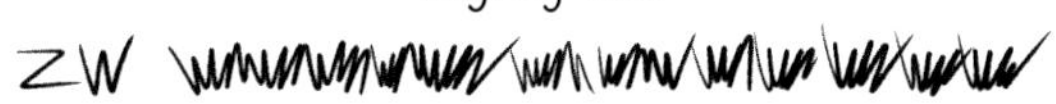

Scalloped line

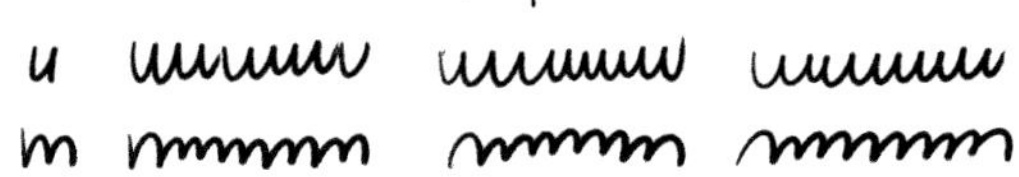

Circular line

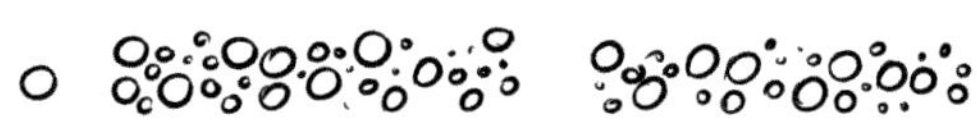

Nervous line

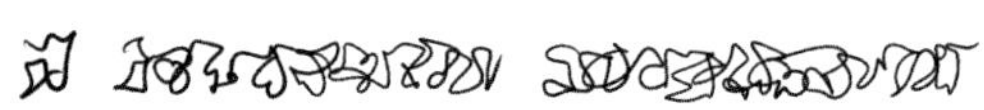

Swirly line

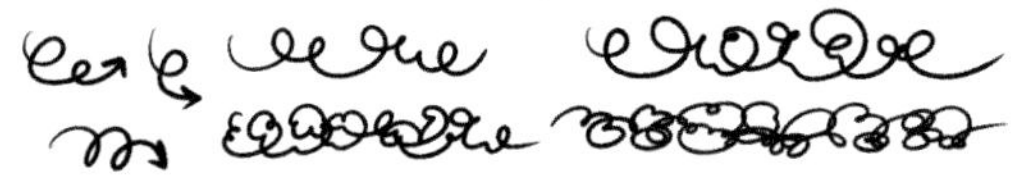

Scan to watch a tutorial.

Simple Straight Line

This is a simple straight line. You can try to make it as straight as you can, but making it a bit squiggly is a good thing—it adds a human touch to your drawing. Also try to break it sometimes, especially when you want to draw textures.

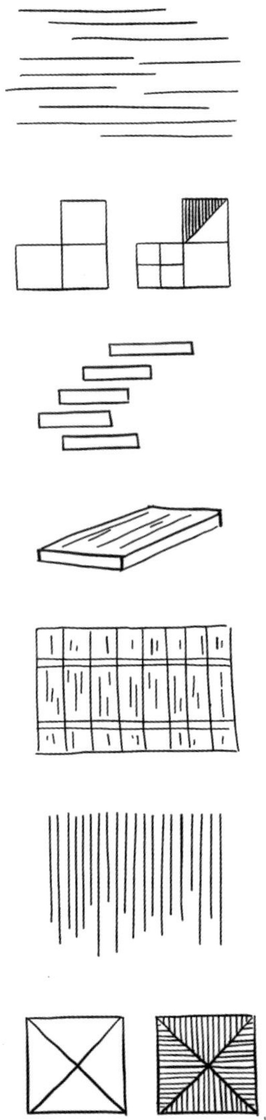

Curved Line

This is a smooth, curved line. Practice drawing it in different directions for different landscape elements and textures.

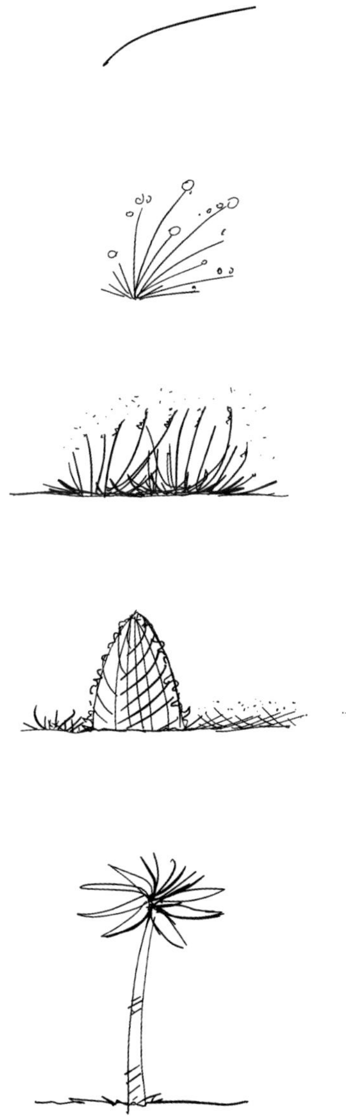

Feathered Line

This line can be used to draw branches and other elements of drawing. Notice that it can be both straight and curved. It has one thick end and one sharper.

When you draw branches, you can use a round template or a dot outline to create a round shape. Next, add the main branches and finally the secondary ones. You can hide the dot outline by adding more dots around the crown.

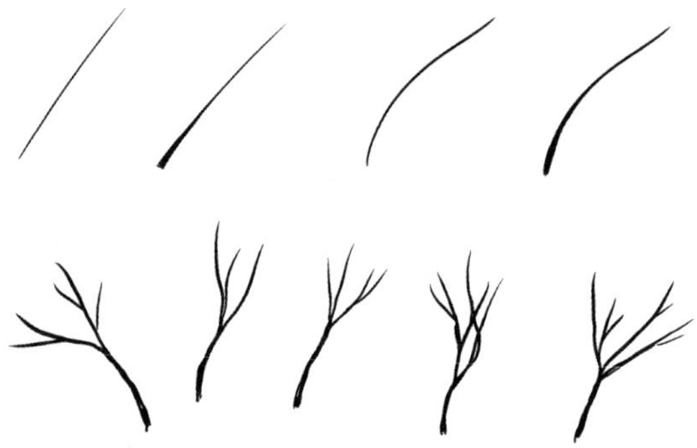

Main branches   Add secondary branches

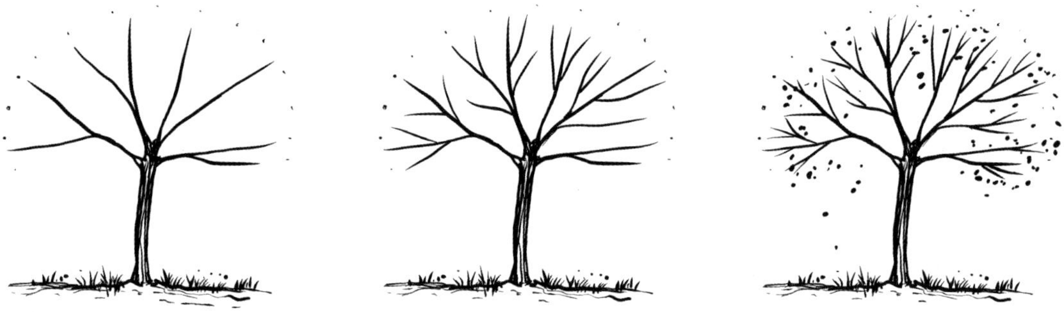

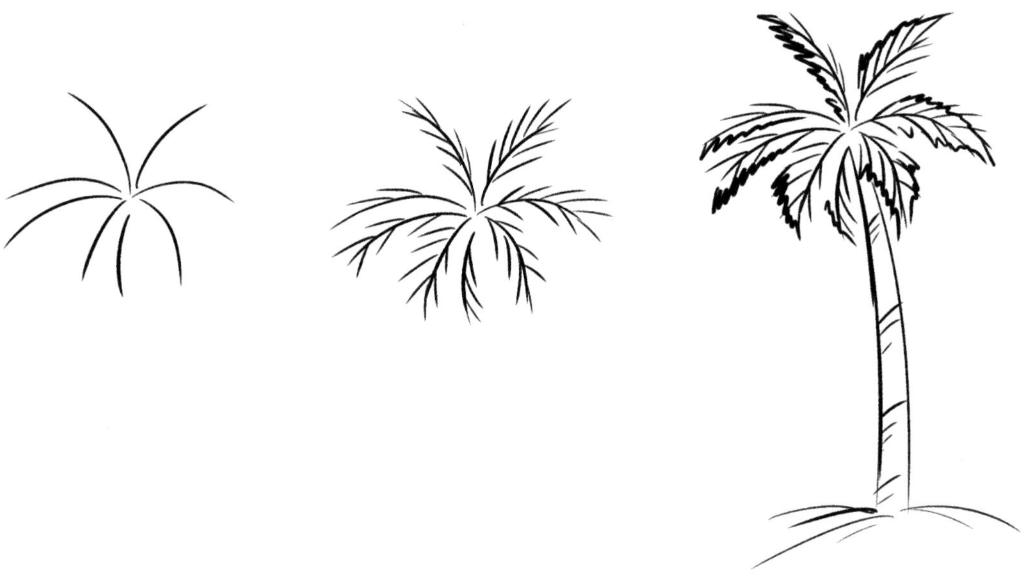

Polygons

Polygons are multisided shapes with more than four sides. They can be used for various subjects, including figures and vegetation, and of course they're especially well suited for rocks and stones.

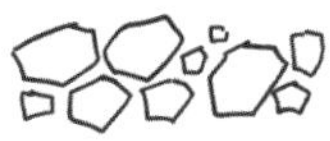

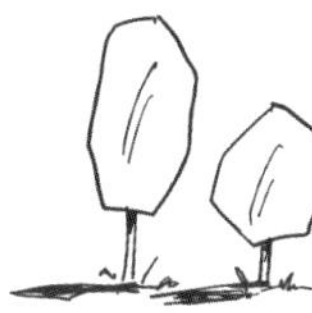

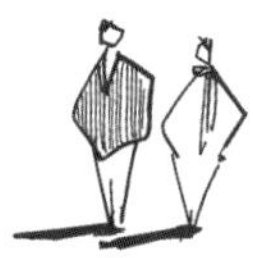

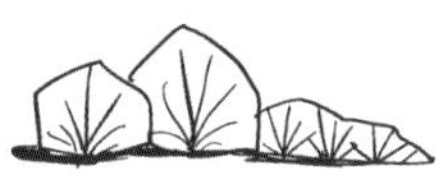

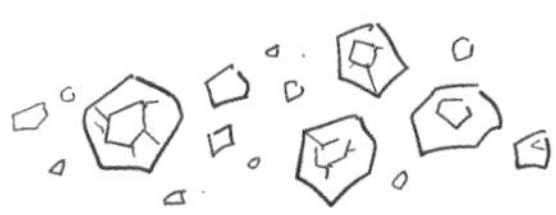

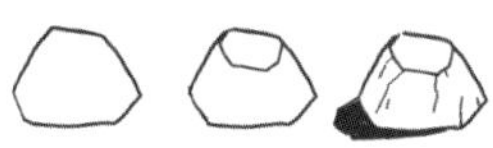

Place the biggest shapes first and then fill in with the medium and small ones:

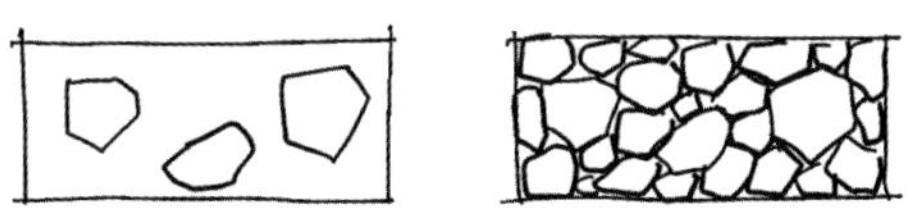

Draw a line inside a box and then add polygons:

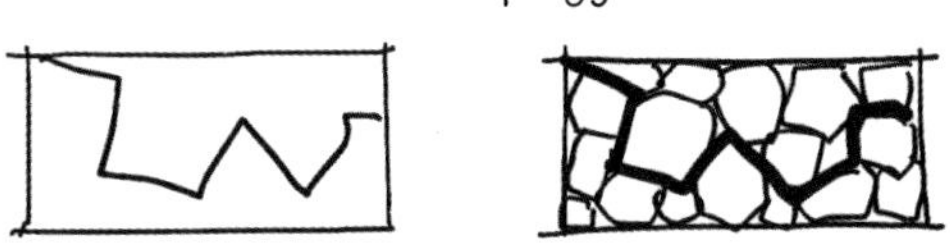

Scalloped Line

Draw irregular scalloped lines by repeating lowercase *U*s or *M*s. With scalloped lines, you can draw deciduous trees/shrubs (ones that shed leaves in the fall) and coniferous trees (ones that are evergreen).

Notice design principles: Add variety by using different lines and shapes while keeping something in common.

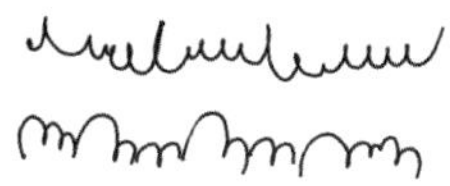

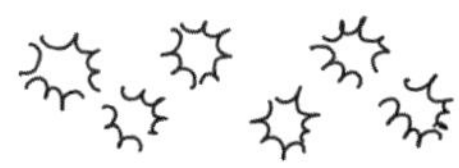

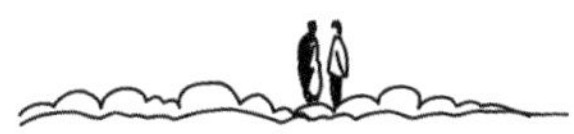

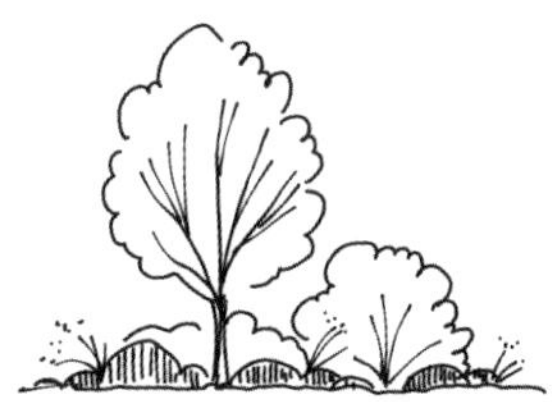

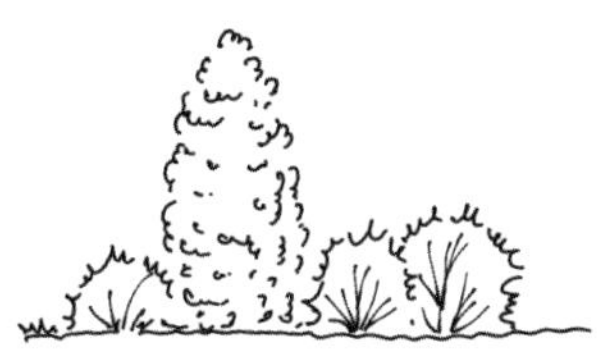

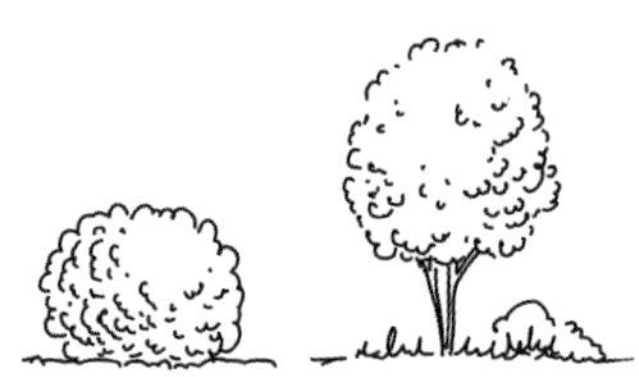

Circular Lines

Draw simple circles or slight ovals. Make sure the shapes have a clean connection. You can also add dotted lines for variety and smoother transitions.

With circular lines, you can draw foliage, pebbles and rocks, flowers, and even people.

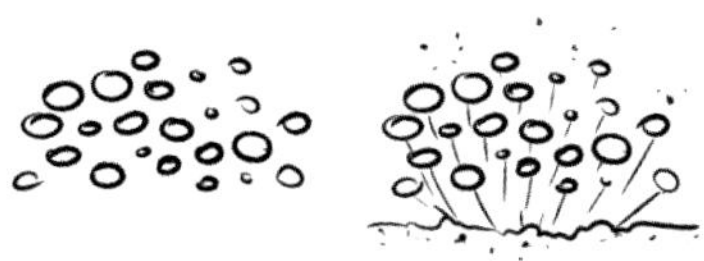

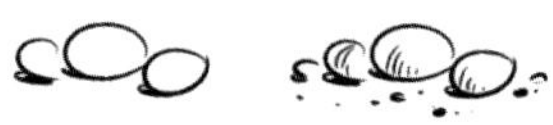

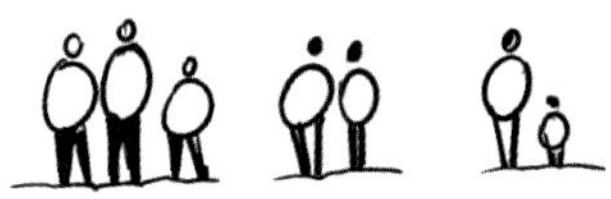

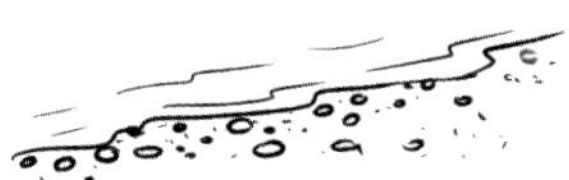

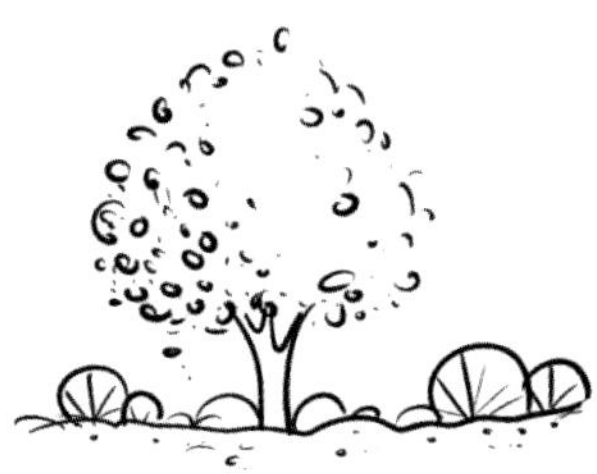

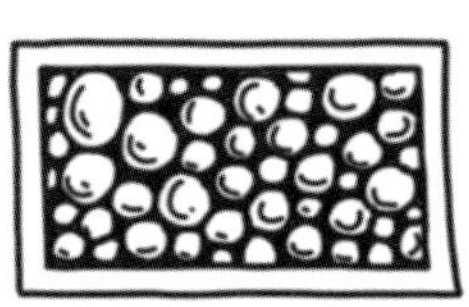

Zigzag Line

A zigzag line is excellent for quickly sketching plants. With just one line, you can create shape outlines and some abstract textures.

Make small back-and-forth movements in different directions. Try to control the length and quality of your line. It should feel as natural as handwriting.

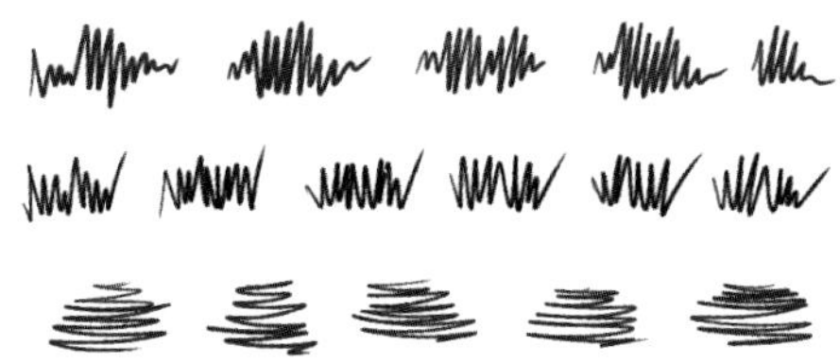

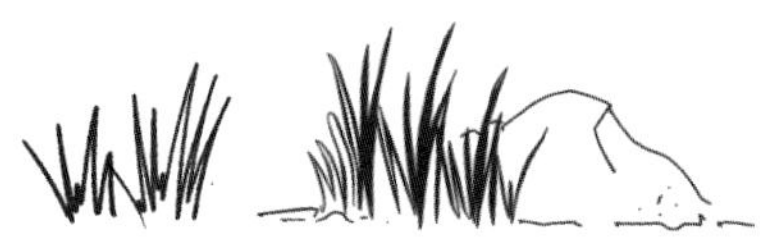

Show the rounded shape of the tree.

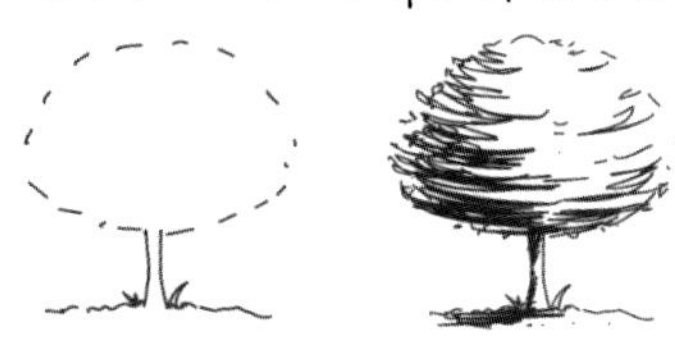

Show the pyramidal shape of the tree.

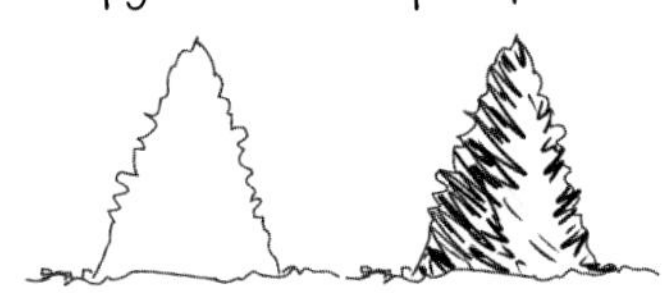

Show the different directions of pine branches.

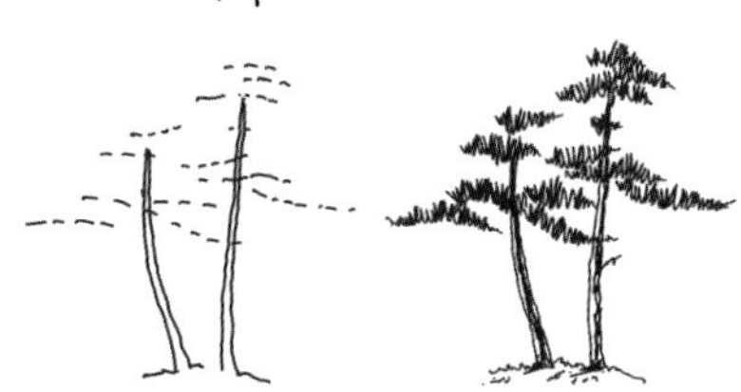

Short Rows

These are basically straight lines drawn in a row. Place them irregularly: sometimes parallel to each other, sometimes slightly angled. Use this line type to draw vegetation, landform (slopes), rocks, textures (soil), and even a bookshelf.

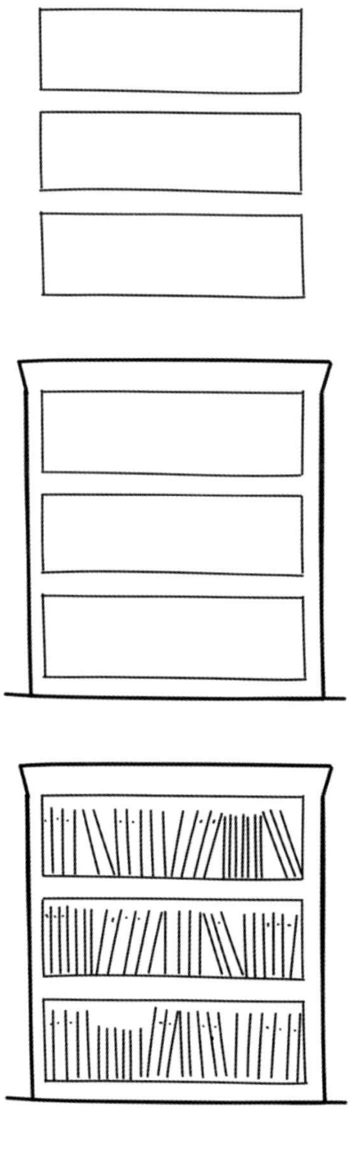

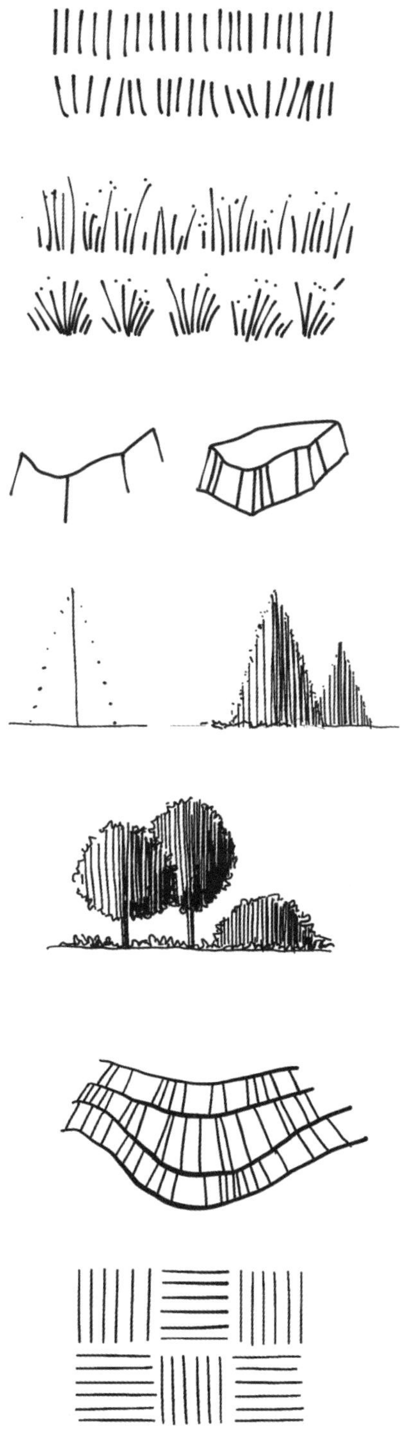

REPETITION AND EVEN SPACING

Repetition in design establishes rhythm, guiding the viewer's eye. It helps create unity and enhance the overall aesthetic. Practice drawing different, evenly spaced elements using basic lines. Do you recognize the lines already? To draw a fence, start with the poles. To divide areas evenly, split them in halves, quarters, eighths, or more.

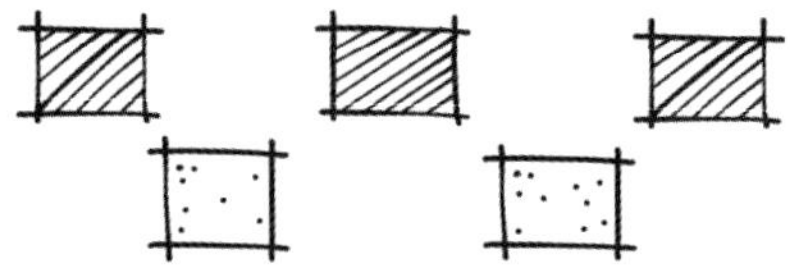

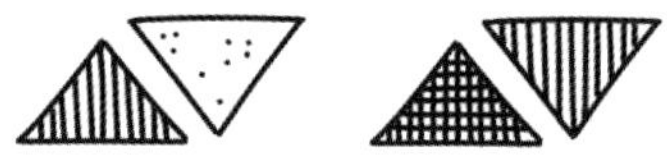

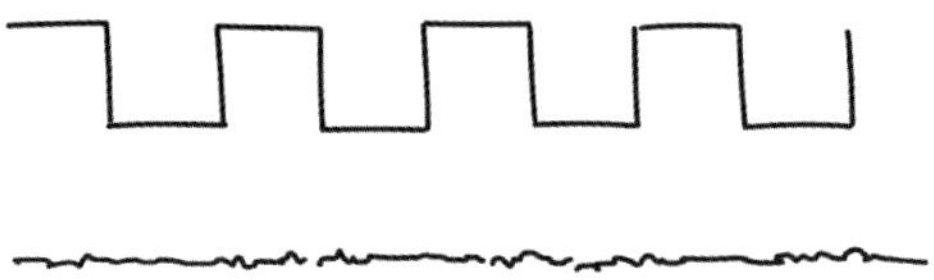

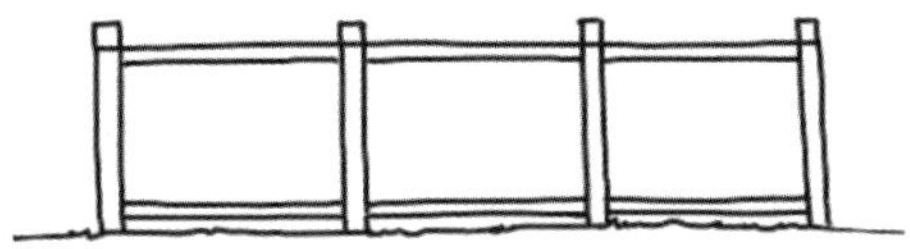

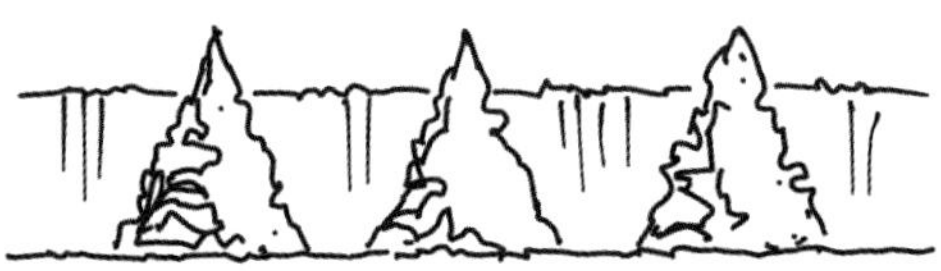

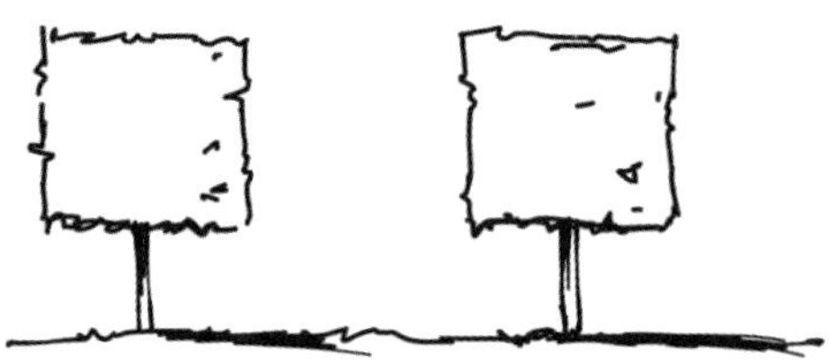

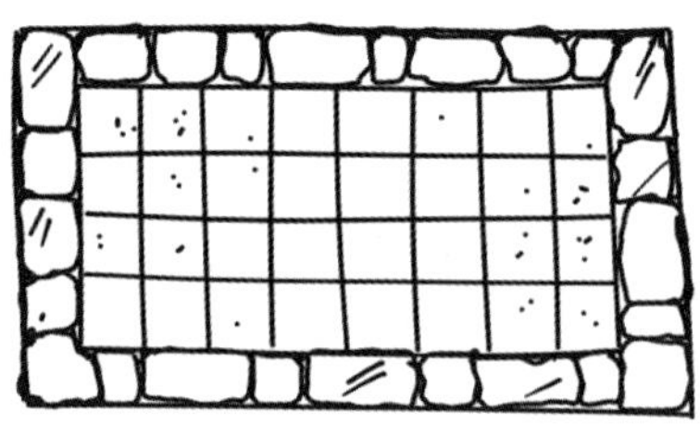

WHY IS HAND-EYE COORDINATION IMPORTANT?

Here are a few good reasons to work on developing hand-eye coordination.

Controlling Your Hand

Drawing requires fine motor skills to control the pressure, speed, and direction of your drawing utensil. With good hand-eye coordination, you can maintain consistent pressure and make smooth, controlled movements, which are essential for creating clean lines and achieving desired effects in your drawings.

Understanding Space

Drawing often involves representing three-dimensional objects on a two-dimensional surface. Hand-eye coordination helps you understand spatial relationships and proportions, allowing you to accurately depict depth, perspective, and scale in your drawings.

Muscle Memory

Developing strong hand-eye coordination through regular practice helps build muscle memory. The more you draw, the more your hand gets used to making certain movements. Good hand-eye coordination helps your hand remember how to draw things so it gets easier over time.

THE MORE YOU DRAW, THE MORE YOUR HAND GETS USED TO MAKING CERTAIN MOVEMENTS.

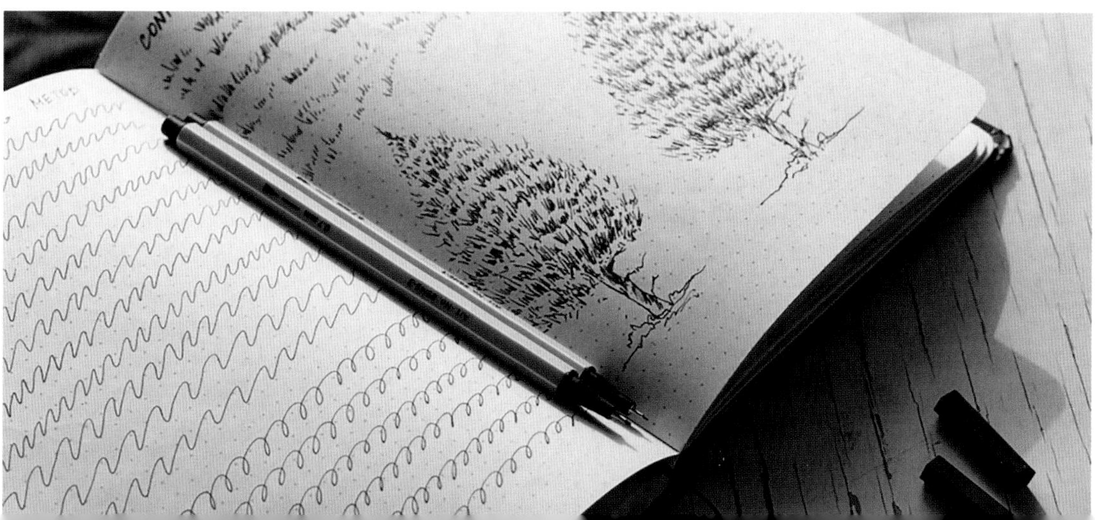

PALMER HANDWRITING METHOD

The Palmer Handwriting Method, popular in the 1950s, was designed to help people improve their handwriting by focusing on smooth, controlled movements that strengthen hand muscles and build muscle memory. These same exercises are also great for drawing practice! They help you develop better hand control, making your sketches feel more natural and confident. I practiced these exercises a lot and found them very helpful, especially when I was building my own drawing habit.

Repeat the lines both slowly and quickly while controlling the movement. The goal is to achieve freedom and looseness in your lines. Remember to relax your hand as you draw. Keep your arm on the surface or table to help stabilize your lines.

If it's too difficult on plain paper, use paper with lines or dots to guide you. You can start on scrap paper or regular printing paper and then practice a few times in your sketchbook to get a feel for it. I personally prefer using scrap paper since I can just discard it after practicing.

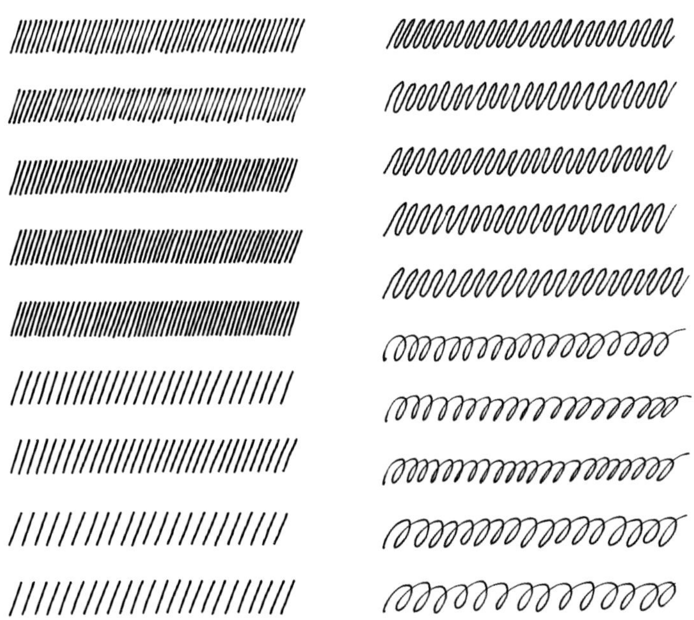

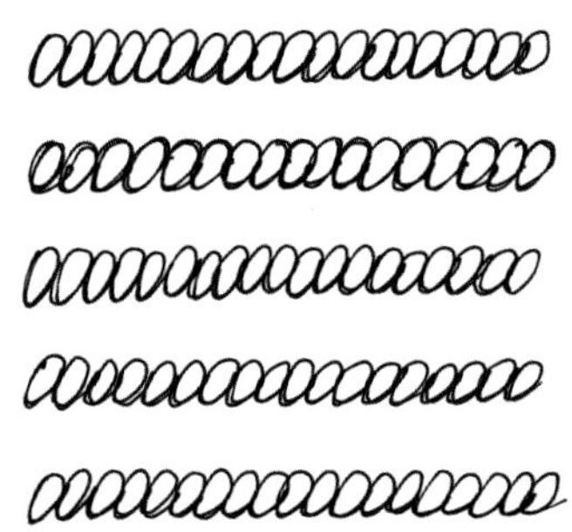

Scan to watch a tutorial.

SYMMETRY

When drawing symmetrical objects, it's helpful to break the process down into simple steps.

Tips for Drawing Symmetrical Objects

Symmetry is all about balance, and we'll use a few tricks to make sure both sides match perfectly.

Start with the Symmetry Line

Draw a vertical line down the center of your flowerpot or other object. This line is your guide to ensure the pot stays symmetrical as you draw.

Mark the Sides

On both sides of the pot, mark little dots at key points. These dots will act as reference points to make sure your lines mirror each other.

Connect the Dots

Simply connect the dots on each side with smooth curves. If you're not happy with the shape, you can always adjust it to make it more even.

Correct with Line Weight

Once you have your basic outline, go over your lines with a little extra weight on the edges. This adds depth and gives the pot a more polished look.

Final Check

Always step back and take a quick look at your drawing to make sure everything lines up. If something feels off, use the symmetry line and dots to adjust until both sides are equal.

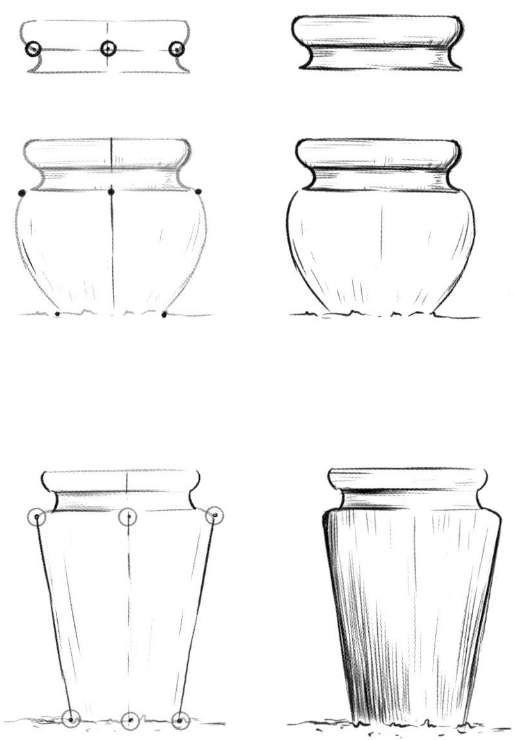

These tips work for any manmade object, like these pots.

Symmetry in Nature

Drawing tree leaves is a great way to practice symmetry. Many natural objects, like leaves, have a symmetrical structure but small imperfections that make each one unique.

I start by drawing the center line and then the left side of the leaf. Then, I simply repeat the right side. The slight variation between the sides gives a natural look, and there's no pressure to get a perfect line.

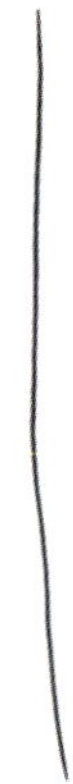

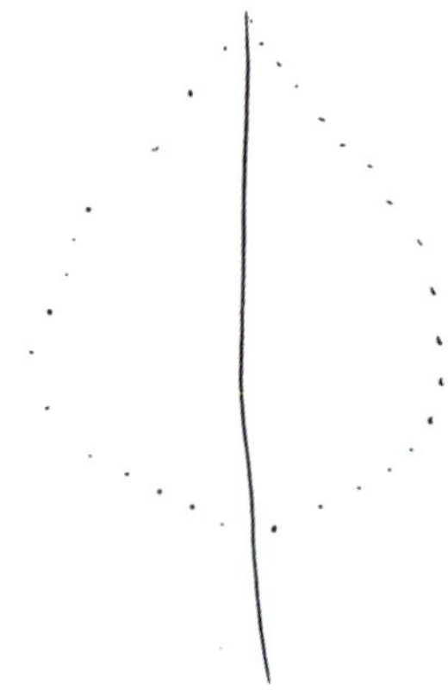

TIP

Have you noticed tree leaves look a bit like miniature trees? Leaves are easy to pick up for reference and serve as a wonderful source of inspiration.

1. Start by drawing a vertical line.
2. Use dots to draw one side of the leaf, then try to replicate it on the other side.

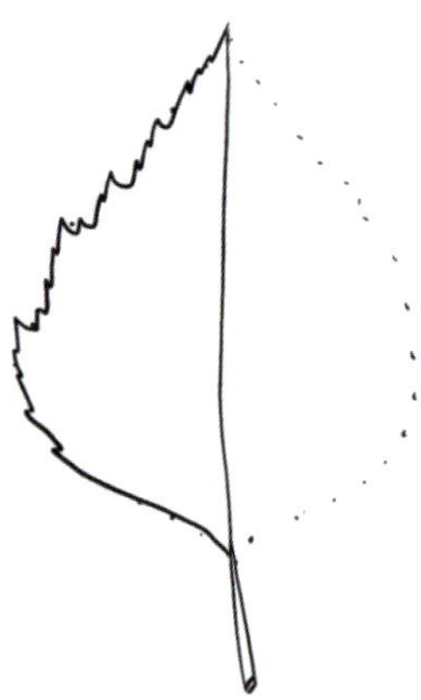

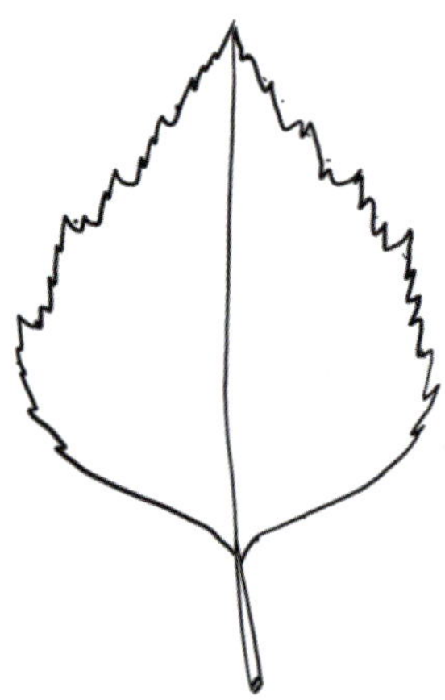

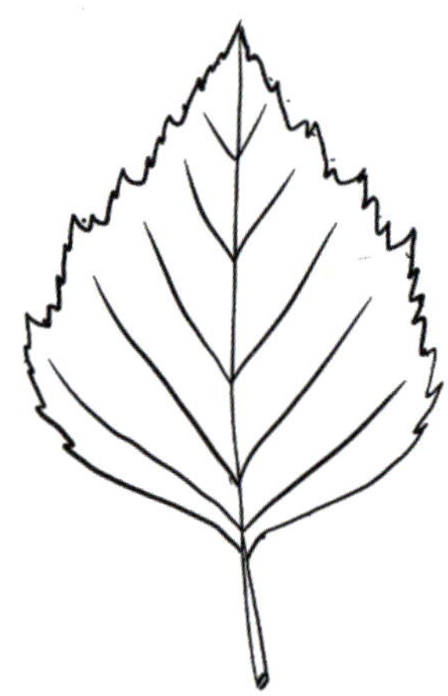

3. Draw a jagged line to mimic the natural edge of a leaf.
4. Repeat the jagged line on the other side.
5. Add lines to create veins of the leaf.

HATCHING

Hatching is a technique of drawing parallel lines that adds a lot of interest to your drawings. You can use hatching lines to create shading, texture, and depth.

Add Hatching Lines

Once the basic shape is in place, start using hatching lines to add texture. You can experiment with different techniques—like parallel or crosshatching—to create varied effects.

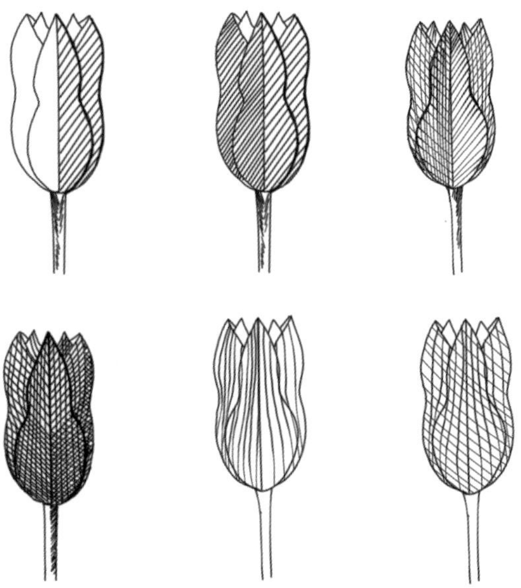

Focus on Coordination

Practicing hatching is a great way to improve precision, control, line quality, and your ability to work with different line weights. Focus on coordination as you draw. Try to match your lines carefully, paying attention to spacing and consistency.

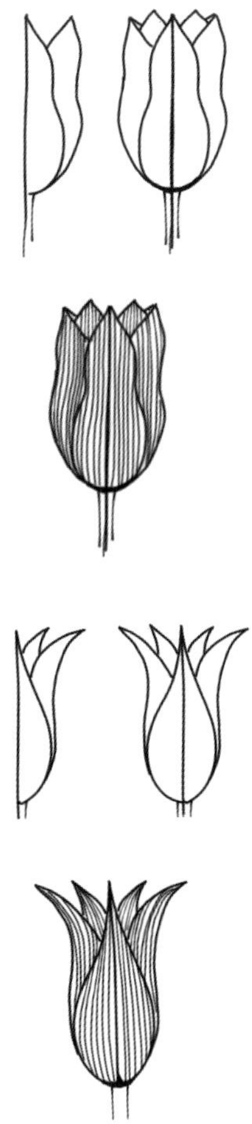

3D BASICS: DRAWING GEOMETRIC SHAPES

Practice these geometric shapes for more realistic and dimensional drawings. They are the basis for most of the objects you will ever want to draw.

As we saw before, hatching lines are a simple yet effective way to create shadows, depth, and texture. By using different types of lines—vertical, horizontal, or diagonal—and combining them in various ways, you can control how light or dark a surface appears.

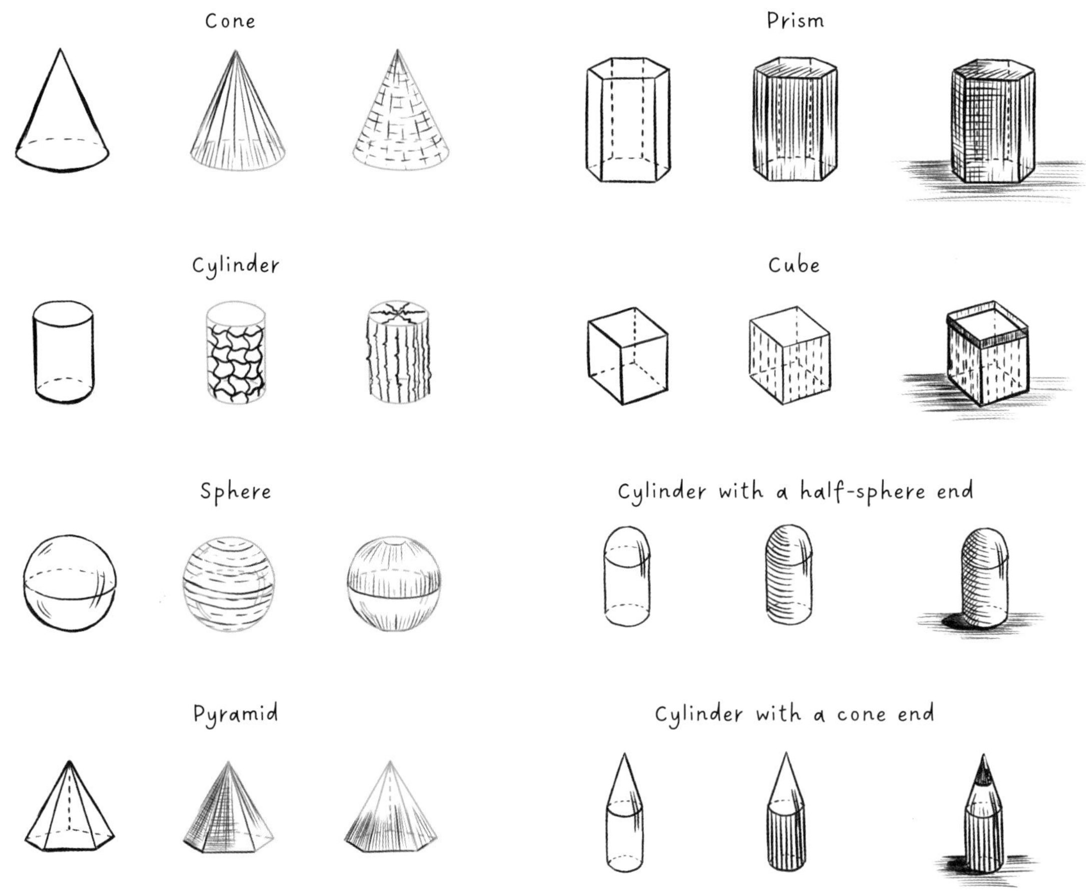

STEP BY STEP:

EVERYDAY OBJECTS

Now that you've practiced basic three-dimensional shapes, try using them to draw everyday objects. For example, a gift box can be made with cubes, a vase with a cylinder, and a lamp with spheres and cones. A ball of yarn is just a sphere. The more you practice seeing how basic shapes make up real objects, the easier it will be to draw them accurately.

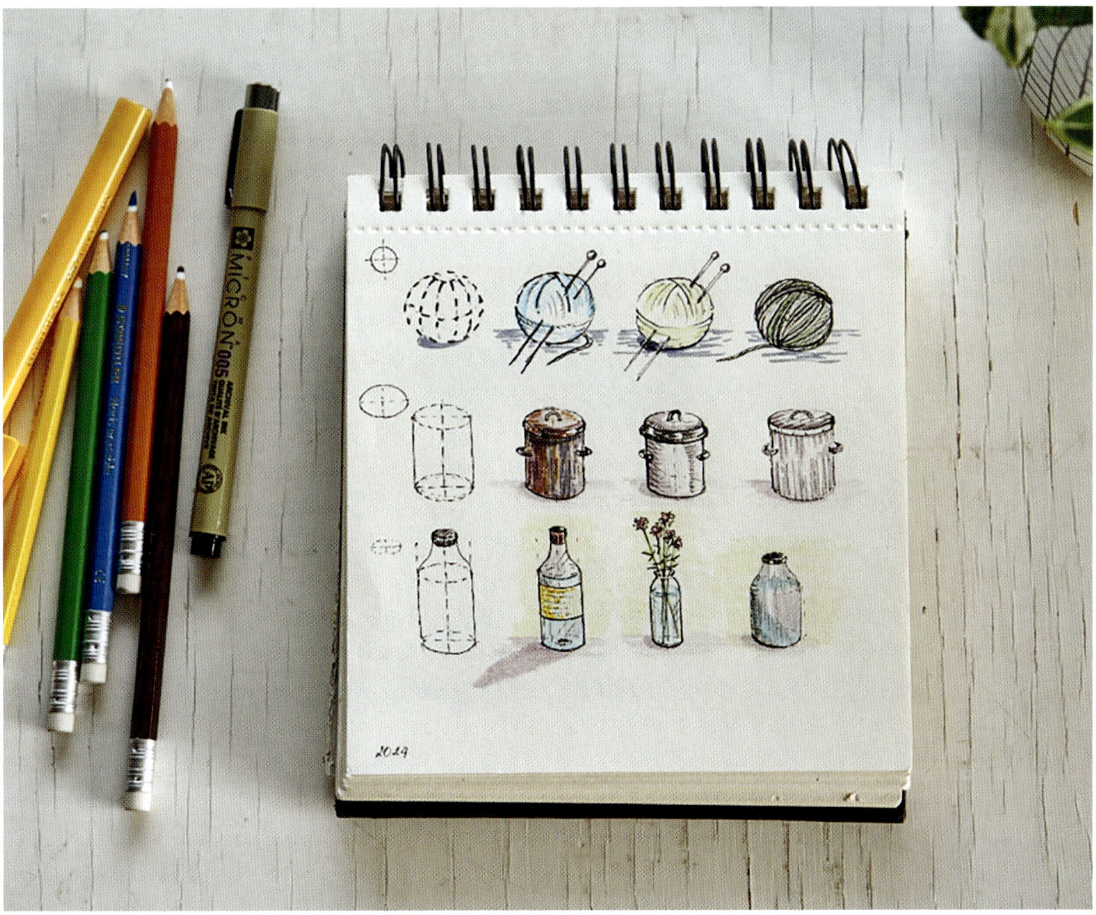

Objects from Spheres

There's no end to the number of subjects you can draw by starting with a sphere or half sphere. Here are a few ideas.

Ball of Yarn

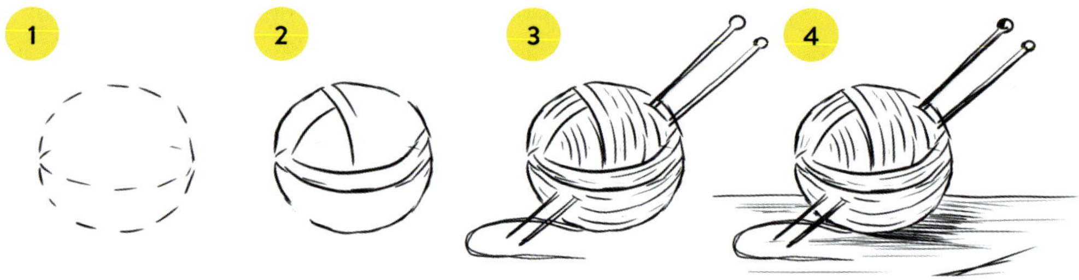

Basket

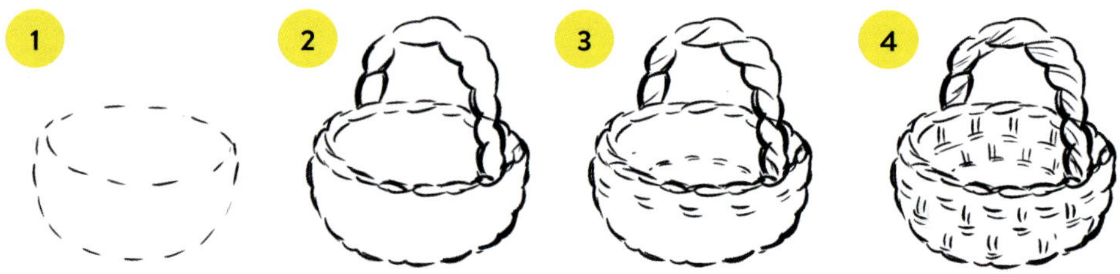

Pumpkin

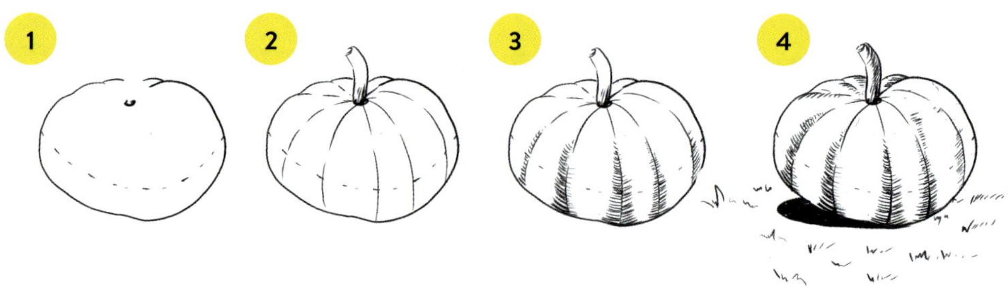

TIP

Draw "contour lines" that follow the shape of the pumpkin to show its roundness.

Object from Cube: Gift-Wrapped Box

This drawing might look a little tricky, but it's simple if you follow a few easy steps.

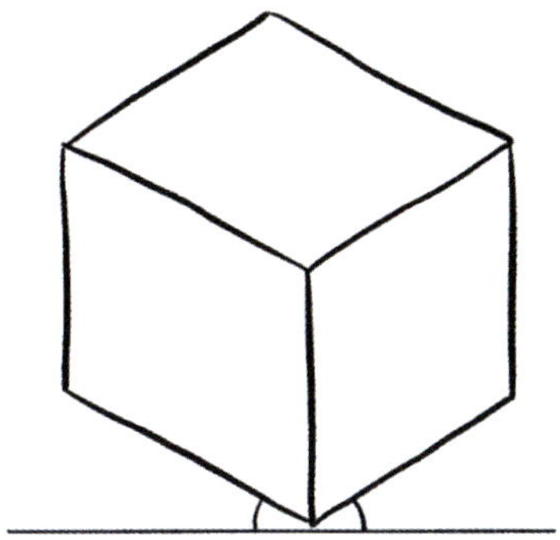

1. Start by drawing a cube turned at about a 30-degree angle. This angle just works well; it's not too flat or too dramatic, and you get a nice view of all the sides.

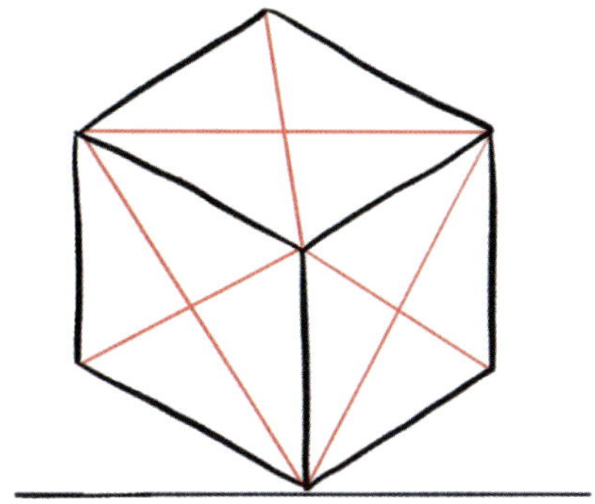

2. Sketch an X on each side.

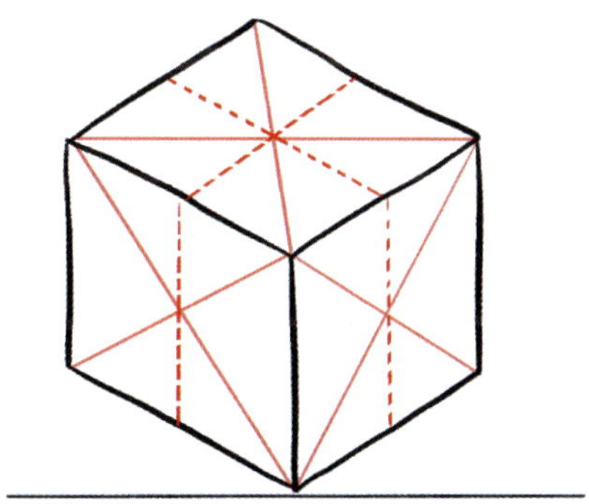

3. Locate the center of each X and draw lines for the ribbons.

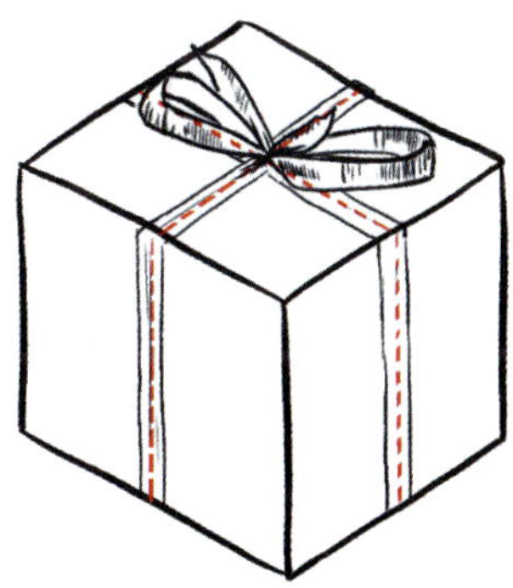

4. Add the ribbon across the cube and decorate your gift however you like.

TIP

You can keep it simple or add extra details like bows and wrapping paper.

Objects from Cylinders

When drawing a cylindrical container, like a jar, the lid follows the same shape but is slightly larger in diameter to show it's separate. You can also tweak the lid's form, but it should still feel like a part of the overall cylinder. This helps you see how the top and body connect.

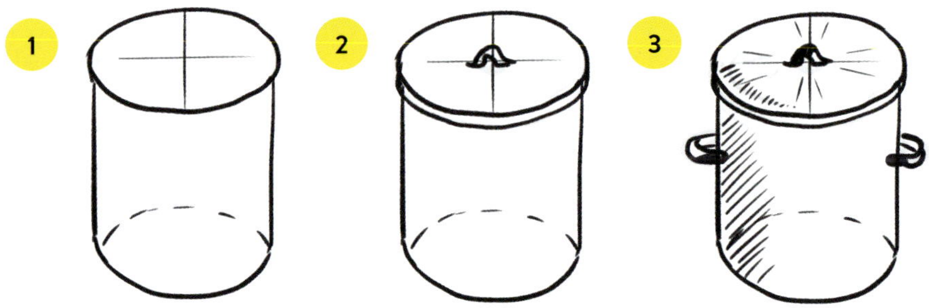

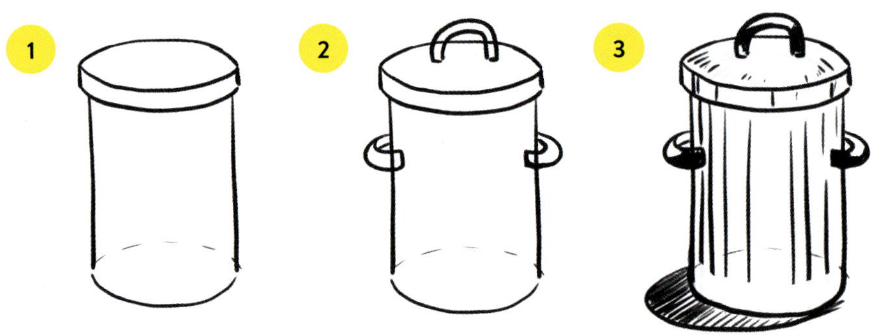

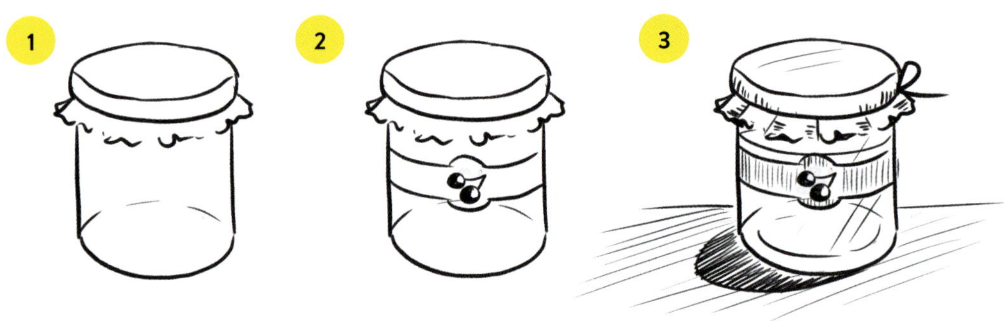

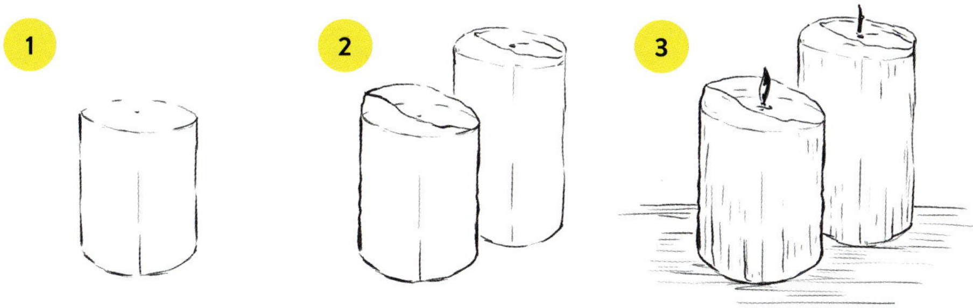
1
2
3

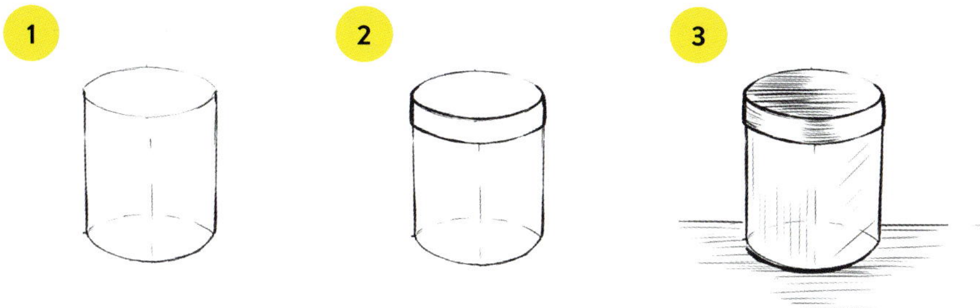
1
2
3

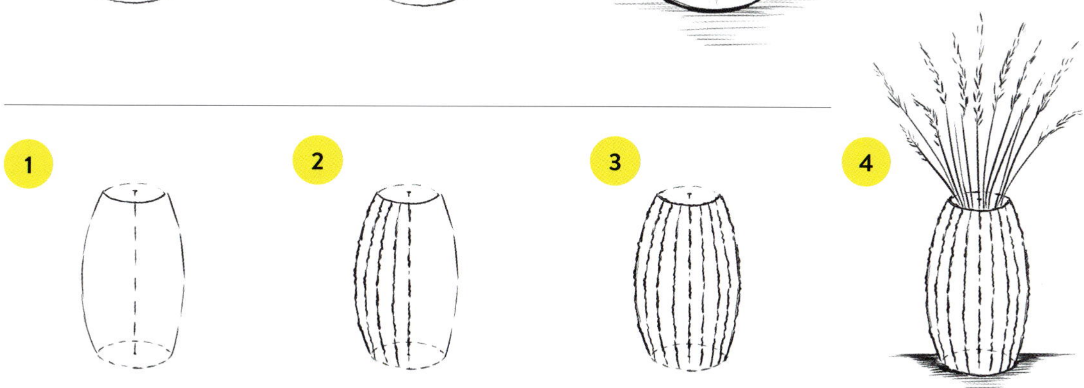
1
2
3
4

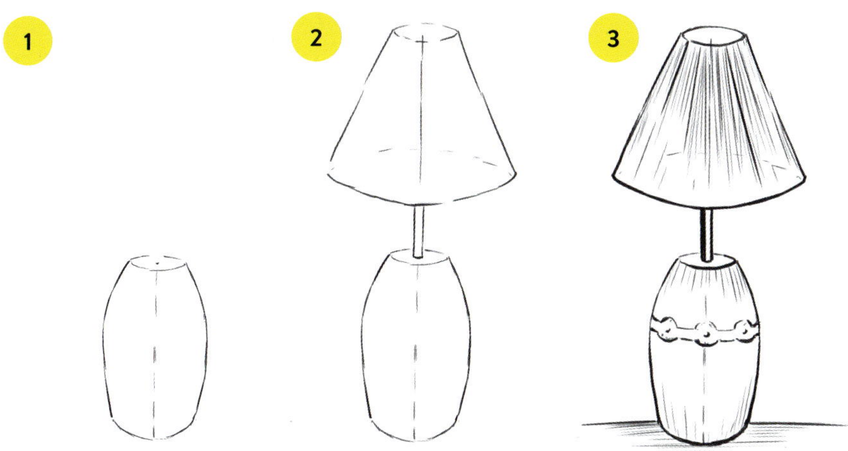
1
2
3

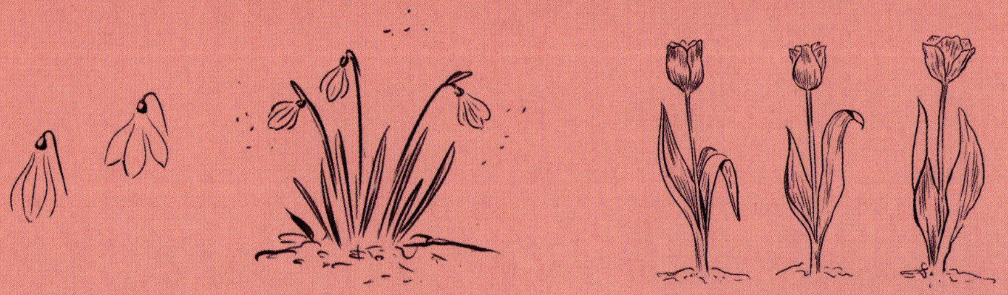

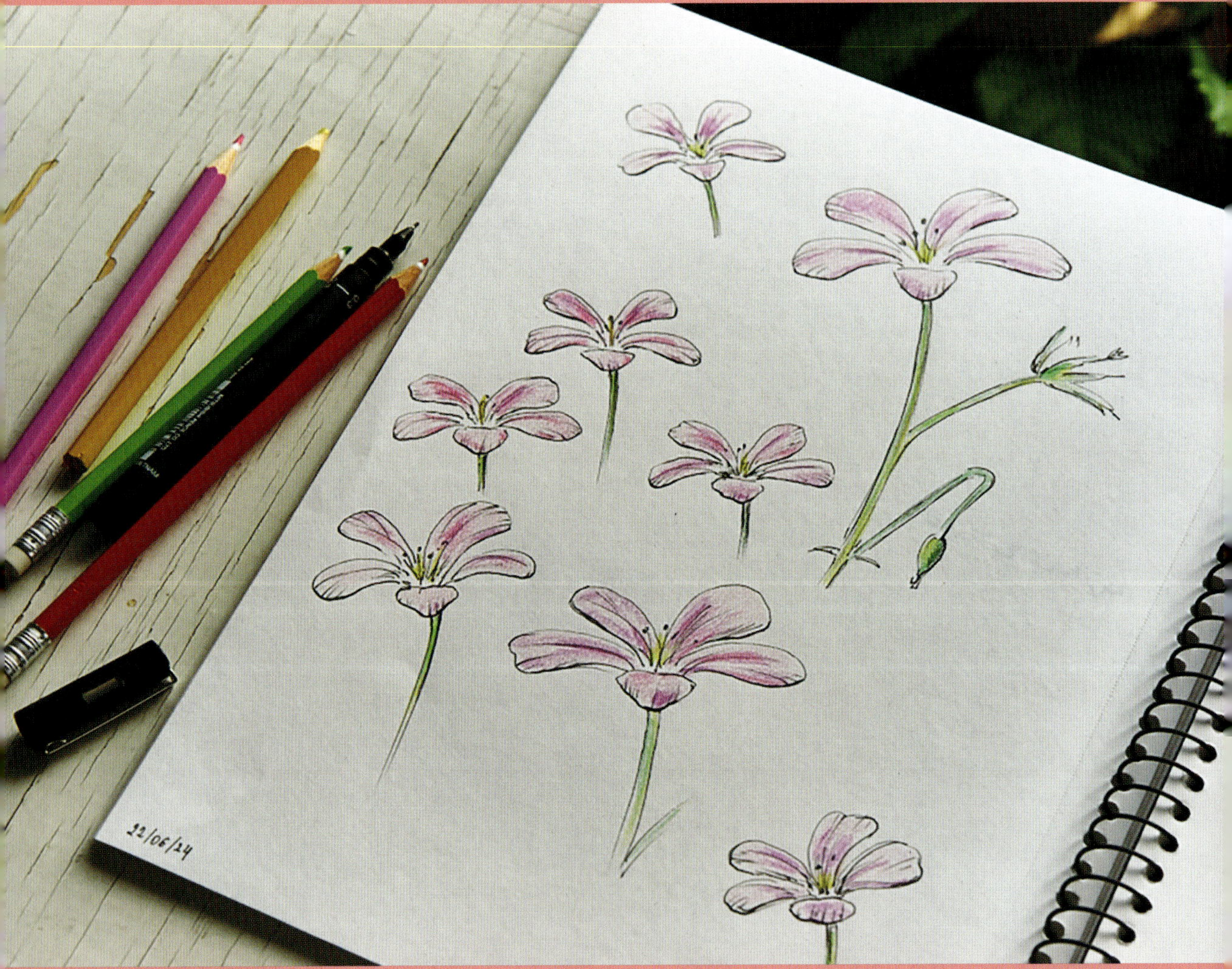
22/06/24

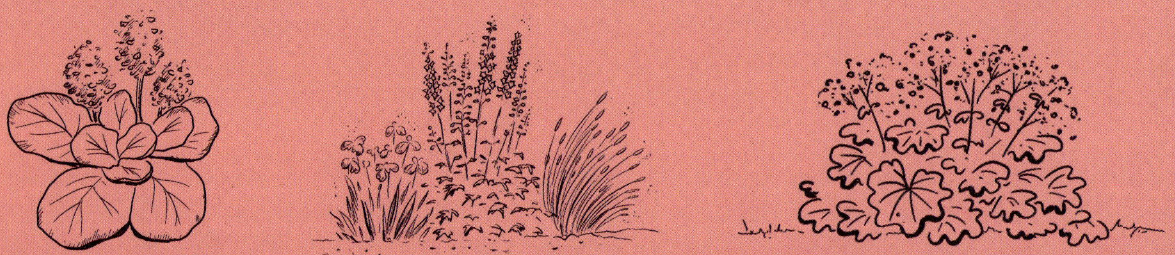

3

DRAWING PLANTS AND FLOWERS

Drawing plants is both a relaxing and rewarding process. Their organic, irregular shapes leave room for small mistakes, making them very forgiving subjects. Every leaf and flower are a little different, and your drawings often feel more natural when your lines and shapes aren't identical. While it's possible to draw plants from imagination, I find it especially helpful as a landscape designer and gardener to sketch real plants. It's a great way to learn more about them and to remember their names. In this chapter, we'll draw garden plants, flowers, grasses, and a few common houseplants. Since we've already practiced the basics in the previous chapter, try to spot those simple shapes in the plants you draw. This will help you keep strengthening your ability to break down forms and draw with confidence.

TIPS FOR DRAWING PLANTS AND FLOWERS

In this chapter, we'll draw a number of flowers and plants step by step. Here are a few useful principles to keep in mind as you draw any types of plants.

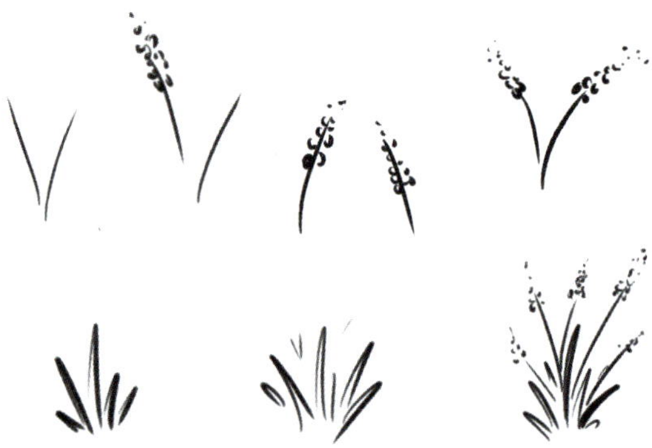

Start with Elements and Lines

Practice drawing parts of the plant, like stems, flowers, and leaves, individually. Once you're confident with each part, try drawing the whole plant. This method also helps you create your own patterns.

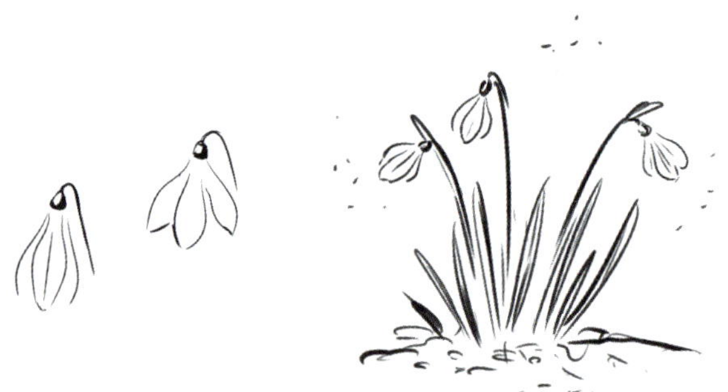

Make It Natural

Try to avoid too much symmetry. Instead, look for a balanced composition that is asymmetrical.

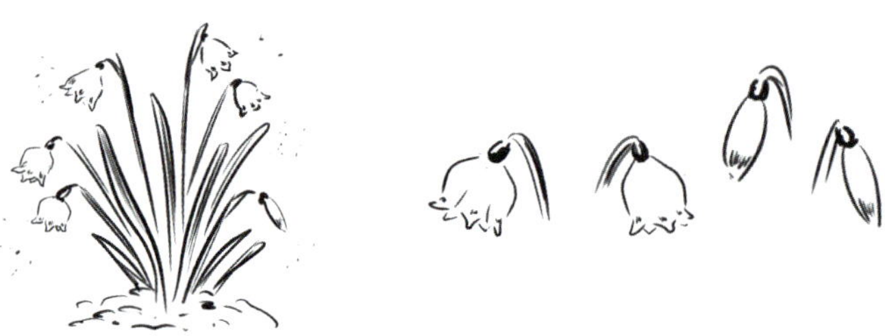

Limit Details

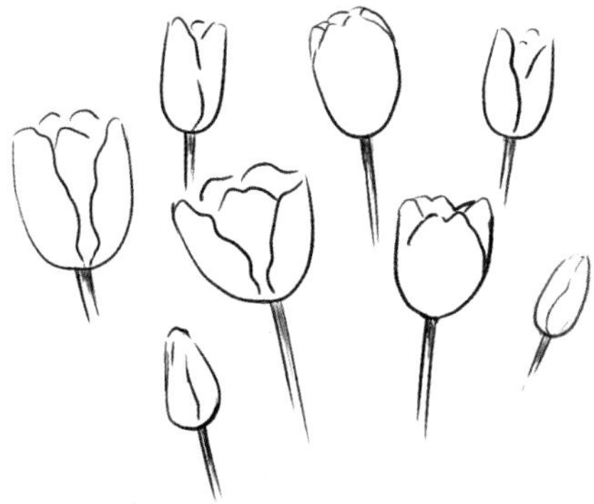

Don't go into too much detail. Try to capture the most characteristic features that show what a plant is like. Include fewer details on the plants in the background to create depth and make the foreground stand out more.

Create Depth

To create a feeling of dimension, overlap the elements and vary their size (small, medium, big). You can add some extra line weight to represent areas of shadow or prominence, while thinner lines indicate finer details.

To do that, you can use pens with different nibs (0.25–0.50 mm fineliners), or simply draw a few times over the same line to make it bolder. Always start your drawing with thin lines first (recommended nib 0.25 mm).

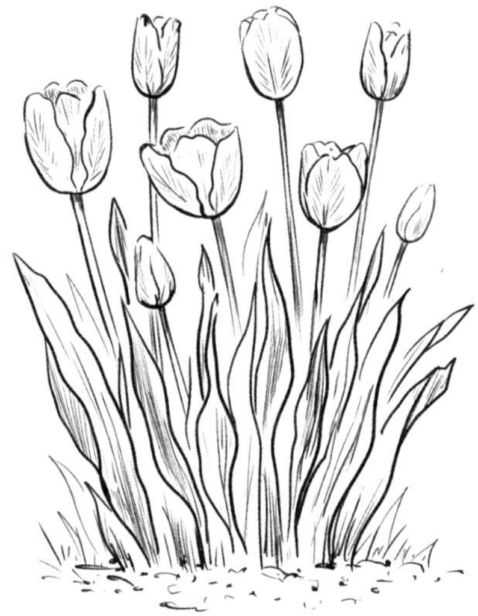

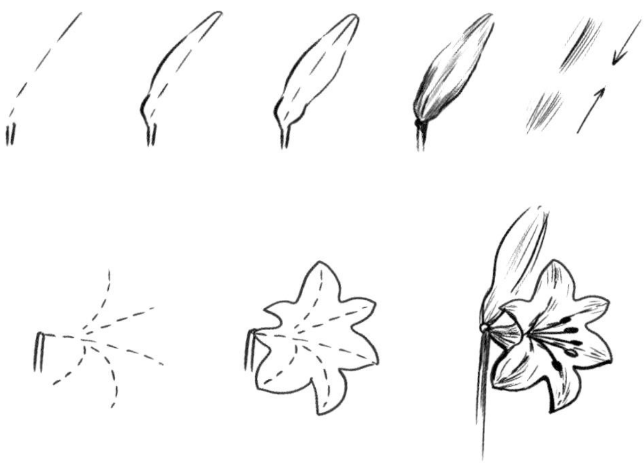

Using Guidelines

Use the guiding or assisting lines to achieve the right proportions and balance. You can use a central symmetry line and draw one side of a plant first, then the other. Also, you can draw the location of the petals. This helps you understand the overall shape and structure.

STEP BY STEP:

HOUSEPLANTS

Houseplants make great subjects for sketching because you probably have a few around the house! When you draw them you can also include the pot, which gives you extra practice.

Cactus

A cactus is a great plant to start with, as it doesn't have any complicated leaves!

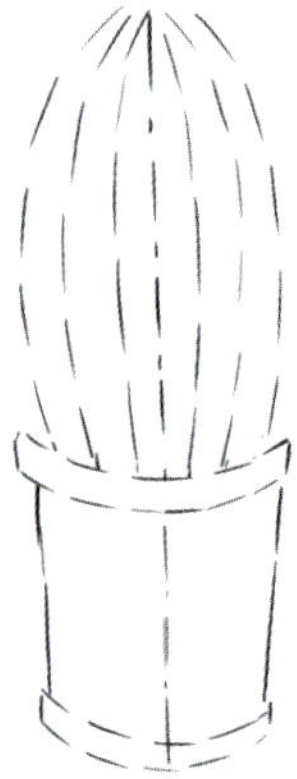

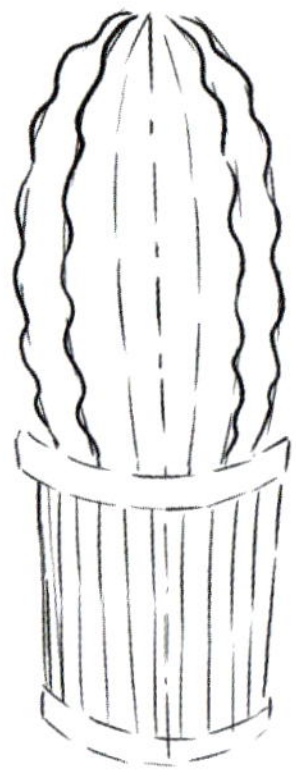

1 Start by practicing symmetry. Draw a central line lightly—it's dark in this example so you can see it better. Gradually make the lines curvier toward the edges to capture the form of the cactus.

2 Fill in the rest of the outline of the cactus and pot.

3 Go over some of the lines and darken them.

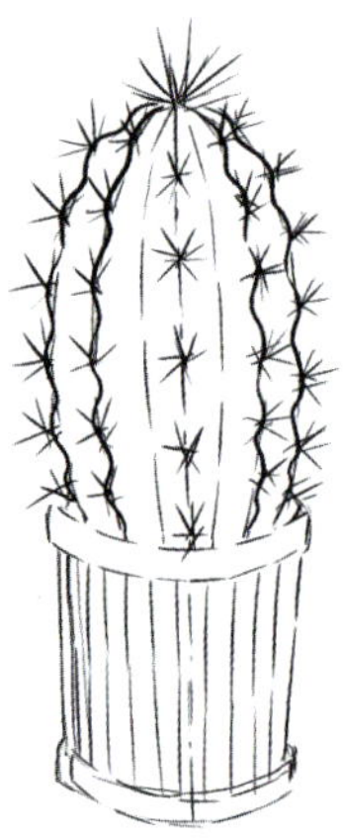

4 Add the prickles with quick, short strokes to create pointy tips. Vary their directions and size, but don't overthink this—keeping it natural is key. Correct the symmetry in the pot at this stage if needed.

TIP

Notice how I corrected the symmetry of the pot. While it's not about the perfection, small mistakes can be corrected. If needed, hide them while adding details and creating texture.

Scan to watch a tutorial.

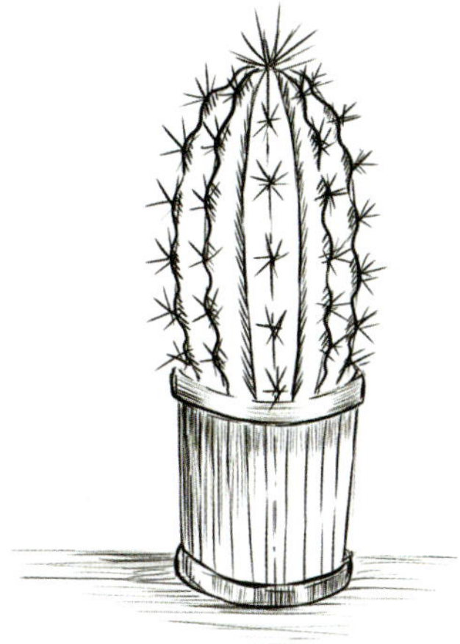

5 Add subtle shading to the cactus and pot, and create a surface for the pot to sit on.

Background and Color

If you'd like, you can color your sketch. For this example, I used two colors: green for the cactus and light brown for the pot. Start by lightly coloring the entire object, then gradually increase pressure to darken areas with hatching lines and shadows. Leave some white space for highlights, especially near dark spots to create more contrast. Once you color an area dark, it's hard to undo, so add color gradually. You can use a white pen or a pencil, but I find it's a good exercise to practice leaving white space naturally.

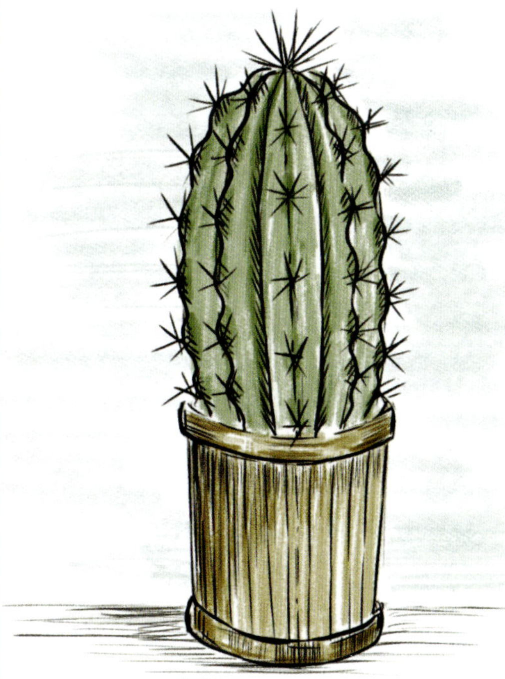

Monstera Leaves

Monstera leaves have such an interesting and impressive look, and they're really fun to draw! I was surprised when I discovered the techniques for drawing these leaves. The main tip is to start with the central line and create an outline of the leaf using broken lines. Then complete the shape with a smooth, curvy line. This will give you the characteristic monstera edge.

Single Leaf

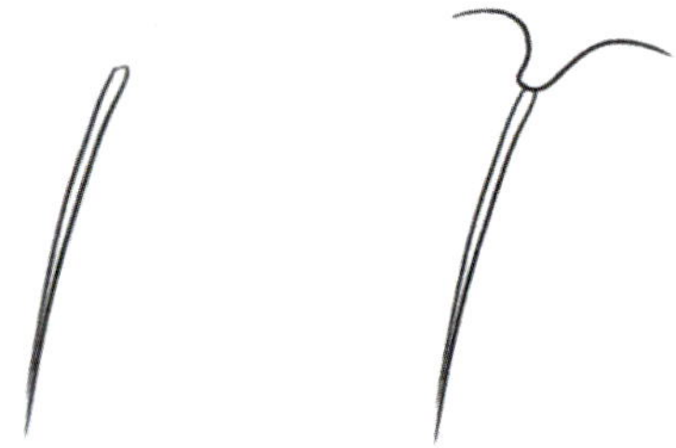

1 Start by drawing a central line of the leaf.

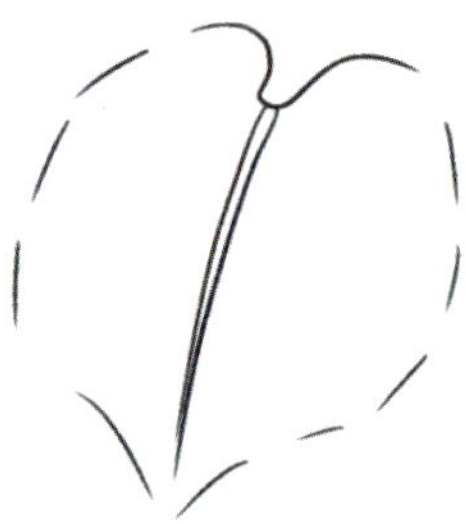

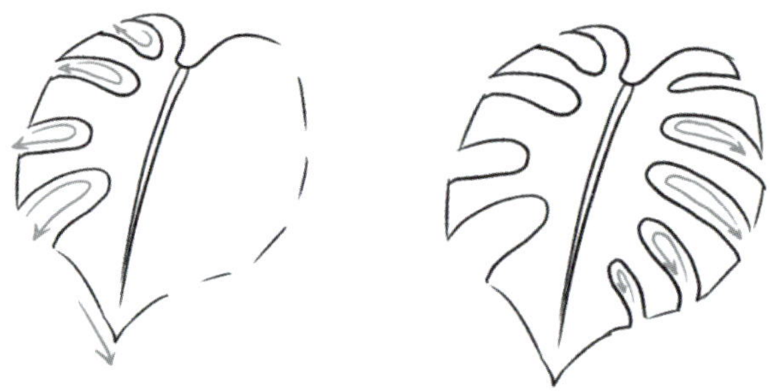

2 Outline the shape with a broken line to give it some flexibility.

3 Create the distinctive edge of the leaf by connecting curves—like *U*s—along the outline.

4 Add veins to the leaf and the holes.

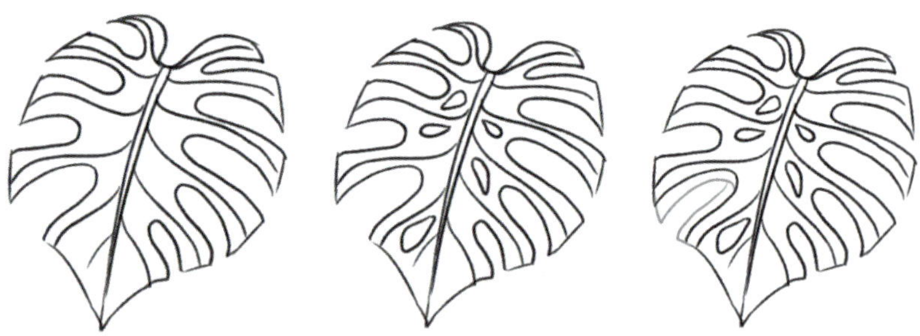

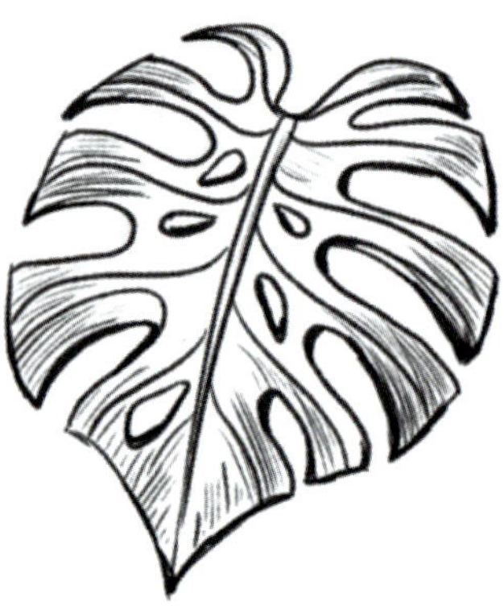

5 Finally, add texture lines along the edges for a more natural look. You can adjust your drawing by adding some extra lines to the edges if needed.

Two Leaves

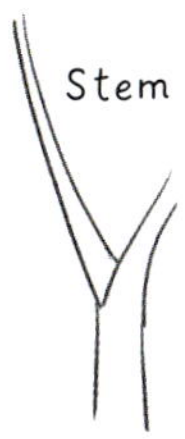

1

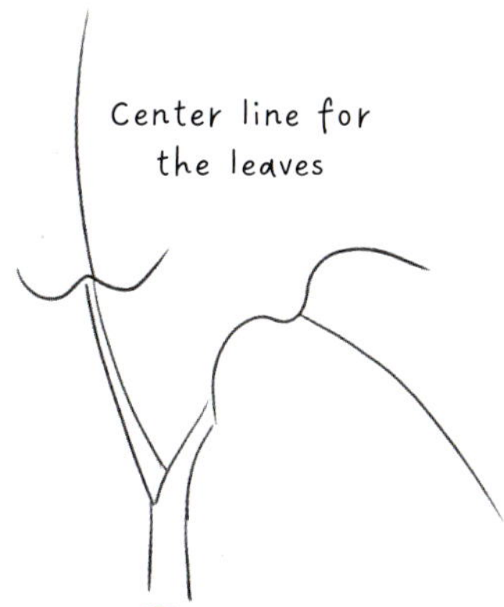

2

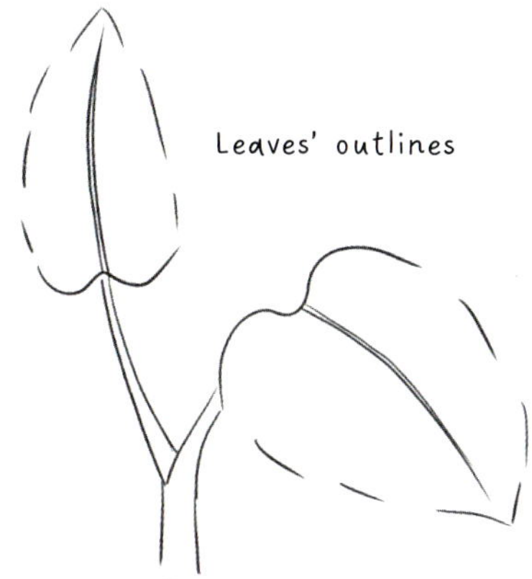

3

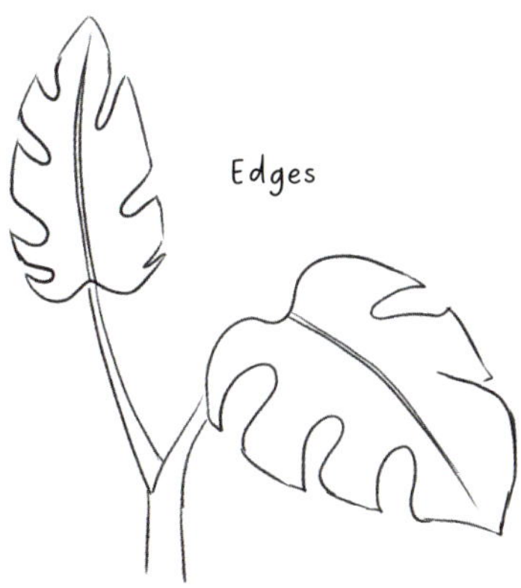

4

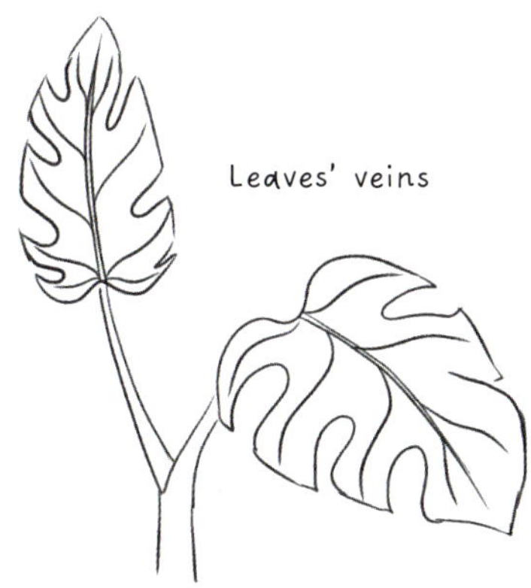

5

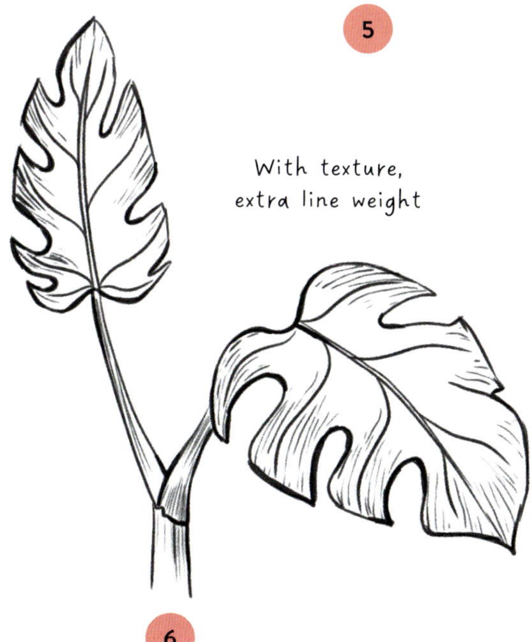

6

Fan Palm

Drawing a fan palm is great for practicing overlapping shapes and creating sharp, interesting plant forms. This exercise will guide you through drawing both individual leaves and a whole plant, which can be used for houseplants or garden plants in landscape sketches.

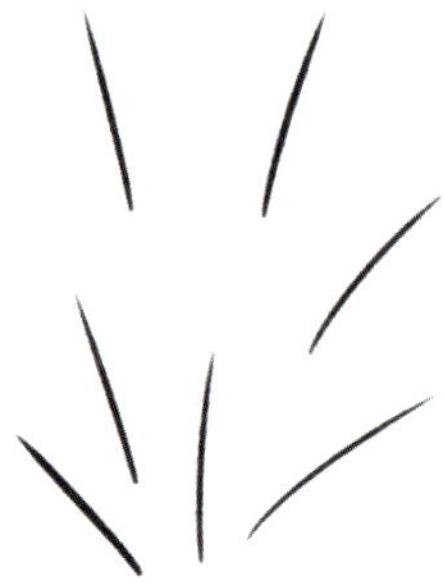

1 Start by sketching the stems randomly with quick, upward strokes. Consider the overall size and shape of the plant.

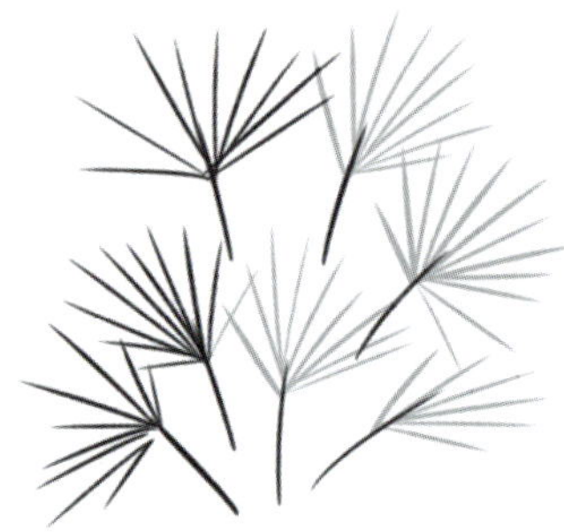

2 Extend the leaves from the stems. You don't always need to start the leaves from the very tip of the stem—you can begin them anywhere along its length. This makes it easy to adjust if a stem ends up too long. Simply start the leaves where you want, and the stem will appear shorter.

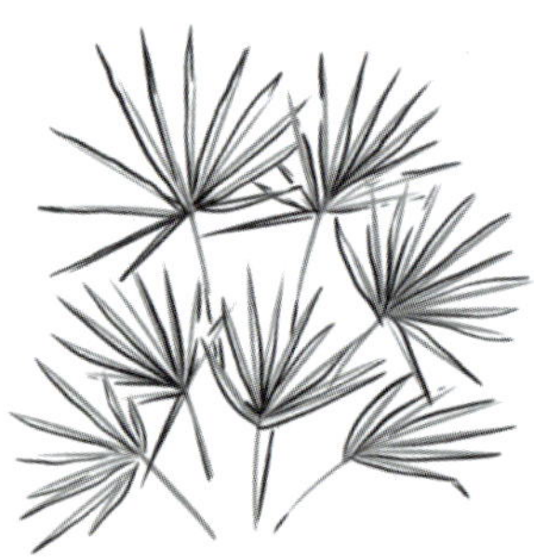

3 Complete the fan-shaped leaves by adding a light curvy line. Pay attention to negative (or empty) space around the leaves as you create them. This helps balance the composition and ensures the plant looks natural. Also add variation to your lines—slight irregularities make the leaves appear more organic and lifelike.

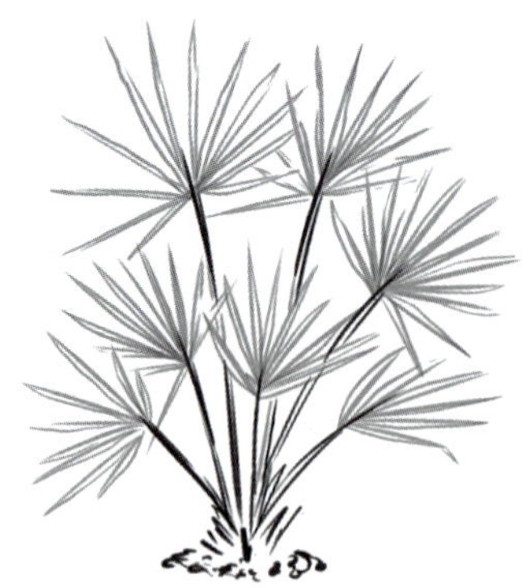

4 Once the leaves are in place, thicken the stems by adding an extra line to each one to make them fuller. Add some soil at the base.

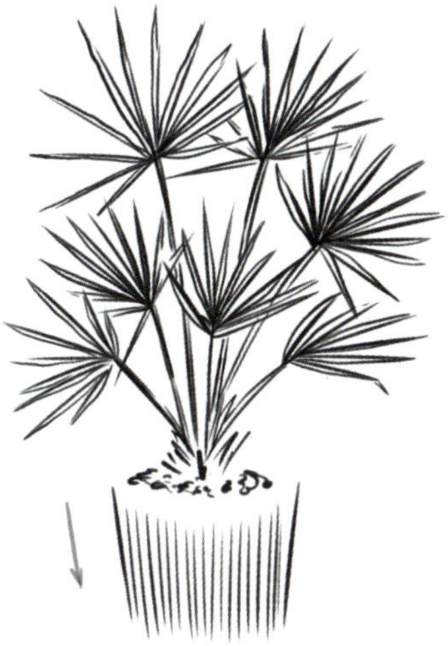

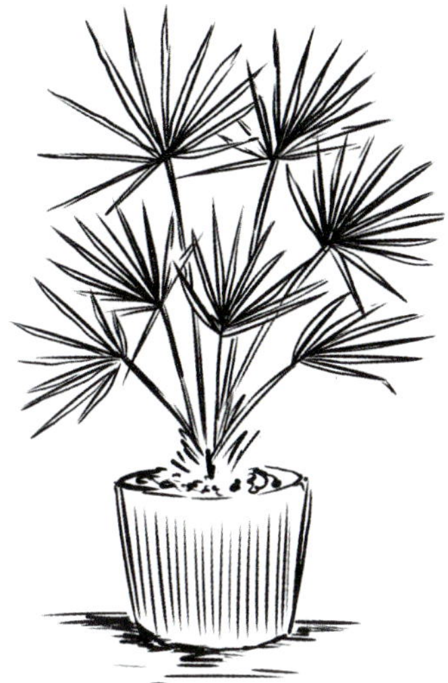

5 If you want your fan palm to be a houseplant, draw the pot. Begin by sketching the front side of the pot with quick parallel lines.

6 Complete the pot and add the shadow to anchor it to the ground.

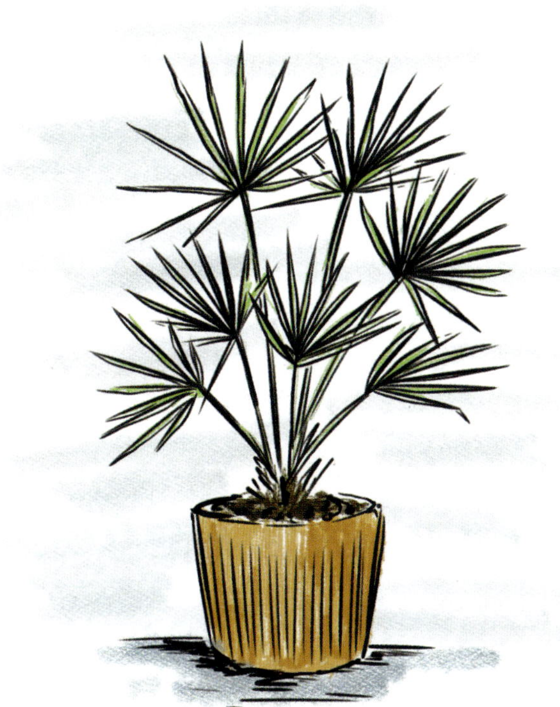

TIP

Try adding subtle color as I did with the cactus.

Scan to watch a tutorial.

Calathea

Calathea has beautiful variegated leaves that are great for practicing organic shapes and textures.

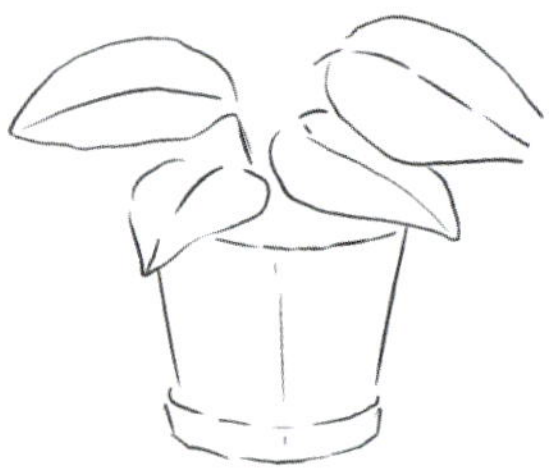

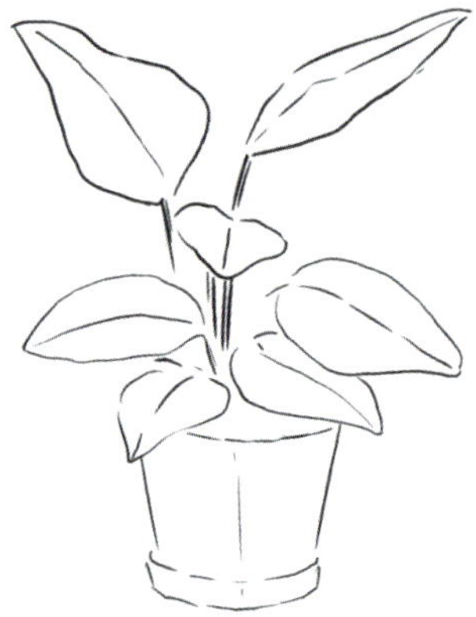

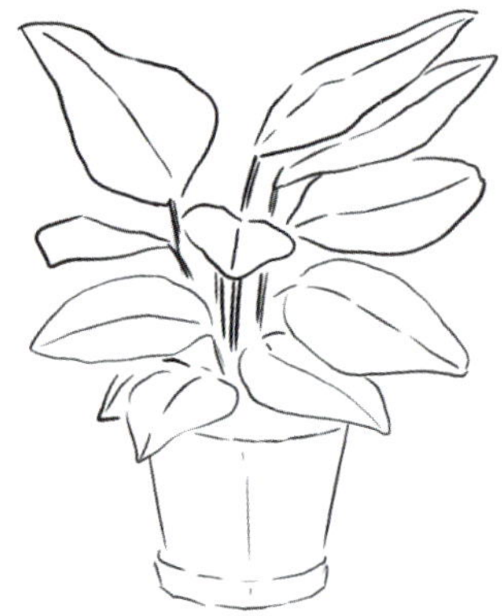

1. Begin by lightly outlining the pot and lower leaves, focusing on the overall shape.

2. Gradually build up the drawing by adding more leaves, overlapping some to create a natural, layered effect.

3. Add veins to the leaves, ensuring they follow the natural flow.

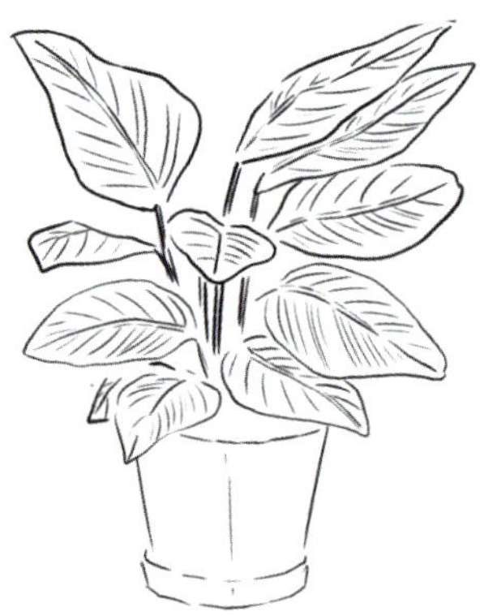

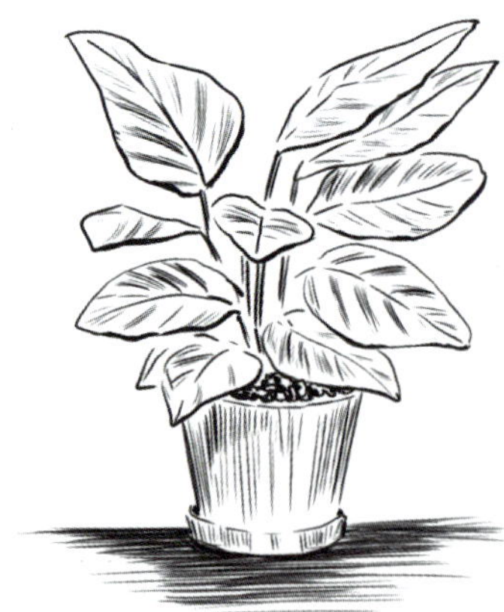

4. Add extra contrast and vary the line weight, especially on the lower edges, to give the leaves depth.

5. Finally, draw the surface the pot is resting on to ground the plant and give the drawing a solid base.

Aloe

Aloe has a pointy structure, perfect for practicing sharp lines and angles.

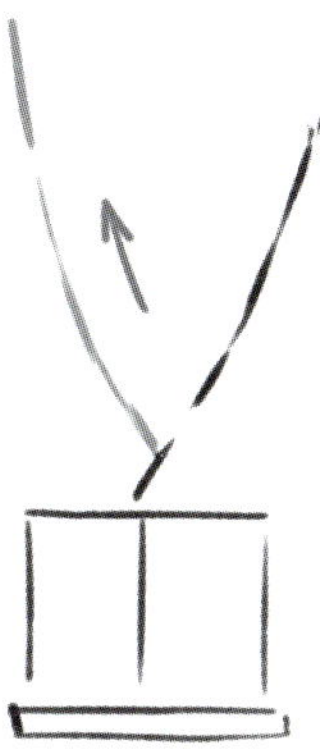

1 Start by sketching the overall shape, like a large V.

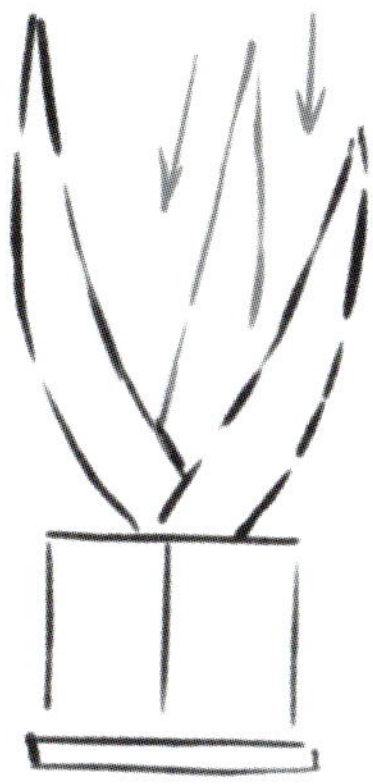

2 Add the largest leaves first.

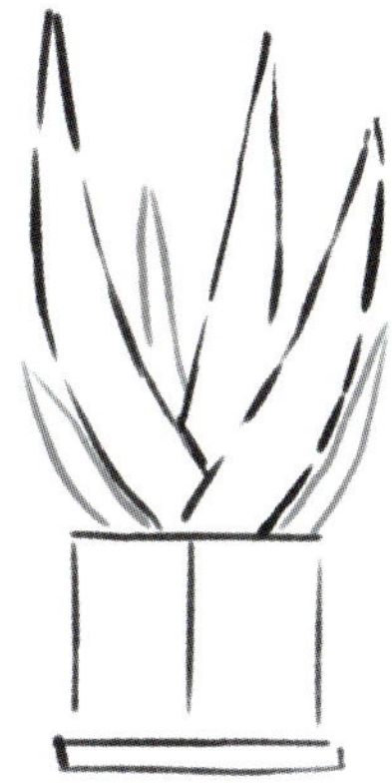

3 Once you have the bigger leaves in place, add the smaller ones in a balanced manner, positioning them here and there to create a natural, layered look.

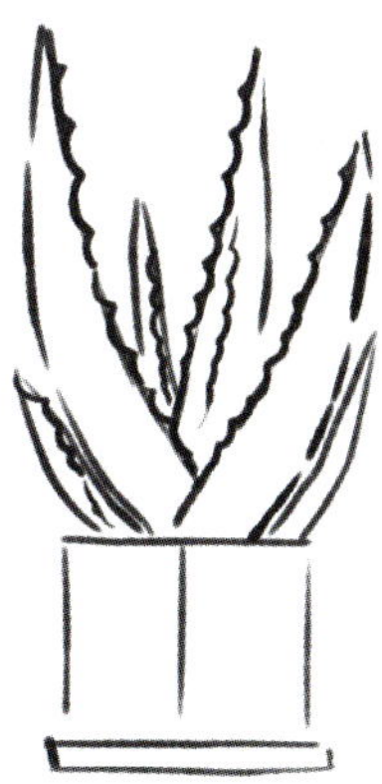

4 One of the most characteristic features of an aloe leaf is its spiky edge. Add a small, scalloped line along the edge of each leaf to give it that distinctive texture.

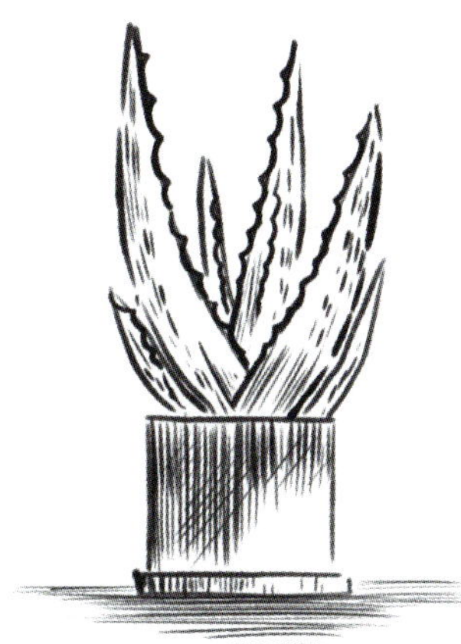

5 Add small marks and hatching lines to create shadows. Don't forget to leave plenty of white space for highlights to bring out the light and depth in your drawing.

STEP BY STEP:

SPRING FLOWERS

Now let's draw a few of the most popular flowers that brighten gardens, parks, and woods after a long winter.

Tulip

Tulips are a great way to show the spring season in your drawings. They look lovely under trees or in flower compositions, and because everyone knows their relative size, they help add scale to the scene.

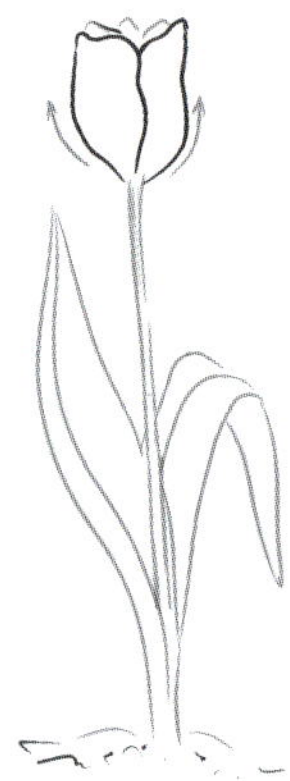

1 Start with the head of the flower using irregular, curvy lines.

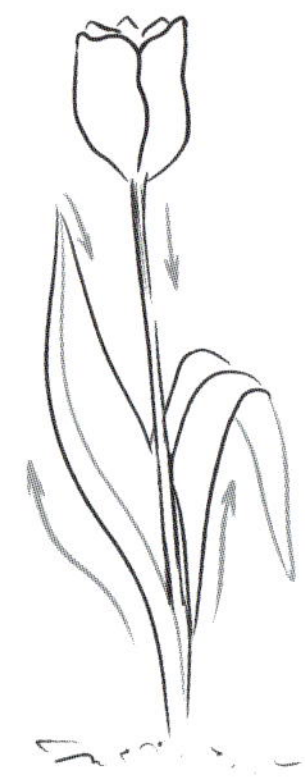

2 Add the stems and leaves, and balance their proportions.

3 For shading, use vertical hatching—drawing lines up and down with varied heights and occasional breaks. This simple technique adds texture, highlights, and a reflective feel. Making a few lines bolder will also enhance volume and depth.

Try drawing some variations on the tulip. You can group them together to create a scene.

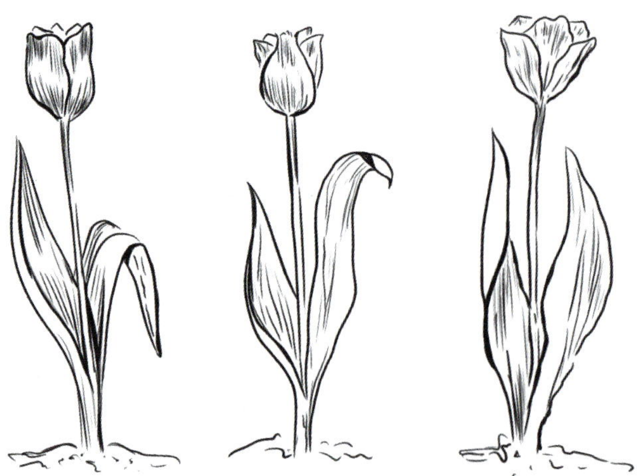

Daffodil

Daffodils are one of my favorite flowers. Their cheerful yellow blossoms are one of the first signs of spring.

1 Start with the center. Draw a few lines to suggest the placement of the petals.

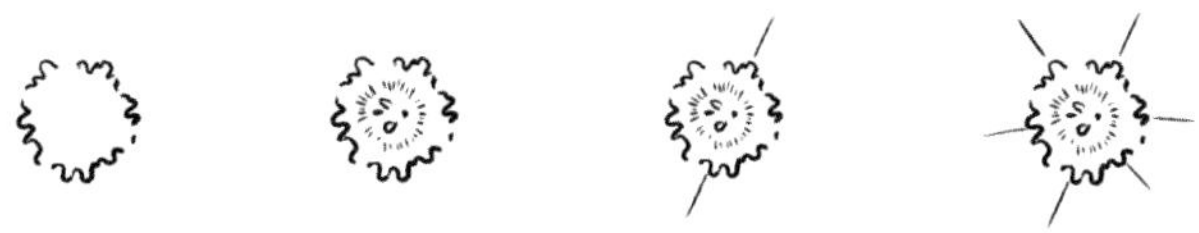

2 Add the petals one by one. Slightly vary the outlines of the petals for a more natural look. Add a few hatching lines with light strokes to create some texture, highlights, and shadows. Draw a stem with two parallel lines at an angle.

3 Add narrow leaves typical for daffodils.

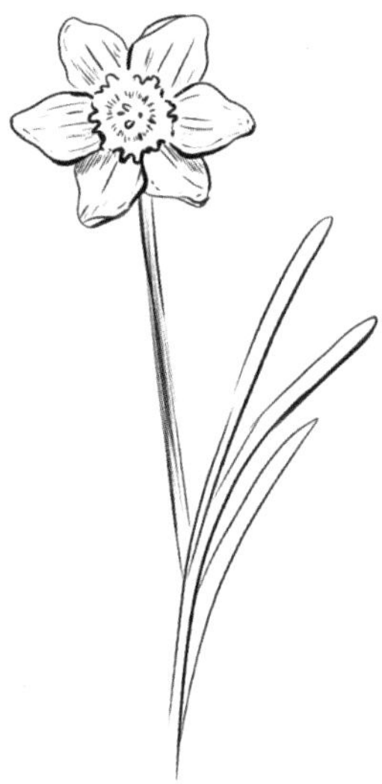

Scan to watch a tutorial.

4 Some extra line weight and hatching lines on the leaves create a three-dimensional and dynamic look. You can also add the bulb, partially visible as if it's growing from the ground.

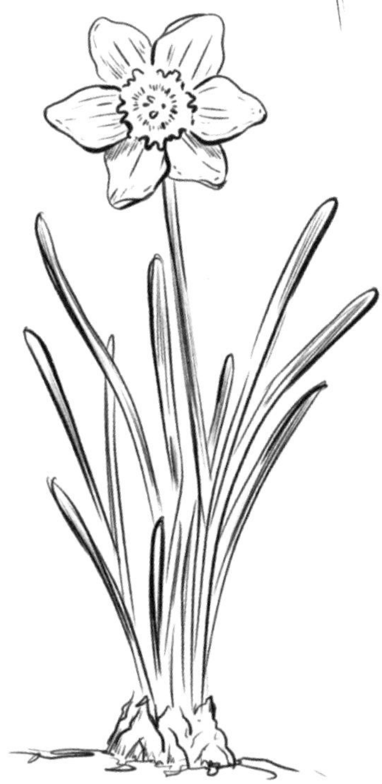

Hyacinth

A hyacinth "flower" is made up of lots of small blossoms. Vary the sizes and directions of the flower doodles. Draw just a few petals to fill gaps or add detail around the edges.

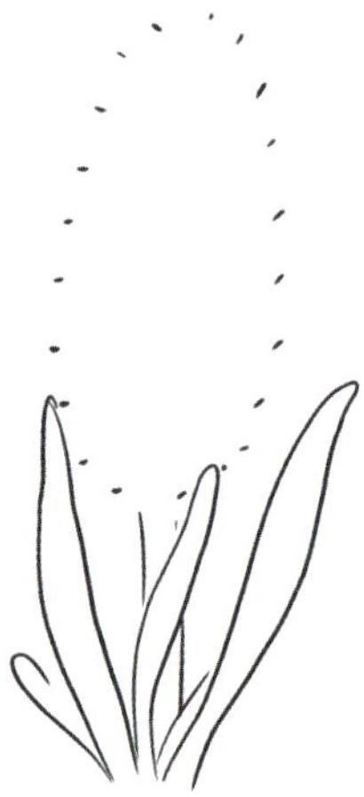

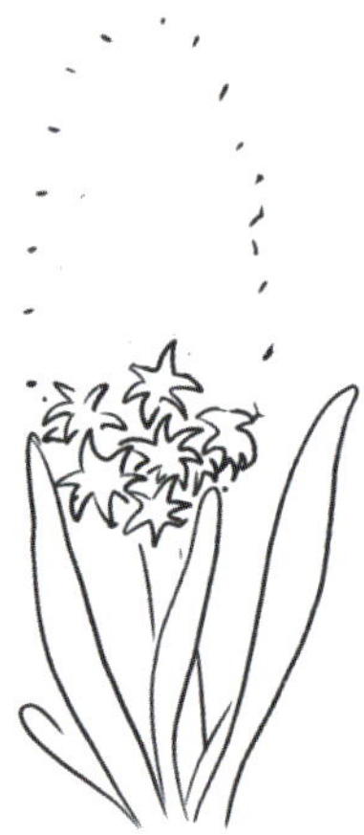

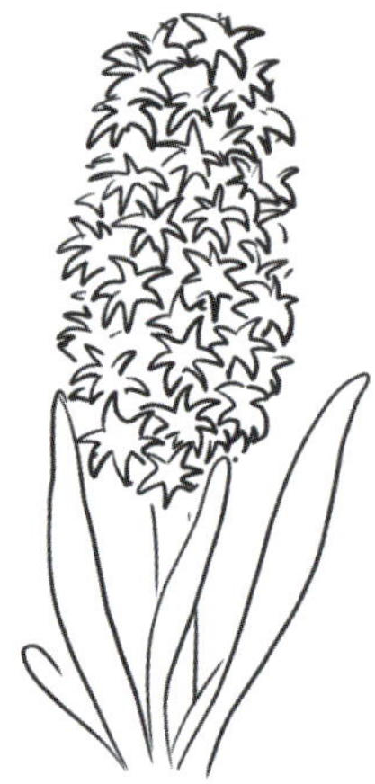

1 Start with the leaves and outline the oval shape.

2 Fill the shape with overlapping starlike flowers. Hyacinth can be starlike with pointy tips or have rounded petal tips, depending on its type.

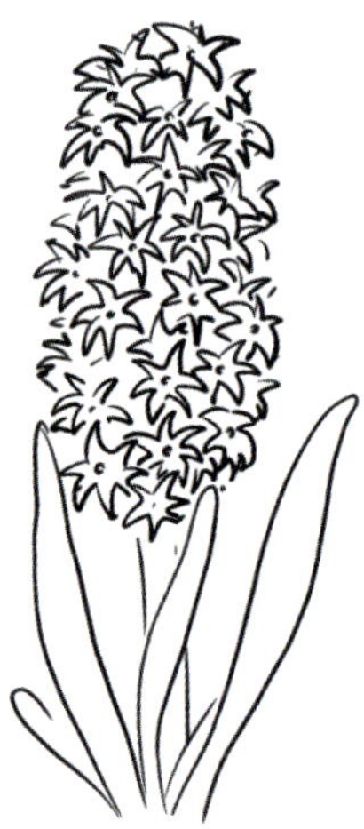

3 Add a circle inside each star-shaped flower.

4 Darken the space around the flowers and add texture to the leaves and the ground.

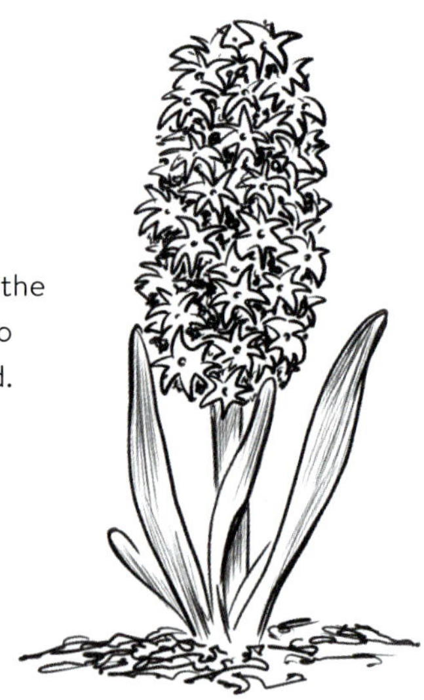

STEP BY STEP:

GARDEN PLANTS

Try your hand at drawing these plants. You'll get to draw many types of leaves and flowers, which will help you build your skills to draw any type of plant.

Geranium

This drawing was inspired by a photo I took during an evening walk. The quality was not the best, but what counts is that I suddenly saw the shape and had an aha moment that I could draw it. It's a good idea to look for subjects you can photograph. Look for contrast in light and shadow and interesting subjects and compositions.

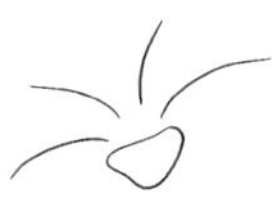

1. Begin by drawing the first petal and adding guiding lines for the other four petals.

2. Create the remaining petals around your guiding lines, ensuring they are balanced.

3. Add light texture lines to the petals to enhance their volume and shape. Draw the center of the flower, including stamens or pistils.

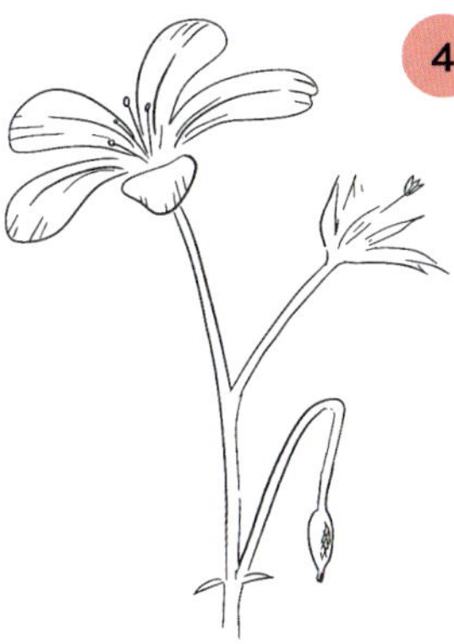

4. Sketch the stem with slightly curved lines and add the other flowers, one with no petals and another as a small bud.

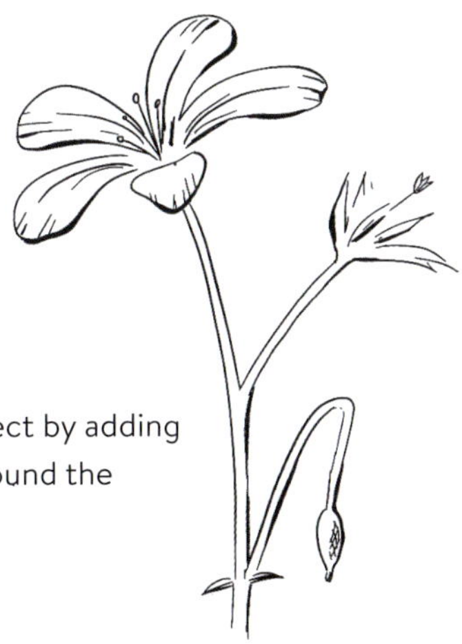

5. Enhance the 3D effect by adding extra line weight around the edges of the petals.

Daisy

Daisies are a great subject for drawing because they are simple yet charming. Their petal shape is easy to draw, but you can add variations to make them look more natural. This makes daisies perfect for practicing texture and detail. They are also easy to remember, so with a bit of practice, you can draw them from memory and doodle them anytime. It's a fun and effective exercise!

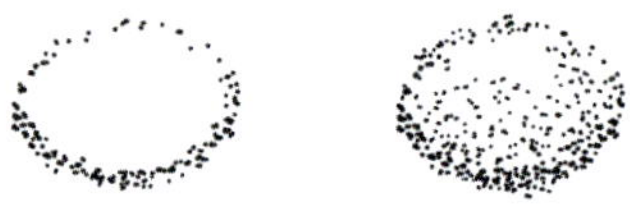

1 Start by drawing an oval for the center of the flower using a dot outline, which is easy to correct. Add more dots on one side of the center for volume and depth.

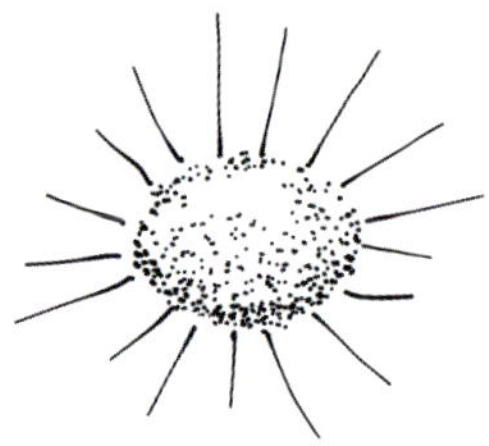

2 Draw guiding lines radiating outward from the circle for the petals.

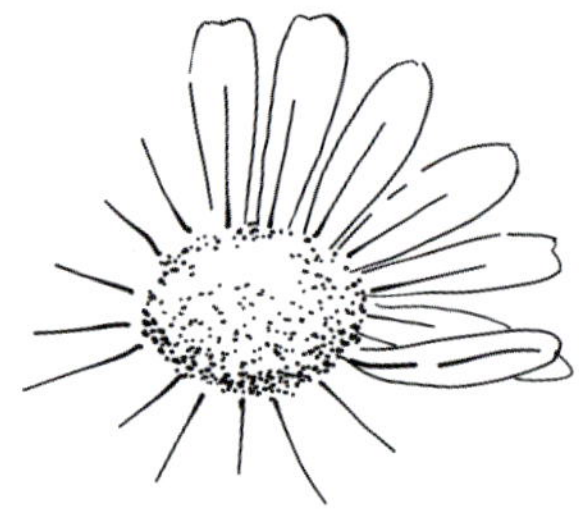

3 Draw the petals one by one, varying their shapes and overlapping some.

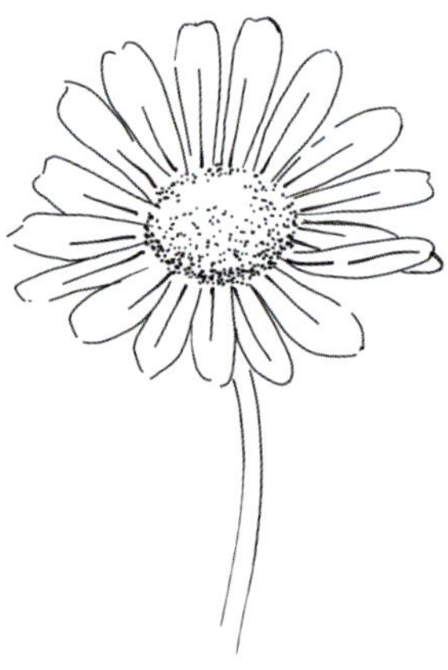

4 Complete the rest of the petals and add a stem.

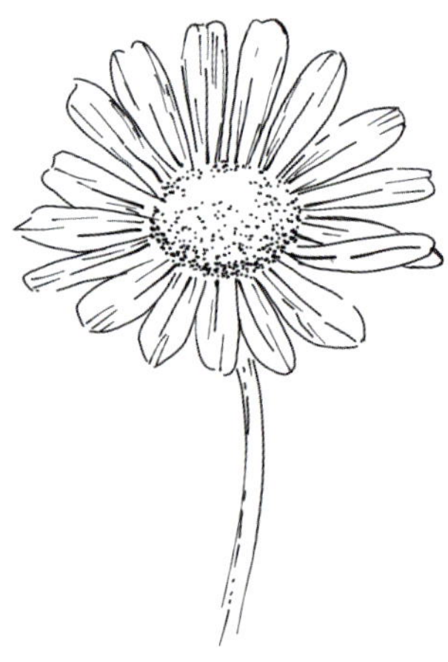

5 Add light texture lines to the petals.

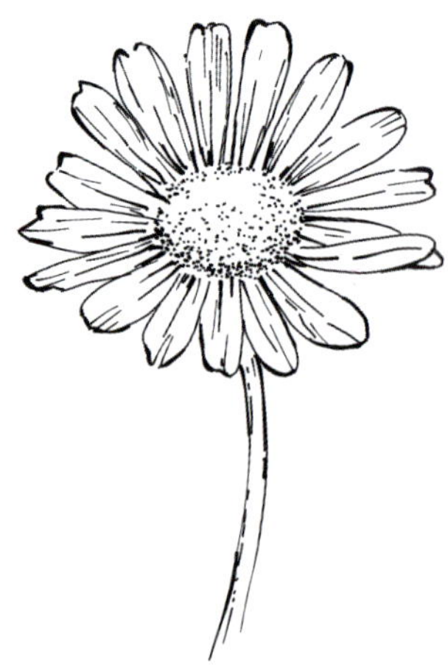

6 Finally, add extra line weight for volume.

A Variety of Flowers and Grasses

We'll now sketch a whole bunch of beautiful perennial flowers and grasses. Use what you've learned with the other exercises to follow along with the step drawings. Remember that practice, not perfection, is what counts—especially with plants!

Purple moor-grass (*Molinia caerulea*)

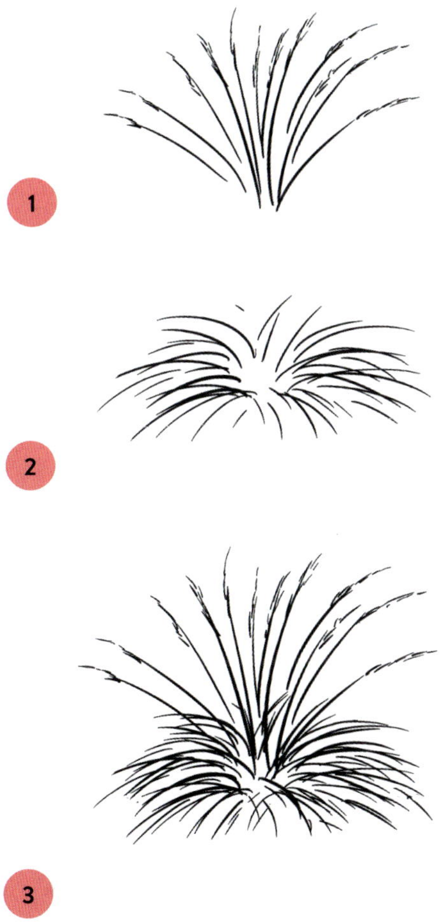

Blacksamson echinacea (*Echinacea angustifolia*)

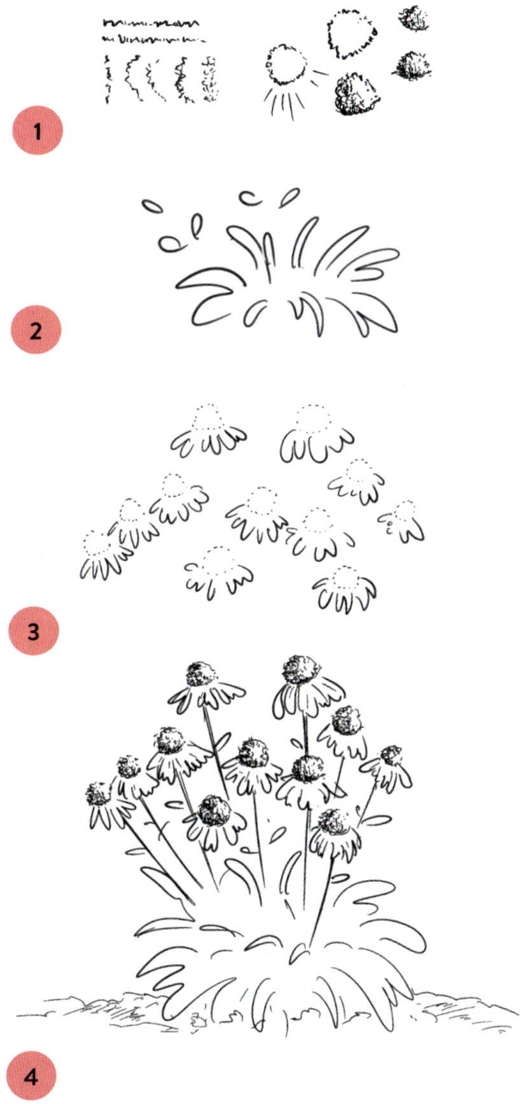

Scan to watch a tutorial.

Elephant ears (*Bergenia crassifolia*)

1 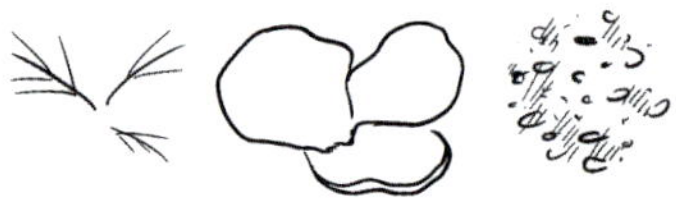

2 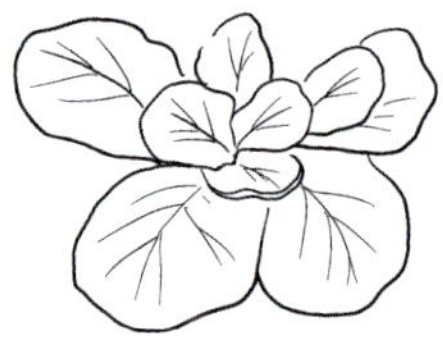

3 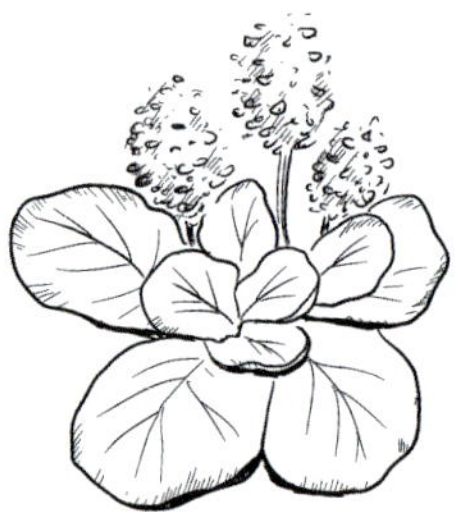

African feather grass (*Pennisetum macrourum*)

1 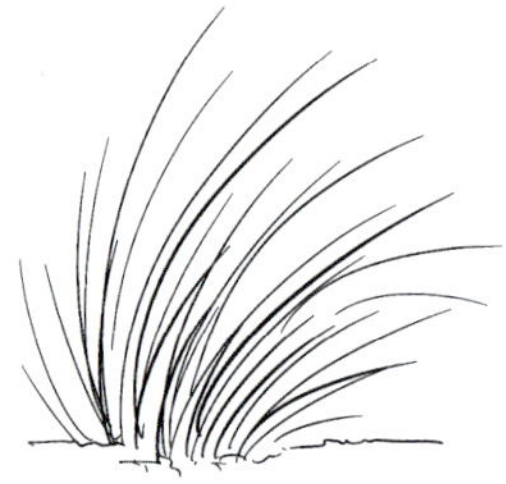

2 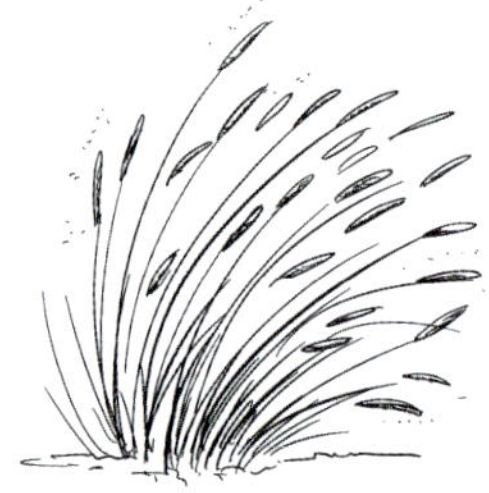

Lady's-mantle (*Alchemilla mollis*)

1 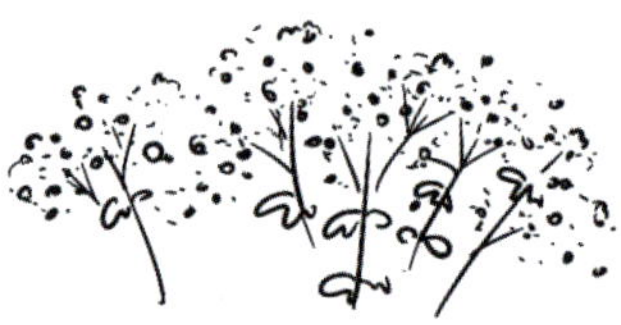

2 

3 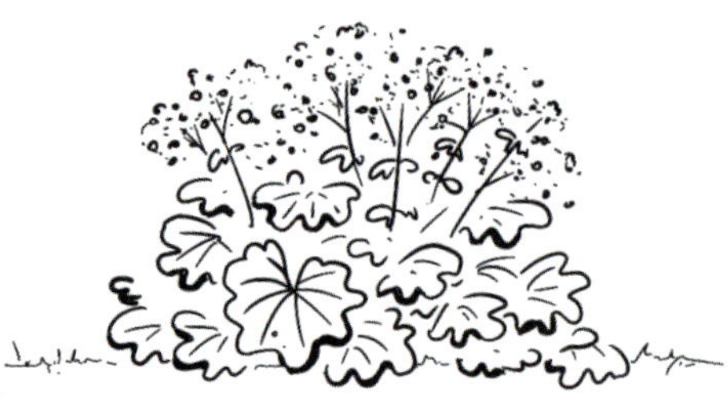

Prickly fescue (*Festuca punctoria*)

1 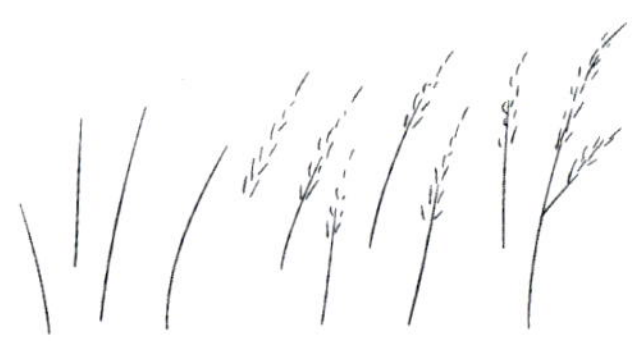

2 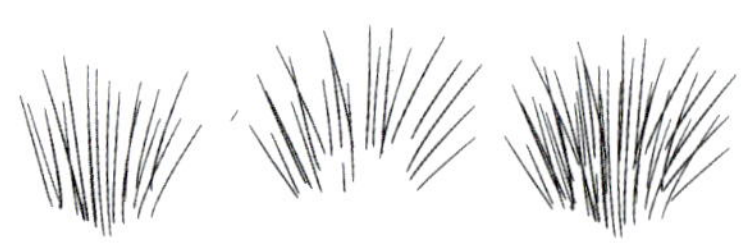

3 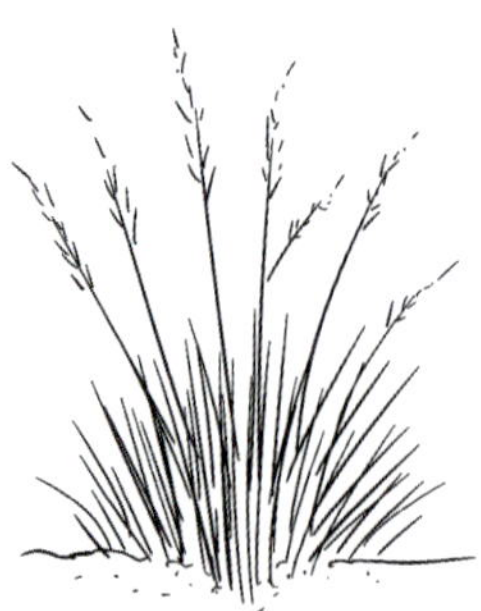

Blue globe thistle (*Echinops bannaticus*)

1 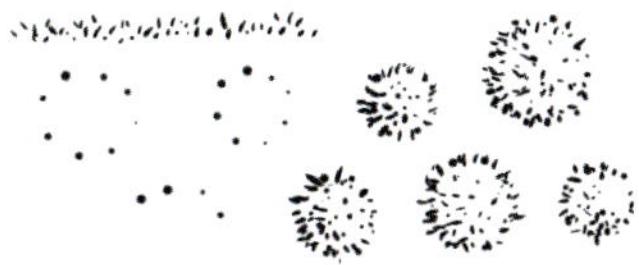

2 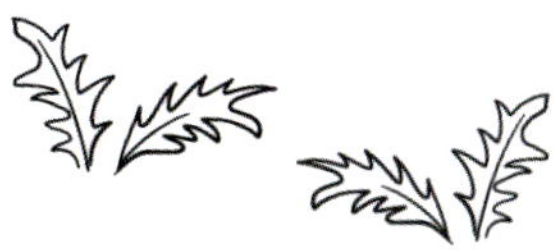

3 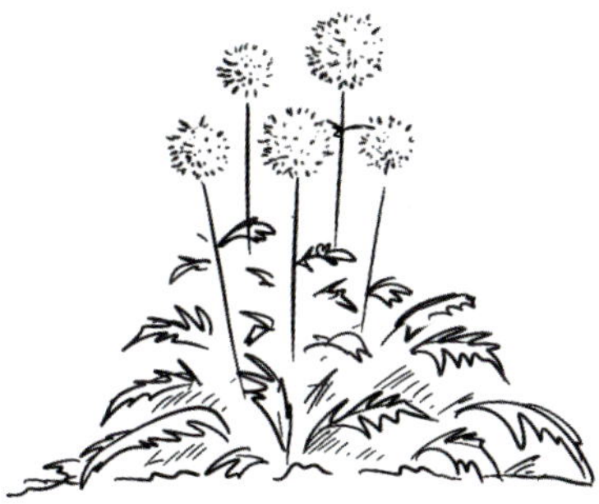

Alpine delphinium (*Delphinium elatum*)

1 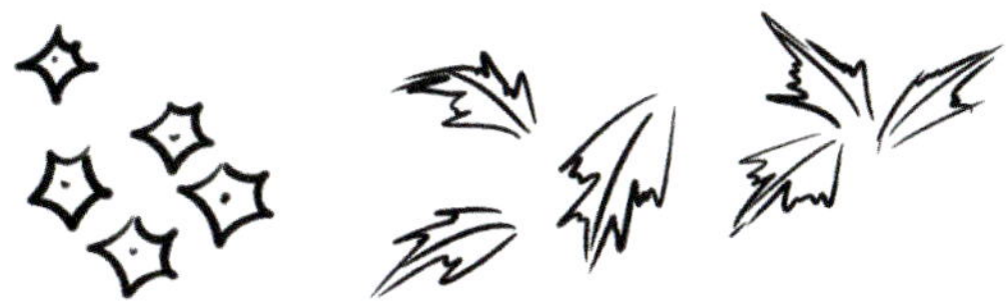

2 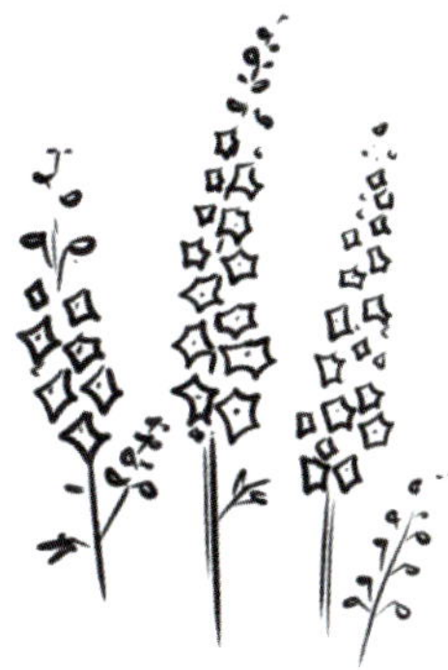

3 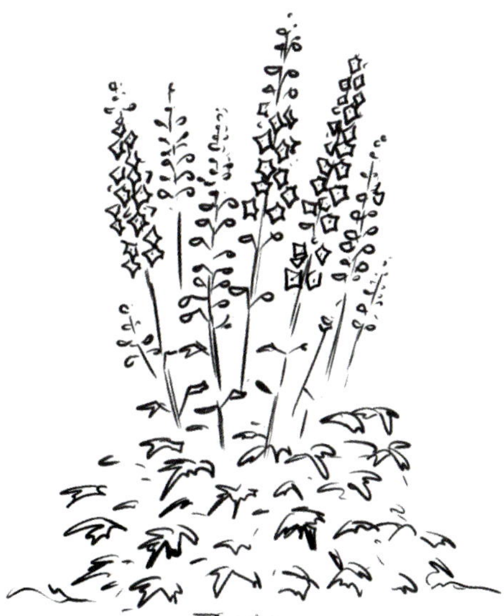

Dwarf beach-head iris
(*Iris setosa* ssp. *Canadensis*)

1 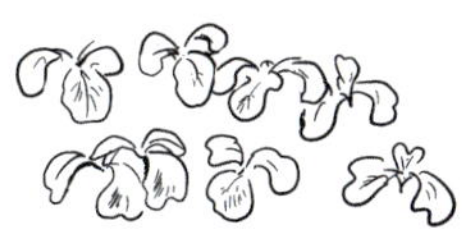

2 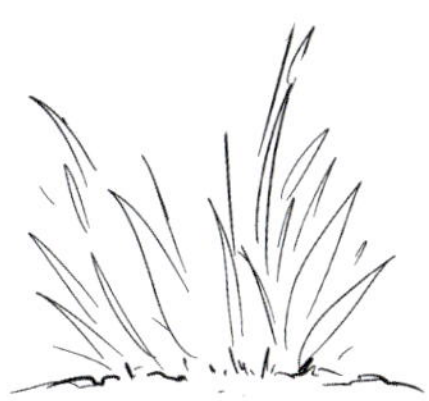

3 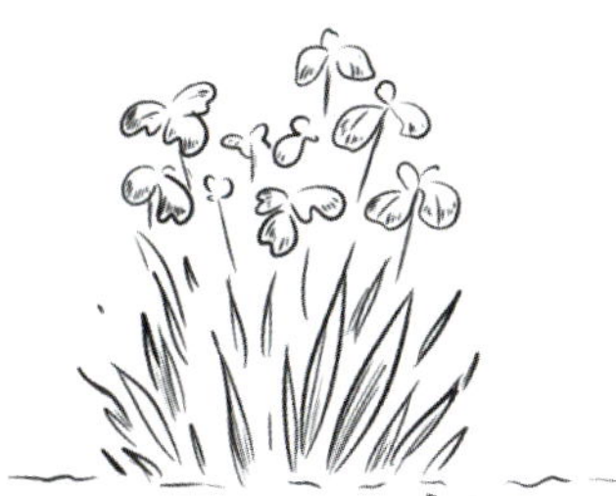

FLOWERS AND GRASSES COMPOSITION

Now that you've practiced drawing different flowers and plants, try putting a few together for a more complex composition. It's actually simpler than it looks! In this arrangement, we mix plants with different shapes and textures to keep things interesting. Even though they're different, they share some similarities. The composition repeats vertical elements like the iris leaves, delphinium flowers, and even the grasses. These plants echo each other through their shapes, creating a sense of unity. The flowers of the iris and the leaves of the delphinium have a similar pattern, which ties everything together.

The composition forms a triangular arrangement with the tallest plant in the center. This helps guide the viewer's eye

1 Start with the iris on the left.

2 Add the delphinium in the center. You can begin with the flowers at the top and work your way down to the leaves or vice versa—whichever feels most natural to you.

3 Finally, draw the grasses on the right.

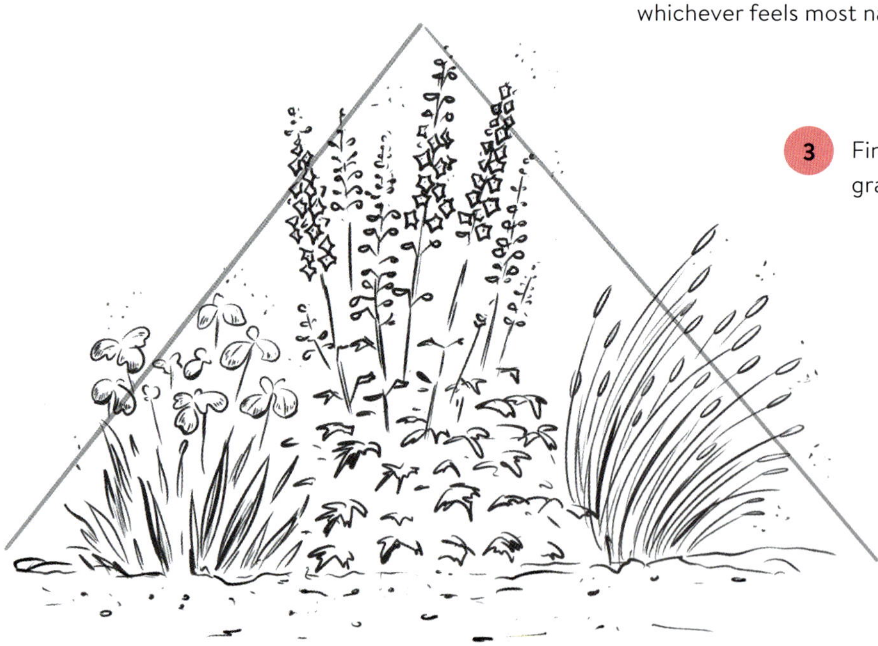

Scan to watch a tutorial.

across the drawing, creating a natural flow and a balanced feel.

Movement is essential to bring the composition to life. The gentle curves of the grasses guide the eye and add fluidity.

Small details, such as tiny dots on the ground or little bugs around the flowers, unify everything in a playful and cohesive way.

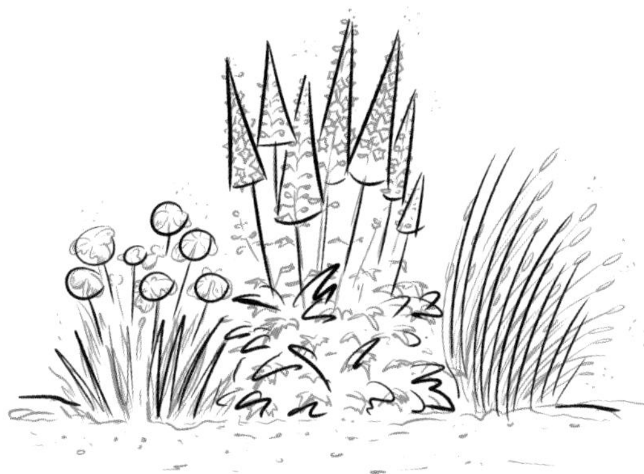

Use a variety of shapes.

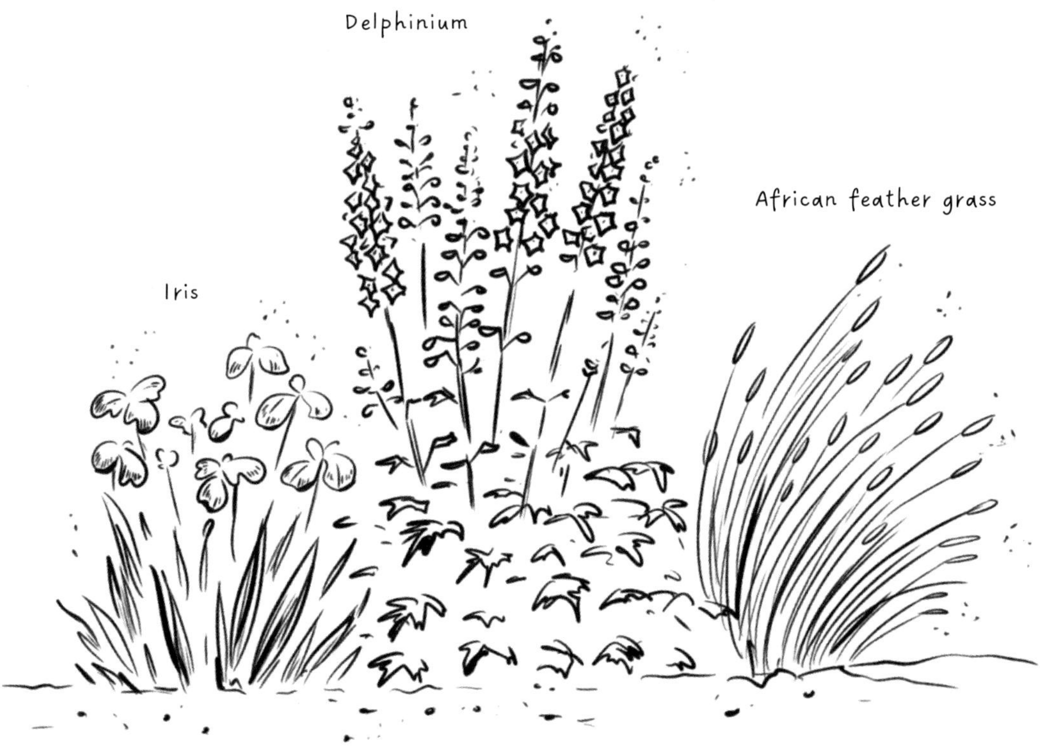

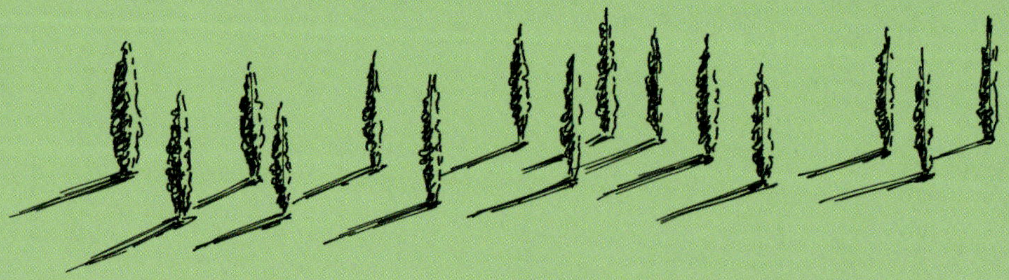

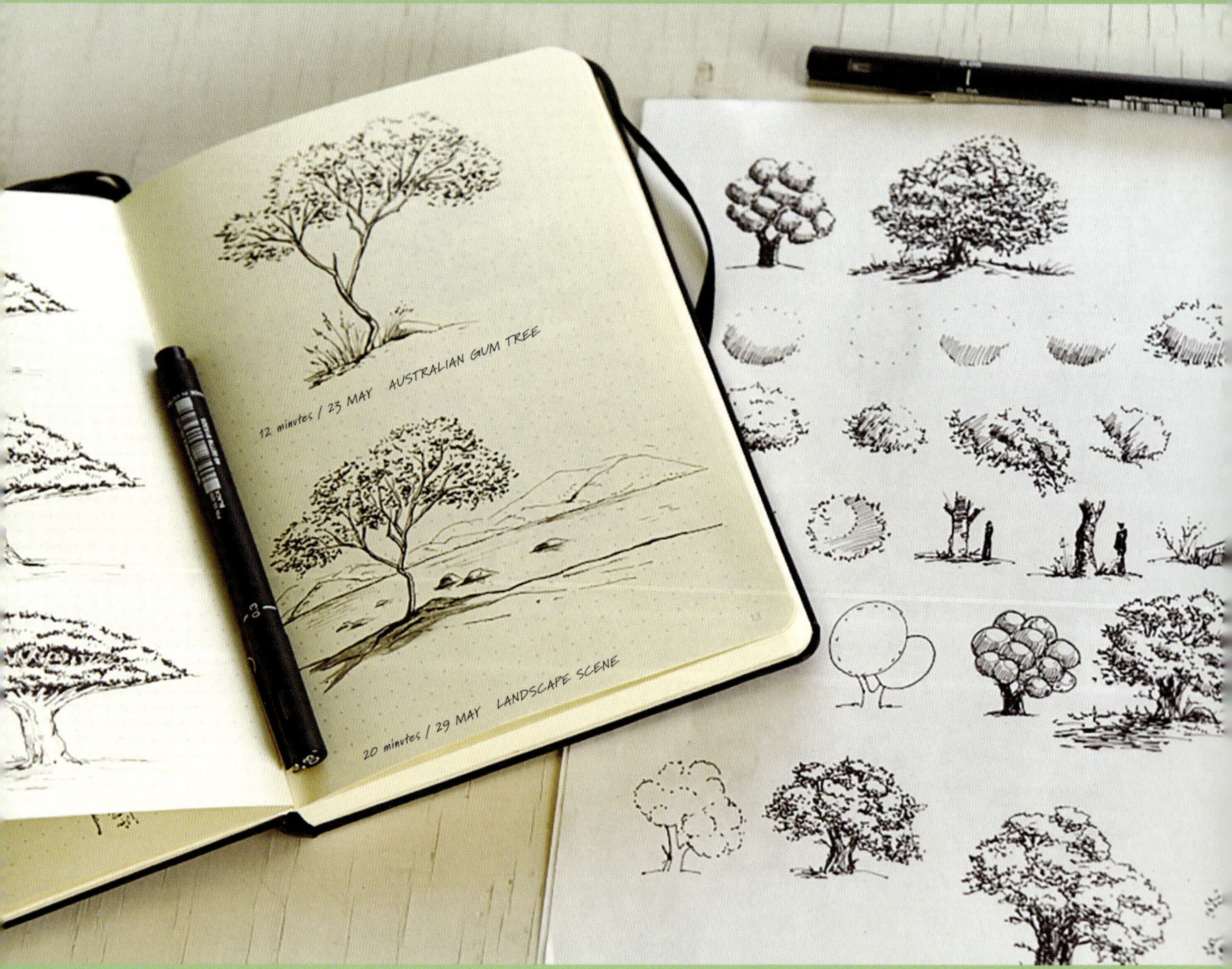
12 minutes / 23 MAY   AUSTRALIAN GUM TREE
20 minutes / 29 MAY   LANDSCAPE SCENE

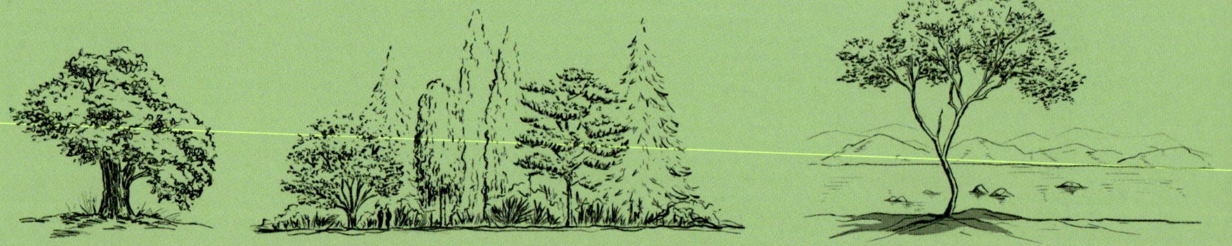

4

DRAWING TREES AND SHRUBS

In this chapter, you'll learn how to sketch trees and shrubs by focusing on their unique shapes, proportions, and textures. You'll explore different techniques for adding depth and volume, as well as capturing the variety of tree forms and foliage. Understanding these details will help you create realistic and dynamic landscapes. As you practice, you'll find that sketching trees becomes more natural, whether you're drawing them from reference or right in front of you outdoors.

TREE SILHOUETTES

First, let's practice drawing silhouettes, or outlines, of common trees, focusing on the proportions and overall shape of each tree. Use a central line to indicate the height and another to mark the width and/or the starting point of the trunk. This will help keep the proportions balanced.

Scan to watch a tutorial.

Cypress

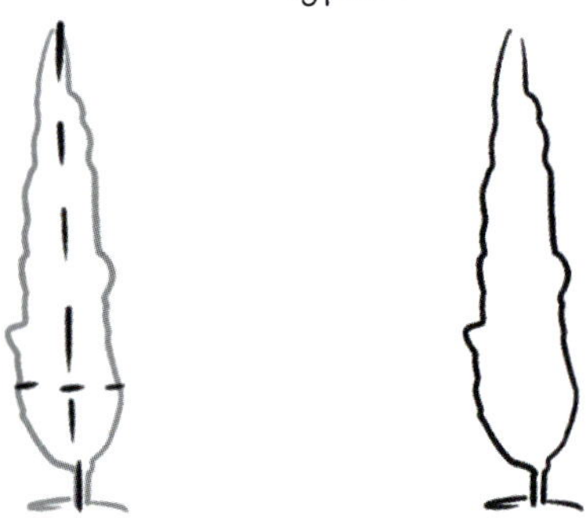

Willow

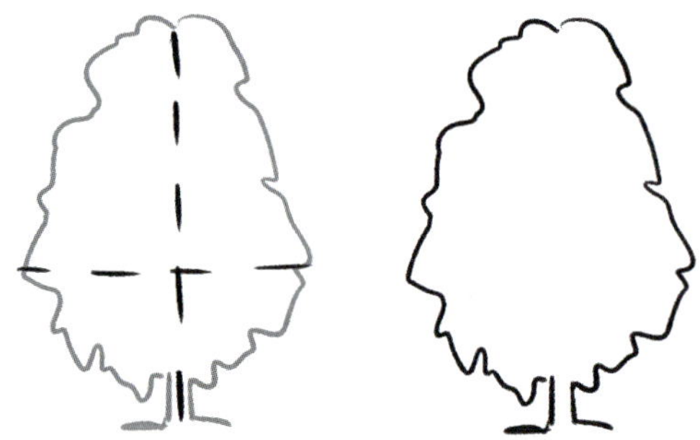

Shore pine

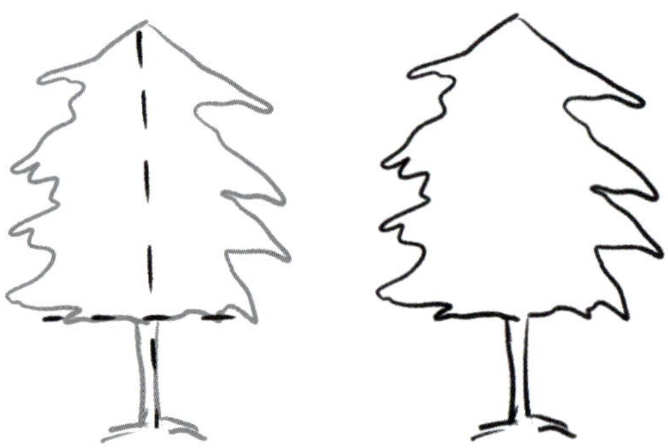

Poplar

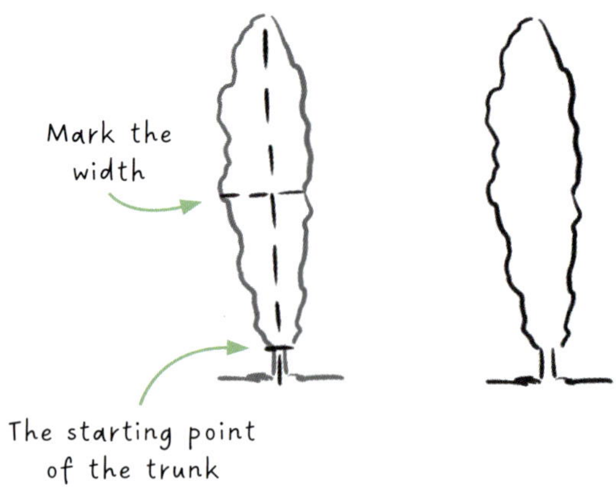

Birch

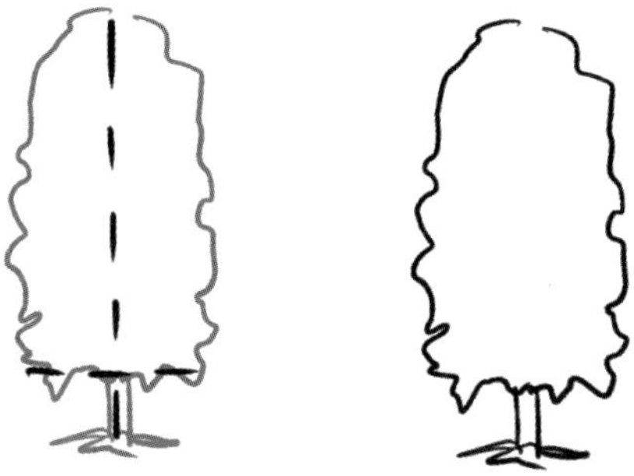

Apple

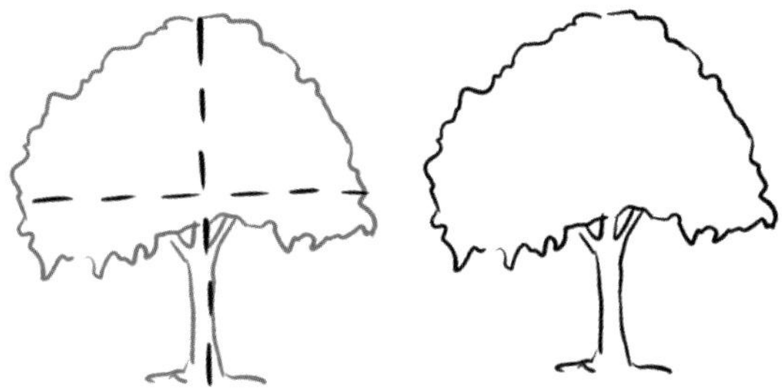

Maple

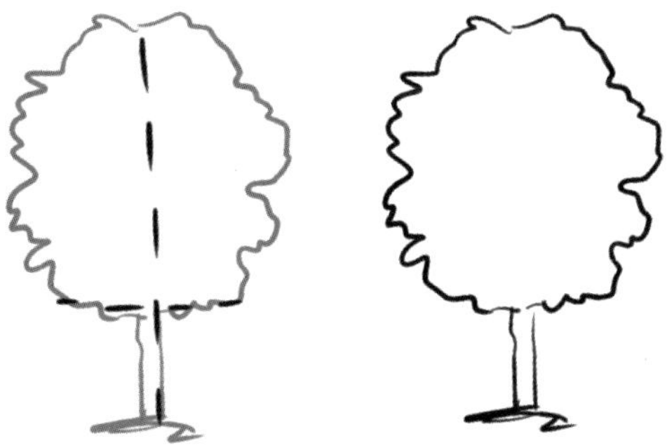

Sequoia

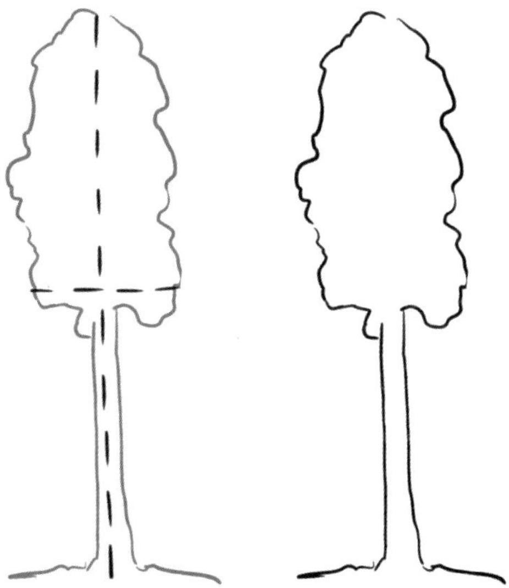

Oak

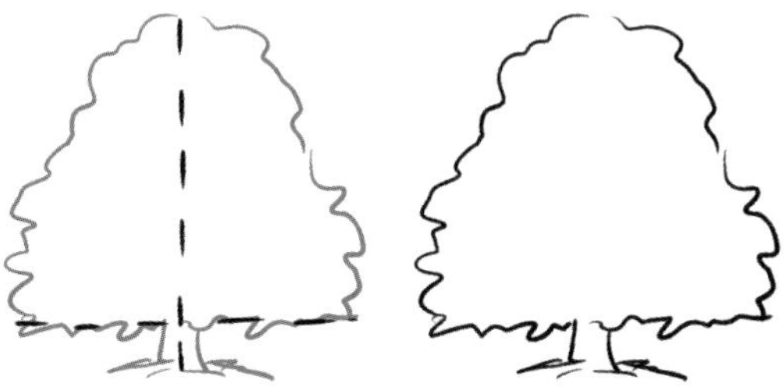

SKETCHING AERIAL VIEWS OF TREES

This practice focuses on drawing trees from an aerial perspective. You'll explore different tree shapes, practice the principle of repetition, and add shadows to create depth and dimension in your sketches. We'll use similar techniques later when we draw people.

Randomly place the trees for a natural, unstructured look. This creates a more organic and realistic composition. Repeat similar tree shapes to practice the principle of repetition. Don't worry about making each tree identical—small differences make the grouping look more natural.

Use light outlines to shape the trees and mark their placement. Try small dots, light strokes, or textured outlines—whatever feels most natural to you.

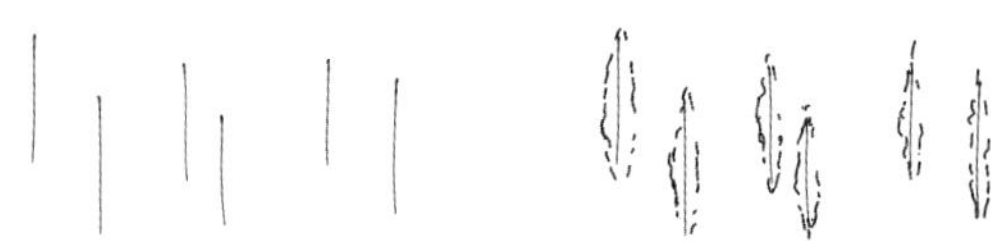

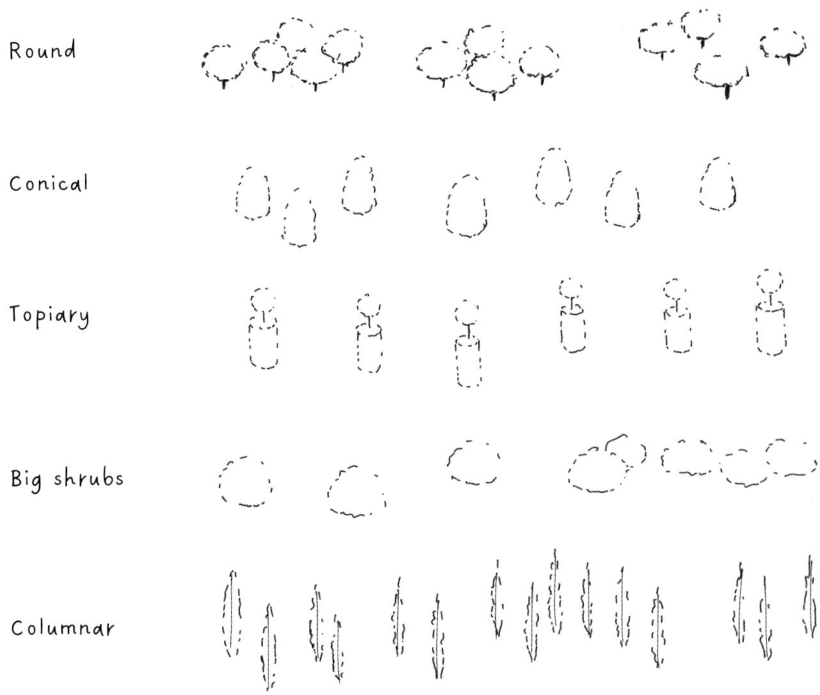

Add shadows to emphasize the aerial view. Shadows should be slightly distorted versions of the tree shapes. Keep them consistent with the light source, which is on the right in this exercise. Let the shadows fall away from the sun, but don't make them overly precise—this is meant to be a quick sketch!

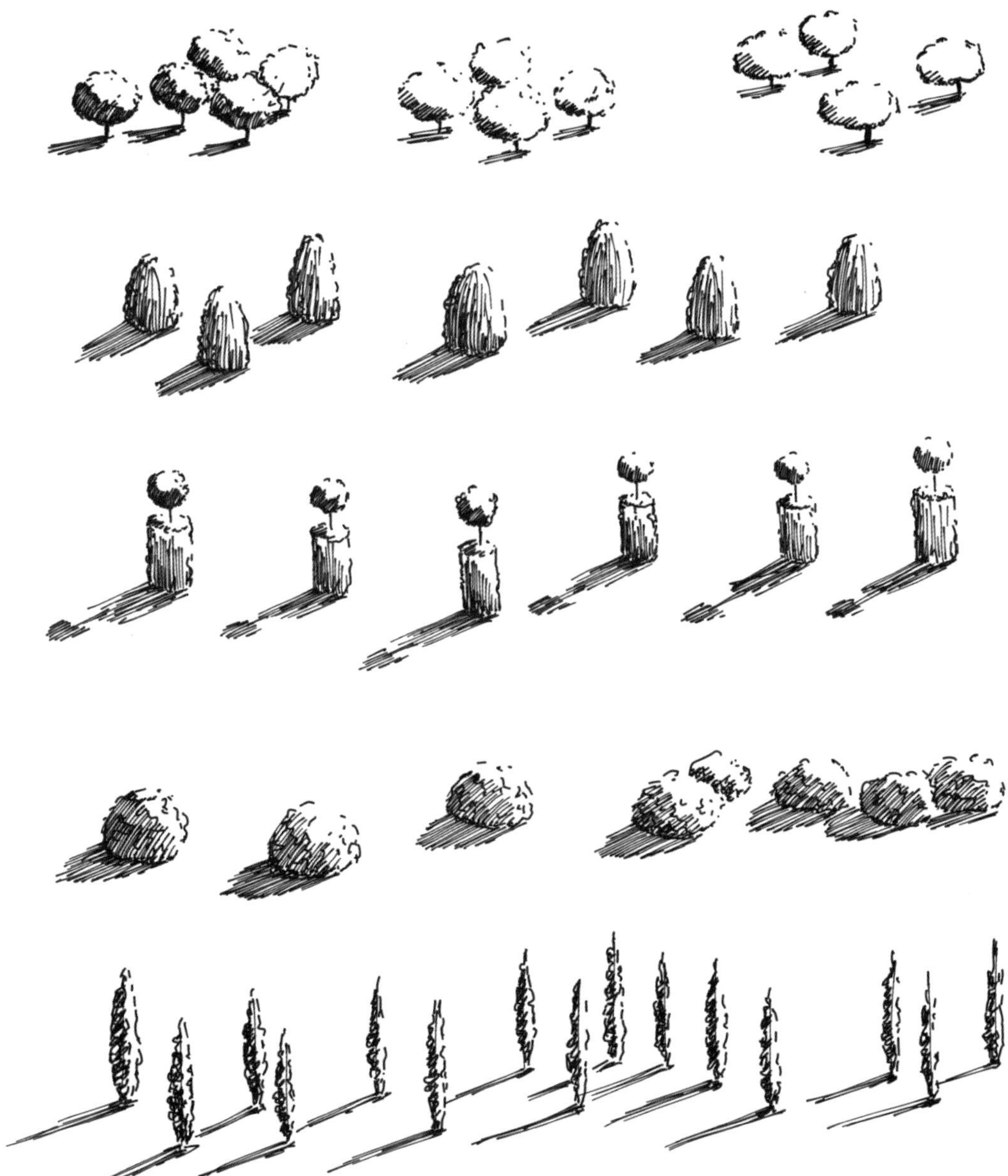

CREATING TEXTURE AND SHADING IN TREES

There are many ways to make your trees look more realistic and interesting. We'll look at a few fun techniques.

Stippling Technique

We'll practice drawing an individual tree and a group of two. Draw clusters of dots close together on the shaded side and use fewer dots on the lighter side. This drawing technique is called "stippling." With dots, you can also add some interest to the drawing; just add a few dots here and there on the ground.

I like this technique because it allows you to correct the outline and is surprisingly easy to use. The only drawback is that it's quite time-consuming, so keep your drawing small if you don't have much time for practice.

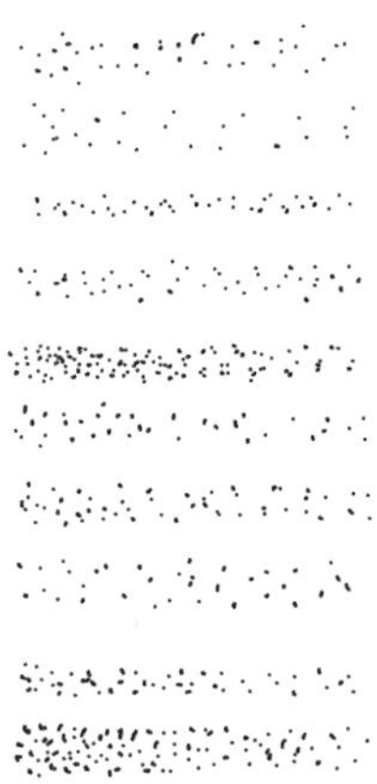

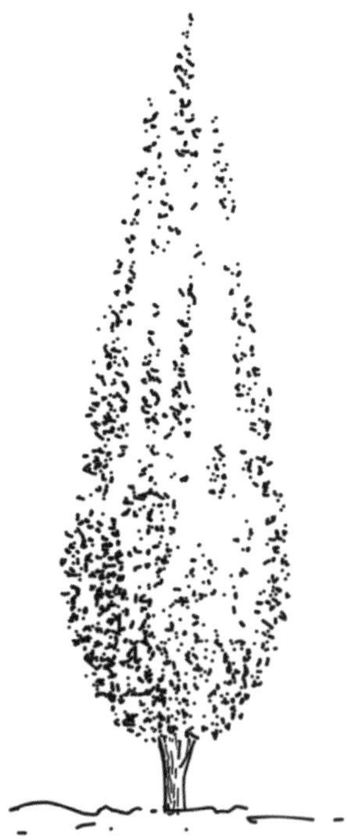

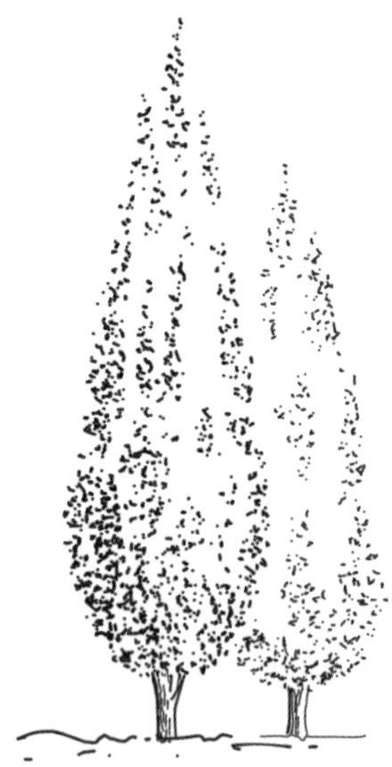

Notice how the tree behind is slightly smaller and lighter in outline. This adds depth to the composition.

Outline Variations

Cone-shaped trees like these are a fun way to practice the various types of lines we learned in chapter 2.

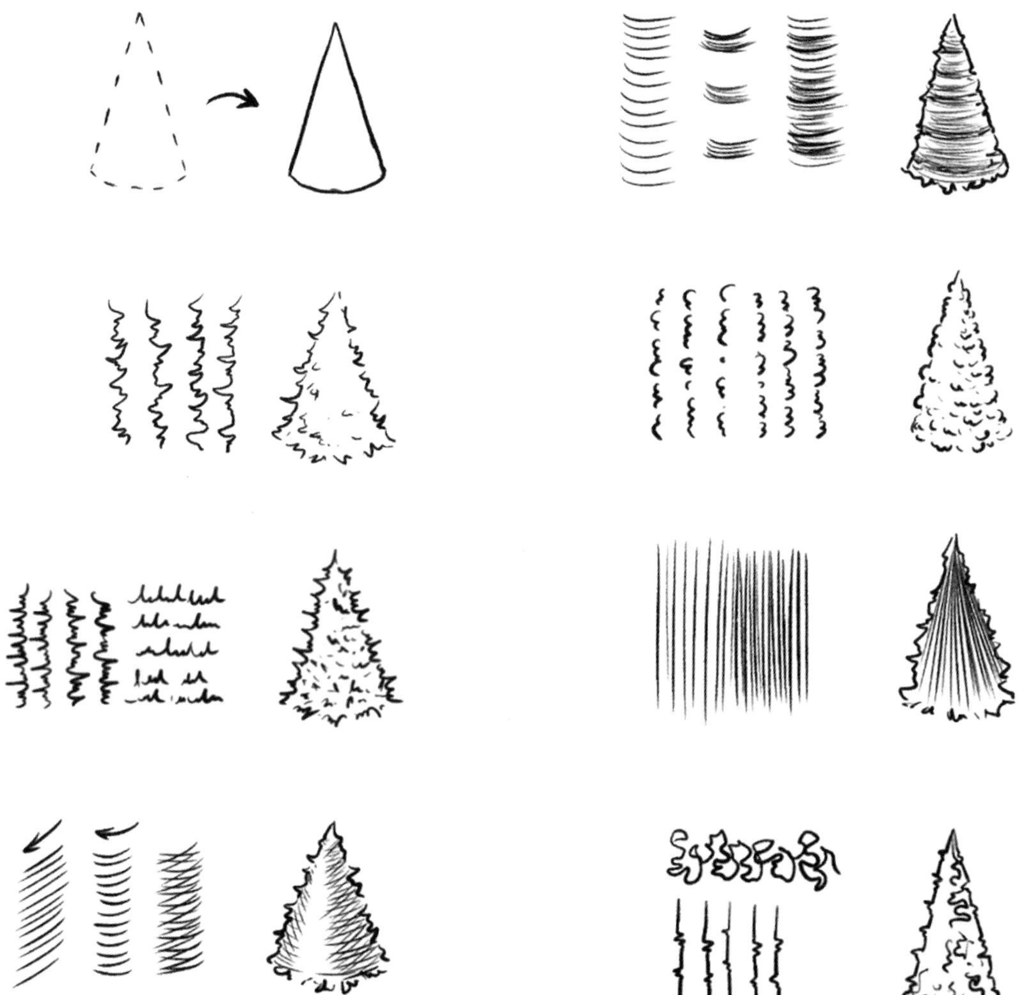

Scan to watch a tutorial.

Shading Techniques

Here are a couple ways to easily add shading to your trees, which will make them appear more lifelike.

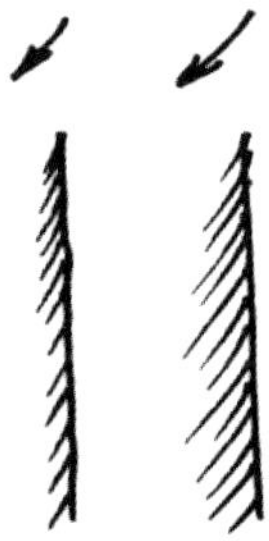

Practice lines following trunk's contour.

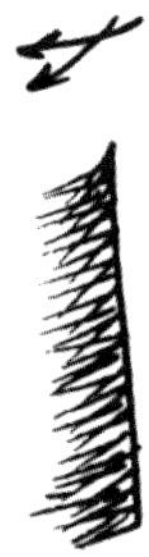

Practice lines following contour plus hatching.

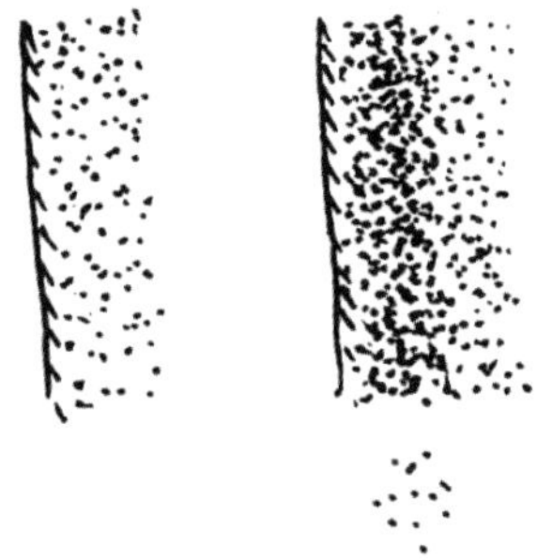

Stipple: Start with a base layer of stippling, using small dots to define the shape. Then, add more dots in certain areas to create contrast and volume.

Modified stipple with short strokes

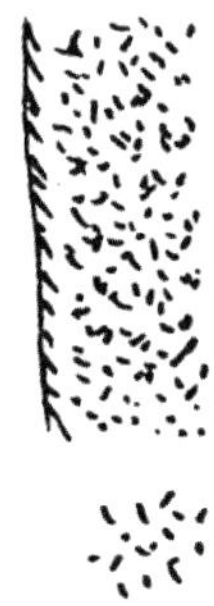

Practice on the trunk and branches.

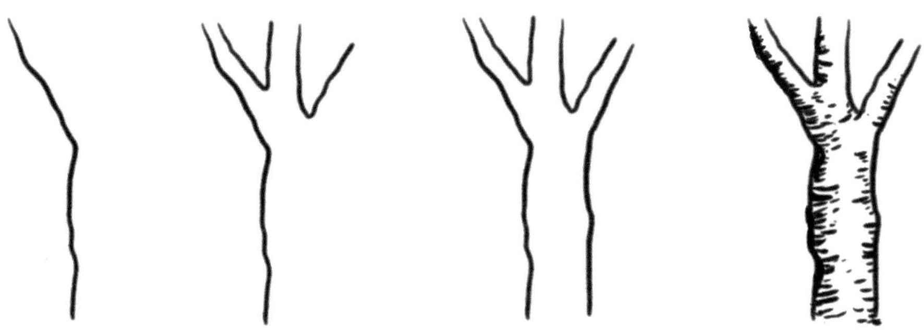

DRAWING A TREE TRUNK

You can practice drawing a tree trunk by using different basic lines like Heartbeat and Flow. Start with simple shapes to form the trunk, and then use these varied lines to capture the texture and details of the bark. Each line adds depth and interest, making your tree trunk feel more natural.

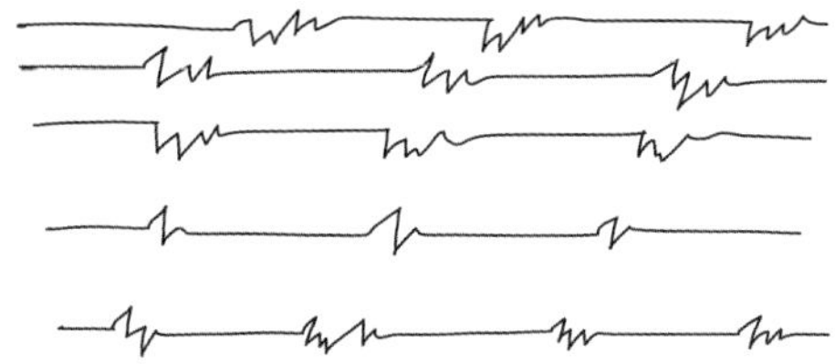

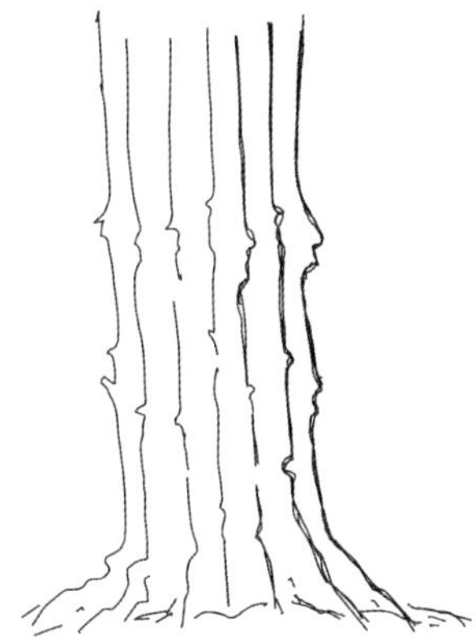

This is the Heartbeat line type. To create it, interrupt a straight line with a blip.

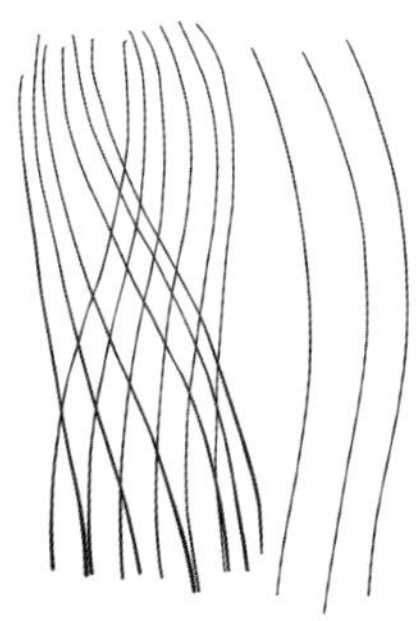

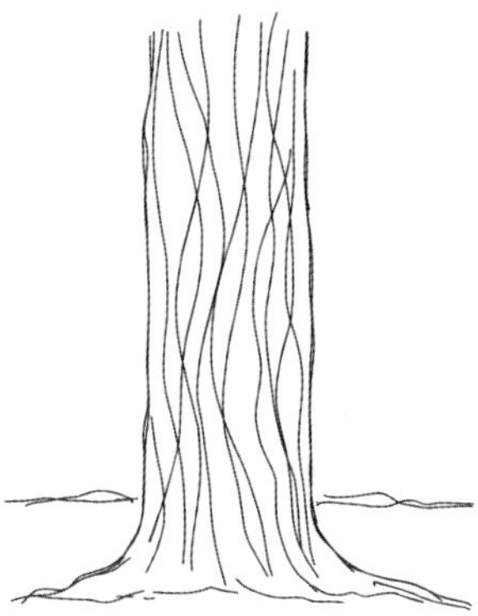

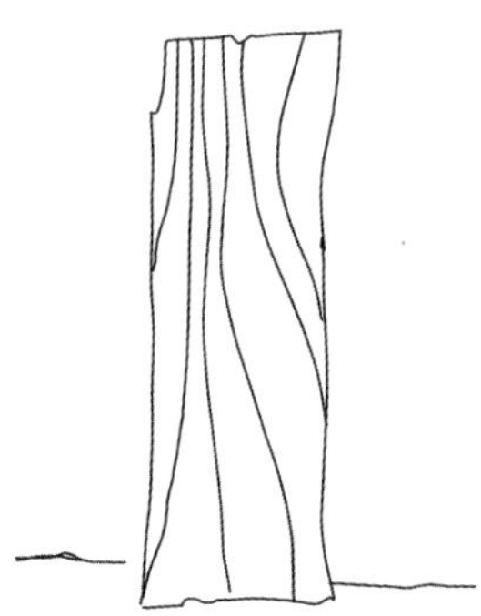

You can also use smooth, curved lines.

STEP BY STEP:

TREES

Now that we have practiced drawing silhouettes and textures of trees, let's put it all together to create some classic and more unusual types of trees.

Deciduous Tree

A deciduous tree is one that loses its leaves every fall. Here we are drawing a classic large deciduous tree. It helps to see a large tree as a combination of simple shapes like circles or organic forms.

Break It Down

First we'll learn to see big shapes before adding details.

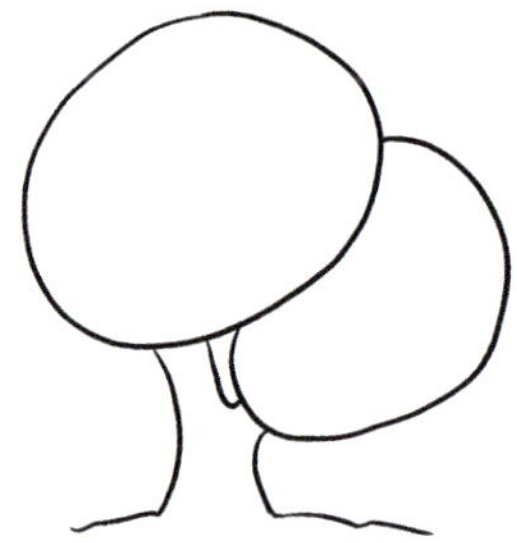

1 Start by dividing the tree into two parts.

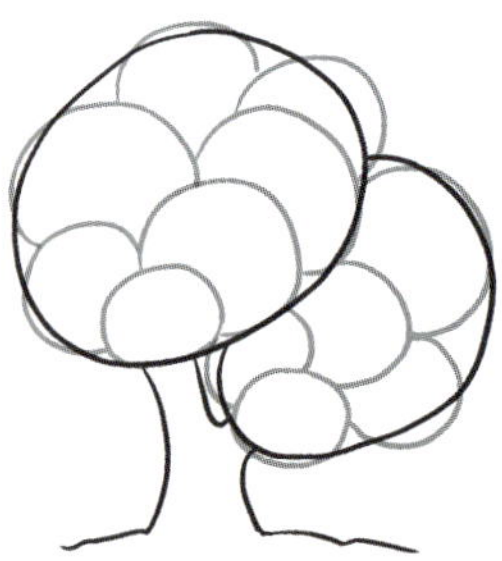

2 Fill in each part with simple shapes, varying their sizes.

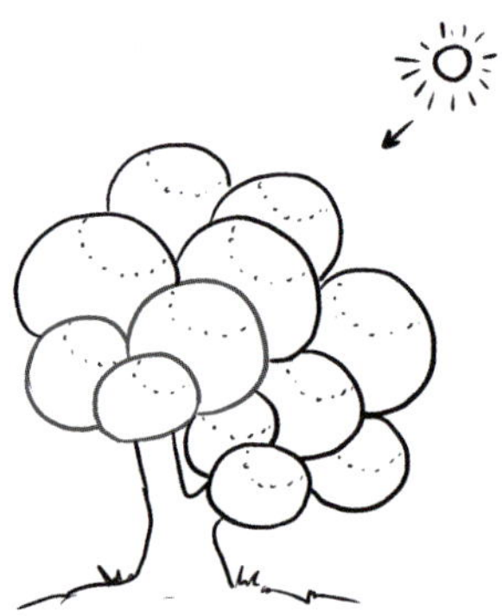

3 Establish the light source.

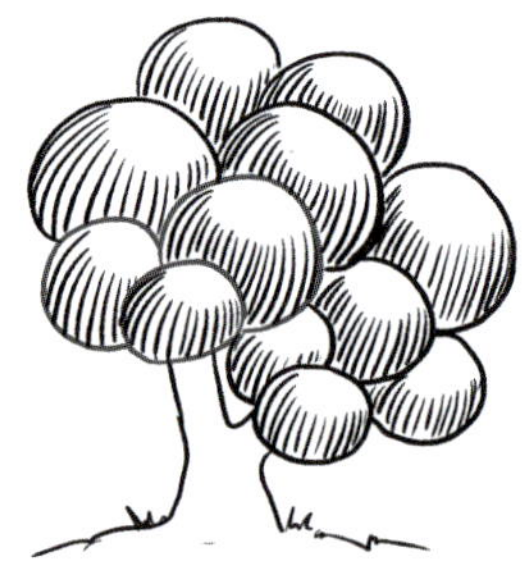

4 Add some hatching, then add more hatching on the lower part for the shadow. Experiment with different shapes and lines to find what works best for your tree.

Try the exercise again, but this time use small doodles to create foliage and a more natural shape. Add shading to the trunk and some grass to complete the scene.

1

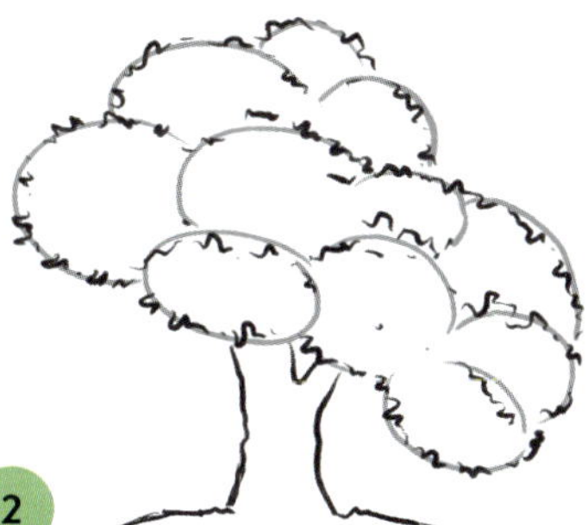

2

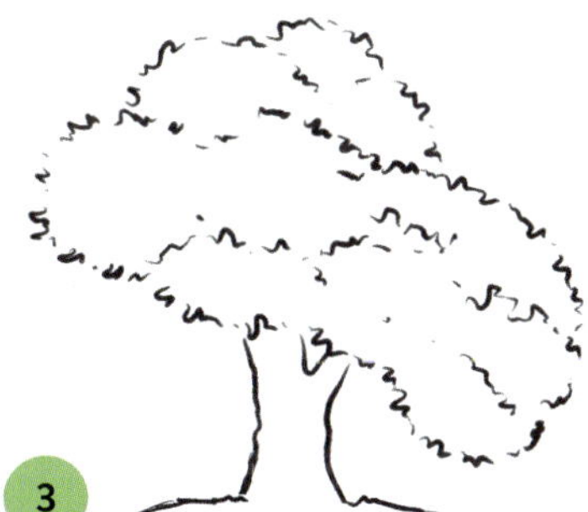

3

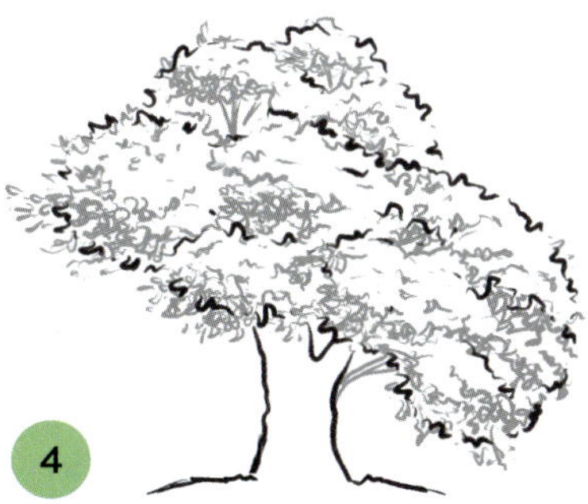

4

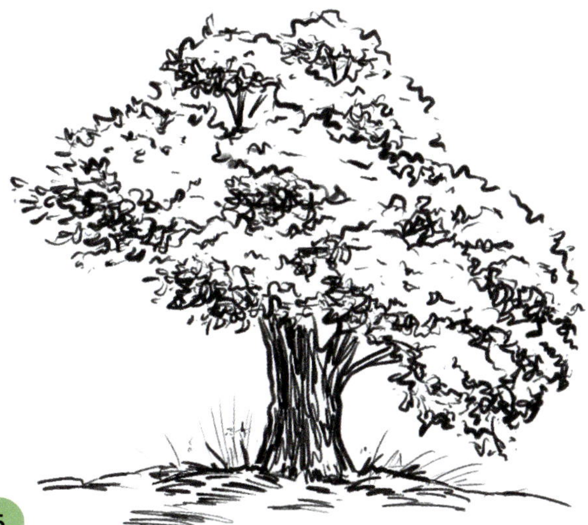

5

Scan to watch a tutorial.

Coniferous Tree

A coniferous tree, or conifer, is an evergreen tree that produces cones. They often have a triangular (cone) shape. The Swiss pine has a typical coniferous tree shape. Create wavy lines to imitate the shapes of the branches. Add separate strokes here and there to achieve a sketchy, realistic look. Notice how much white space you need to leave to make the appearance of the branches with needles.

Start by practicing your line work with short, controlled strokes. Keep them close together, following the natural flow of the branches. These same short strokes can also be used to create vegetation, like grasses or small plants, adding depth and texture to other areas of your drawings.

Focus on layering the strokes from the trunk outward, capturing the tree's unique shape and texture.

Swiss pine

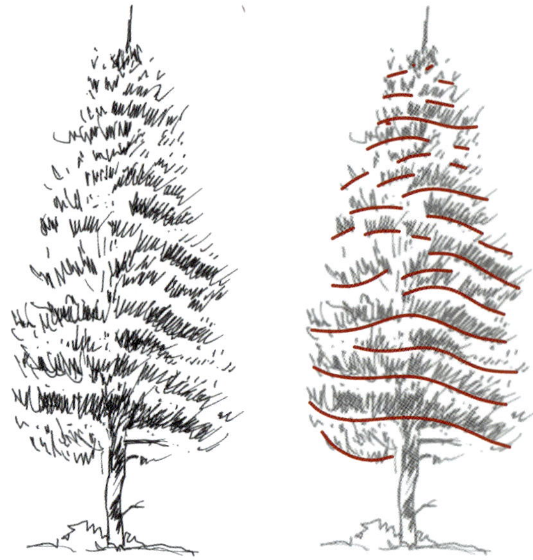

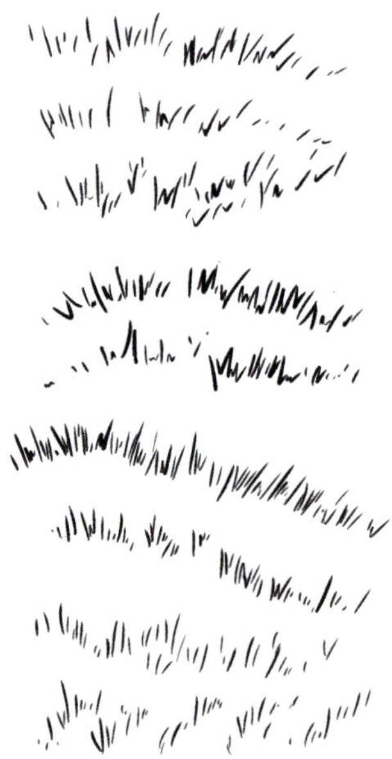

TIPS

- Strive to avoid rigid line-up doodles, like the ones shown below, unless they're part of the style you want to achieve.

- Remember to vary the direction and size of the strokes. Draw lightly from the top up and/or from up down.
- Add some line weight to create volume and contrast between highlights and shadows.

Weeping Tree

A drooping, or weeping, tree is drawn with a similar structure to the deciduous tree we drew earlier. The big difference is in the leaves, which create a beautiful cascade effect.

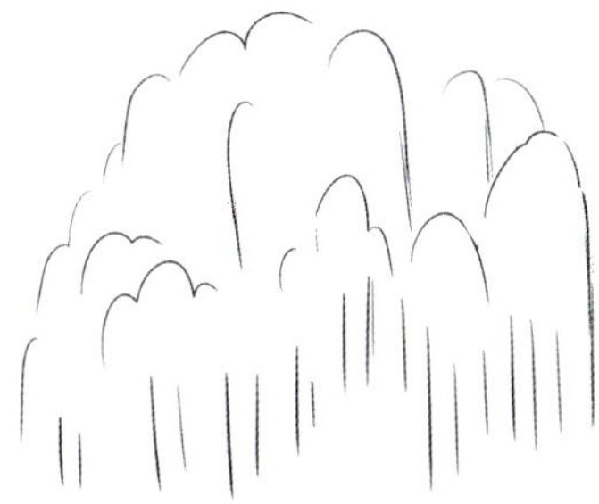

1. Start with a simple, light outline of the tree shape. Keep it loose and basic, just suggesting the tree's form.

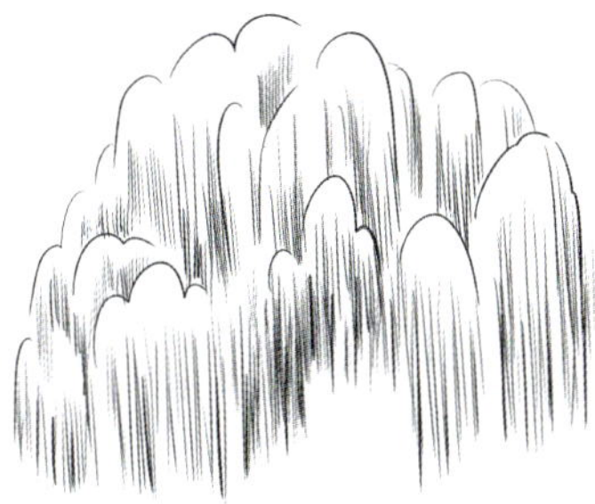

2. Begin adding more lines to the tree crown, making them random to mimic the natural flow of the branches.

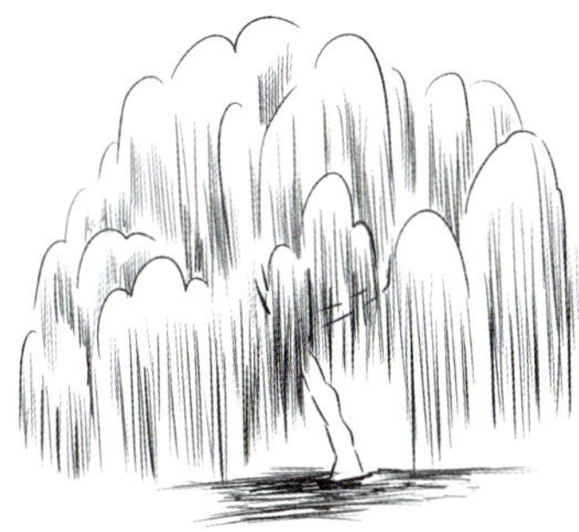

3. Begin adding foliage by creating light, feather-like strokes to represent leaves. Keep the strokes light and varied, leaving space for highlights. Add a trunk.

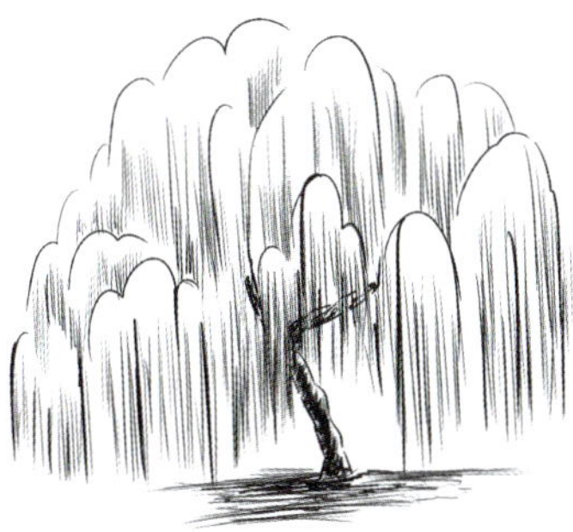

4. Darken the tree trunk for contrast and detail (leave a bit of highlight there). Add shadows on the ground beneath the tree to give it a grounded appearance.

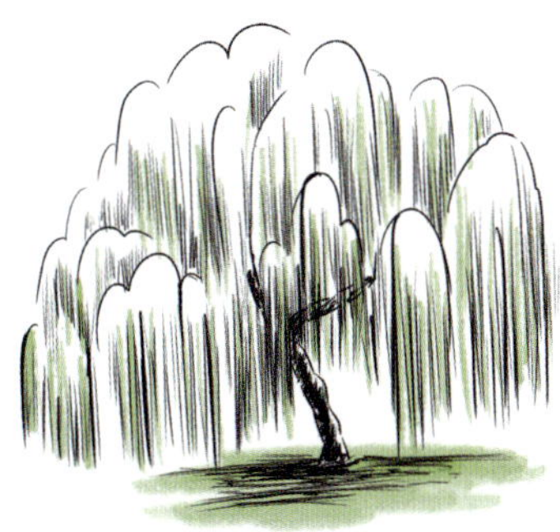

5. Lastly, if you like, you can add color to bring the foliage to life.

Eucalyptus Tree

Eucalyptus trees, also known as gum trees, are famous for their tall, curvy trunks and cloudlike foliage. Their unique shape makes them a great accent tree in a landscape. When drawing, focus on the long, sweeping trunk and the rounded canopy. You can experiment with making the trunk thicker or trying different shapes for the foliage.

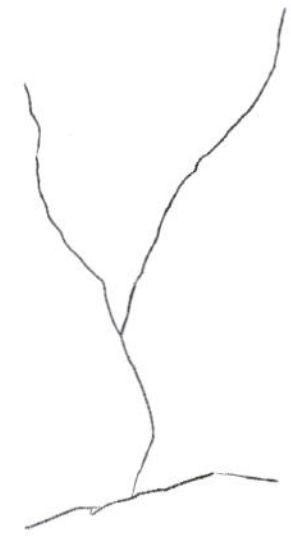

1. Start with the overall trunk shape. Draw an asymmetrical V shape as the foundation.

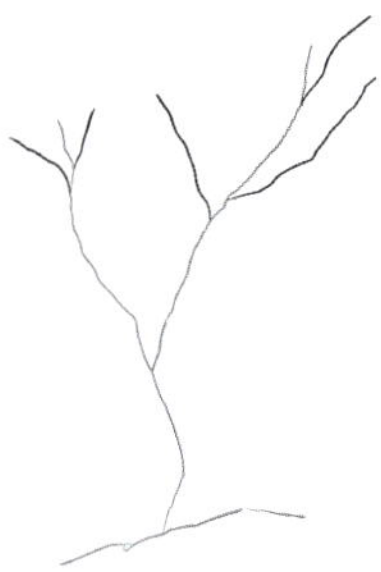

2. Add more branches extending from the trunk, keeping them in asymmetrical or irregular V shapes.

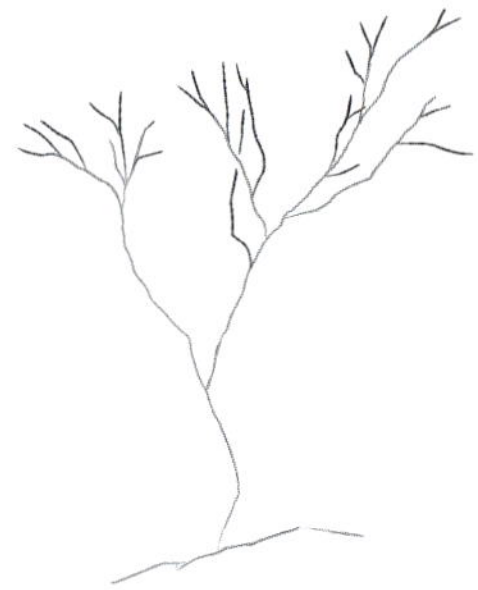

3. Keep adding branches as you go, but don't worry about perfecting them—you can always add more later.

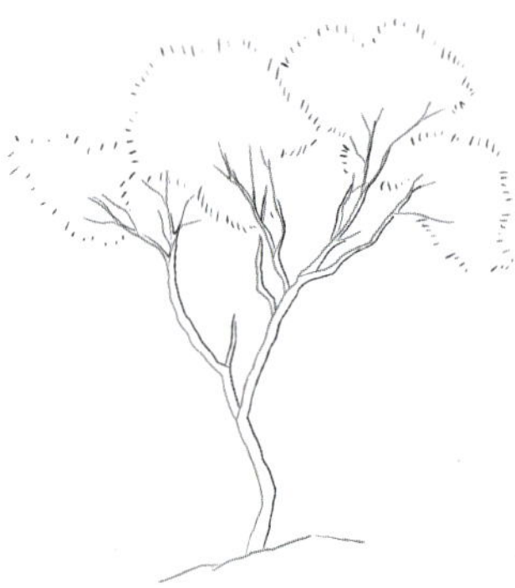

4. Lightly sketch a rough outline for the foliage, keeping it loose and doodle-like.

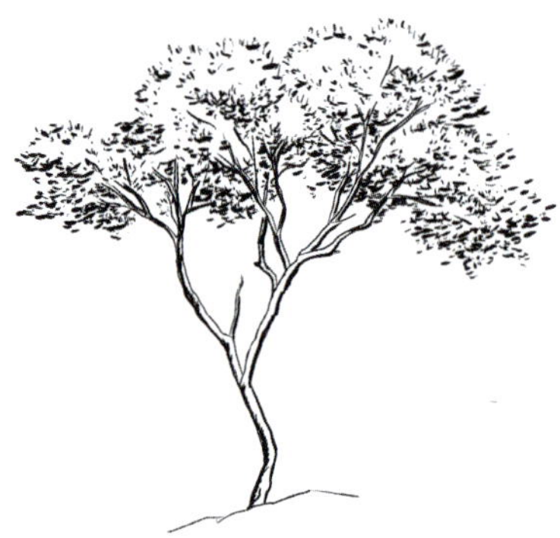

5. Adjust the trunk as needed and add shadows along it while making corrections. Then, add more foliage doodles to the crown to build up the shape.

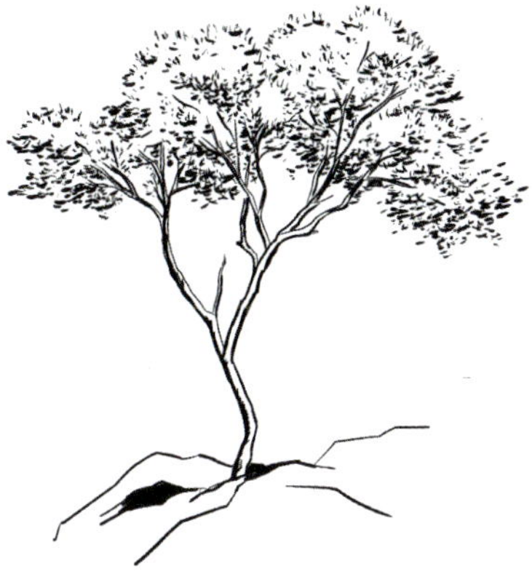

6 Add rocks to give the tree a firm setting.

Practice Landscape Scene

When drawing a landscape, consider the **foreground, middle ground, and background.** In the foreground, place an accent tree. In the middle ground, add some rocks, and in the distant background, sketch mountains. The distant mountains should appear softer and lighter in tone, creating a sense of depth. Use light and shadow to define shapes and add dynamic contrast to the composition.

I took inspiration for this landscape scene from *The Esterel Mountains* by Claude Monet but featured a eucalyptus.

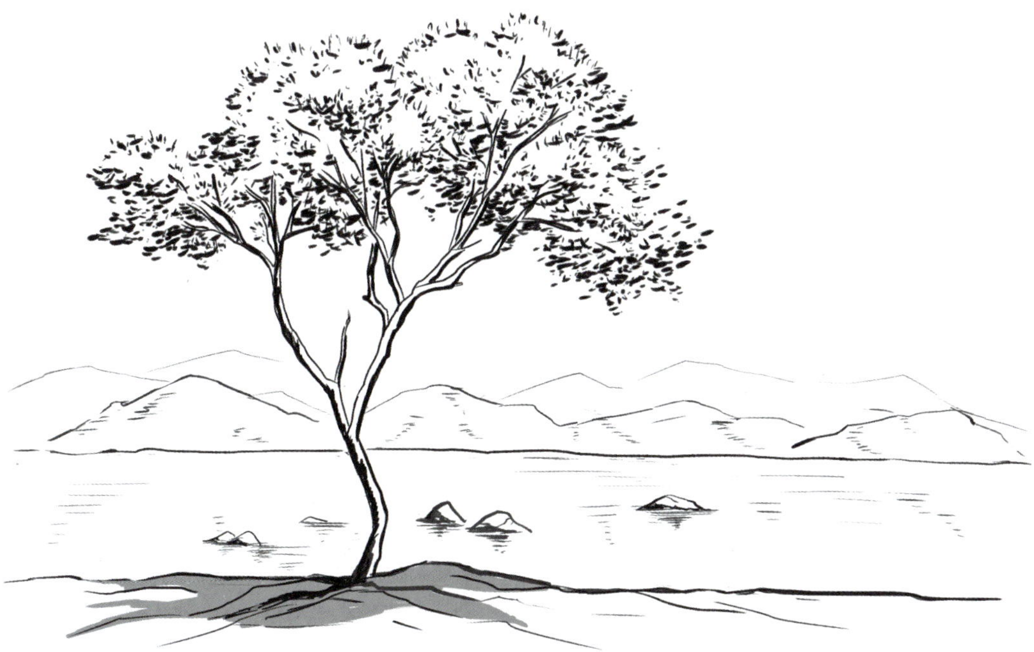

Australian Grass Tree

An Australian grass tree looks like a fantastic combination of a palm and grass. The soft texture and flowing movement of its grass-like leaves add life and interest.

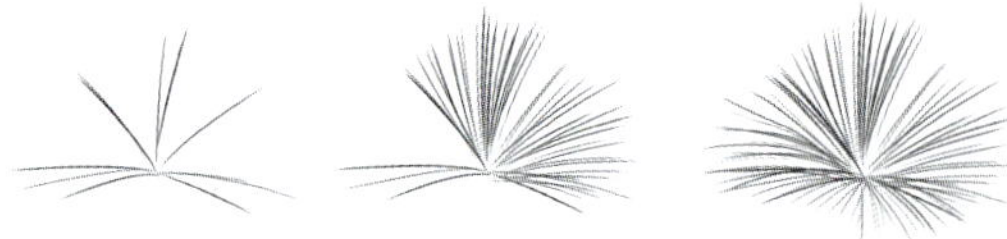

1. Start with a few lines coming from the center. Move to one side and then another to complete the shape.

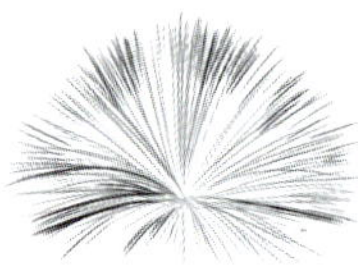

2. Add shorter lines to define edges and create contrast. Layer more lines quickly from the center outward, varying the direction and placement.

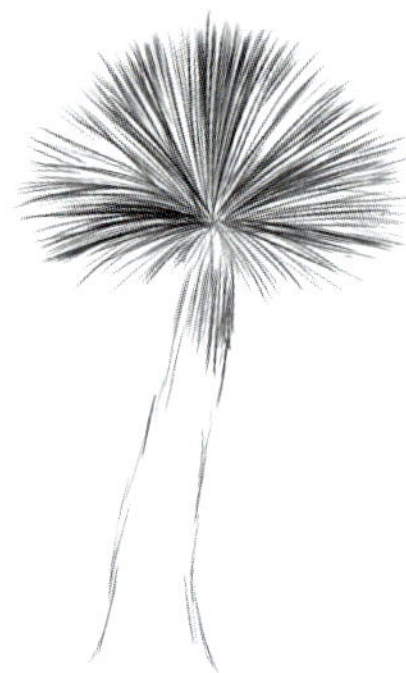

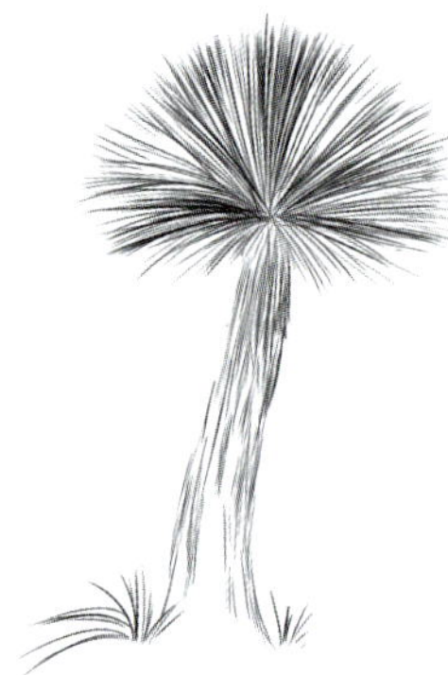

3. Add more lines to the top of the tree. Add the trunk with short, light strokes.

4. Finish the drawing by adding more lines for shading to a the trunk and some grasses coming from the ground.

Try creating a composition with three grass trees. Tie it all together with some grasses and marks to indicate the ground.

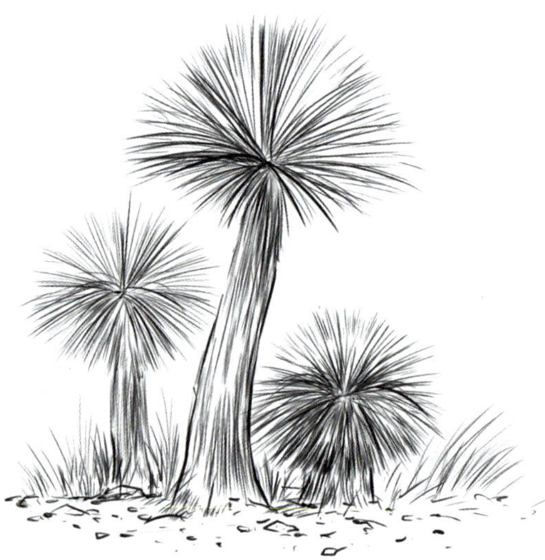

TIPS

- Use your whole arm to make swift, gliding movements. This helps control your line and creates a more natural, flowing effect.
- When creating a composition, vary the size of the plants—use smaller, medium and larger ones. This adds depth and draws the viewer's eye across the entire composition.
- To create more contrast and interest, add different textures to the ground, like small stones or gravel.

DRAWING DIFFERENT TREE LEAVES

This exercise helps you practice drawing different types of lines and shapes while learning how to draw a variety of leaves. Use what we've learned so far about symmetry and line types to create natural-looking leaves.

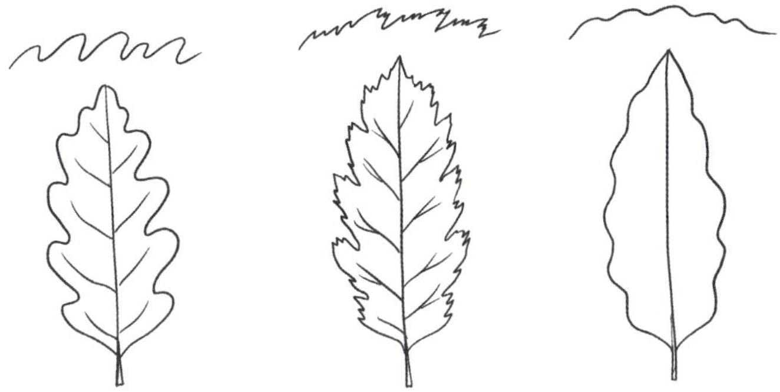

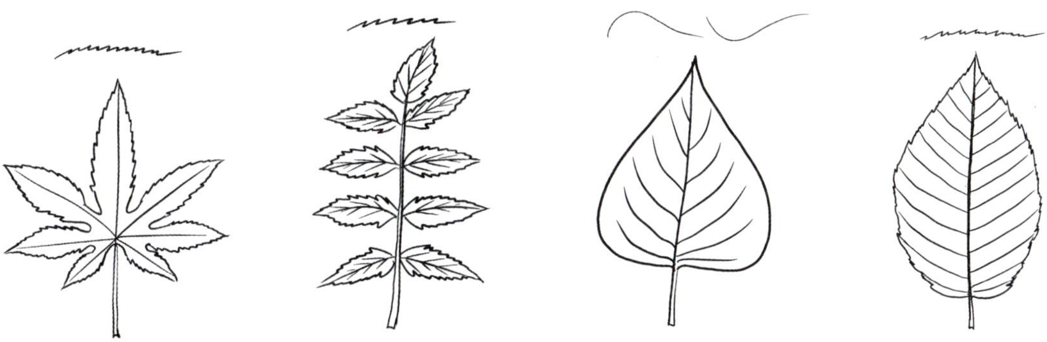

Scan to watch a tutorial.

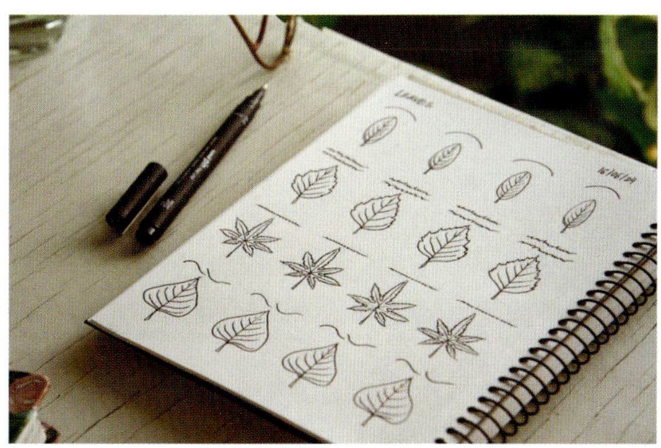

STEP BY STEP:

GROUP OF TREES

In this exercise, you'll be working with a group of trees, which gives you a chance to combine all the tree types you've practiced. You can experiment by mixing different shapes and foliage. Additionally, notice how the sketch is layered: We have the canopy layer, middle layer, and ground layer. We'll explore how to emphasize these layers using techniques like varying line weights and adding depth. This will help bring the trees to life and create a more dynamic composition.

"Cloud" Tree

Here's another simple approach to drawing a tree.

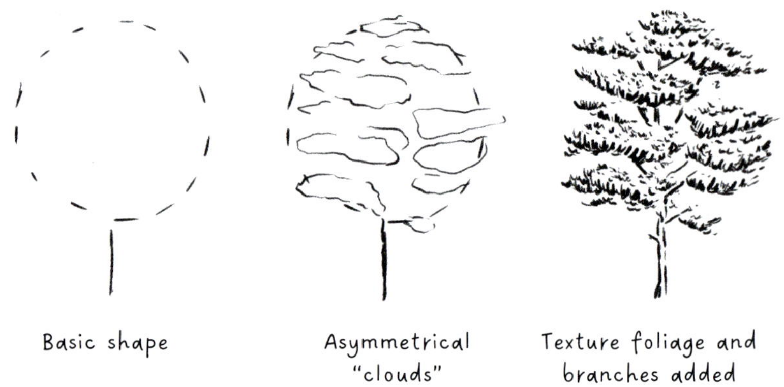

1 Start light and loose: Begin with basic outlines and build up gradually.

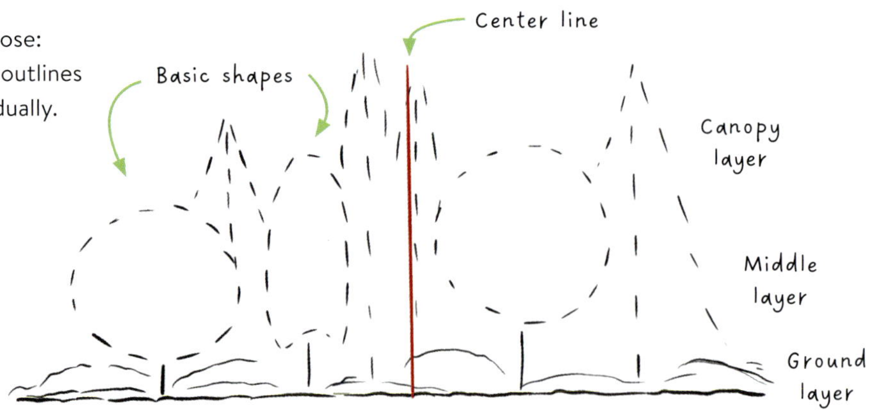

2 Add the foreground trees. Texture is key: Build up texture slowly for a natural, balanced look.

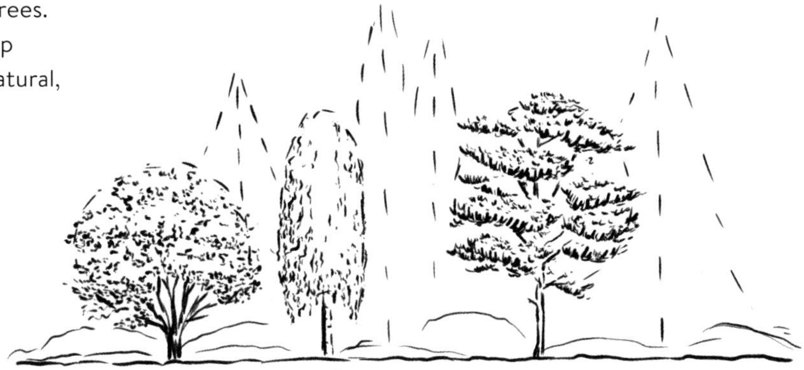

3 Add background trees. Balance light and shadow: Keep highlights light at the top, shadows darker at the bottom for depth. Let background trees stay subtle to make the foreground trees stand out.

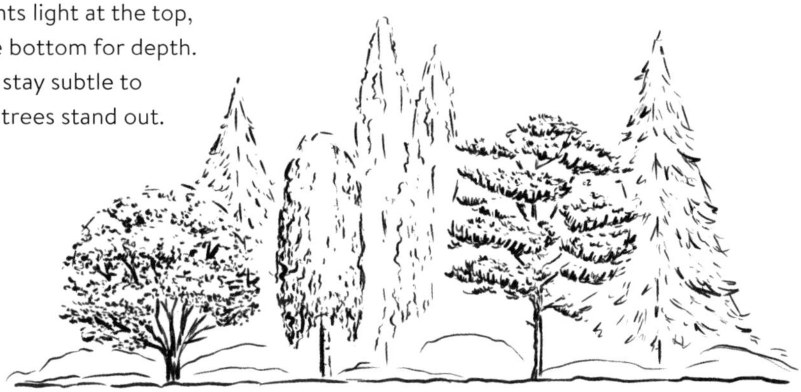

4 Add more texture and shading to complete the drawing.

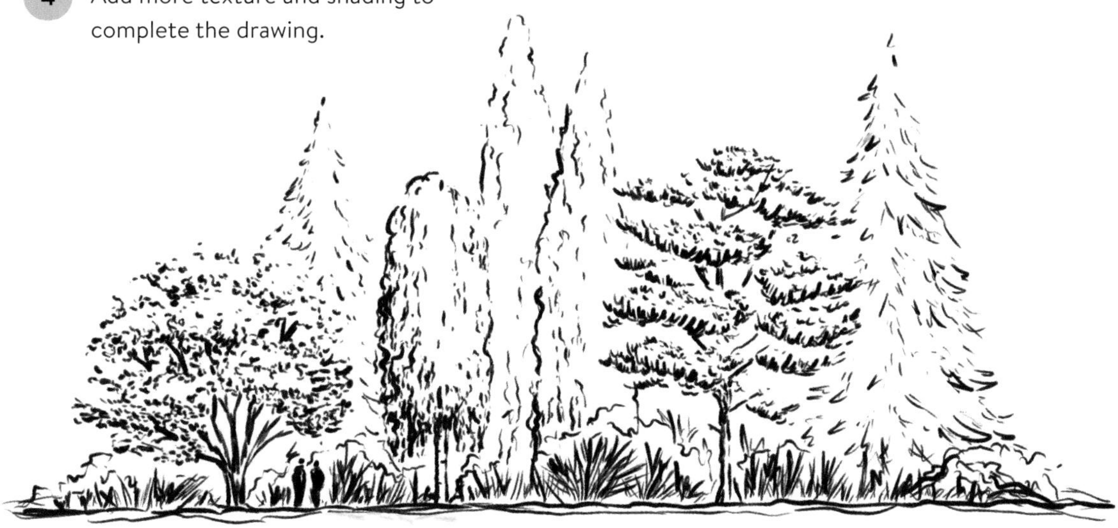

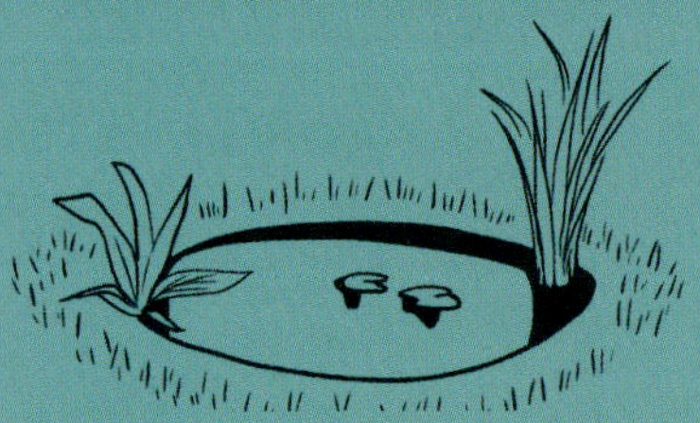
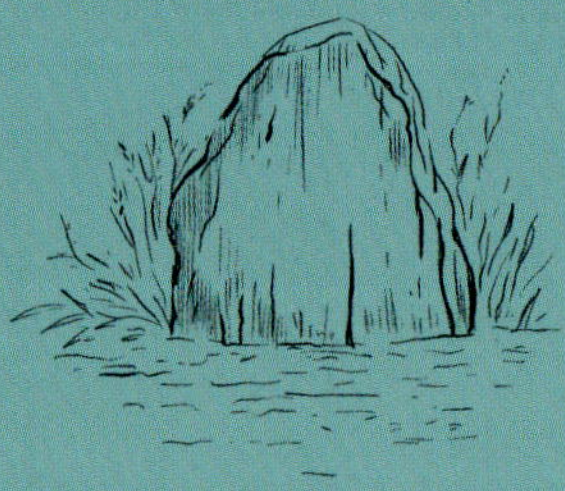
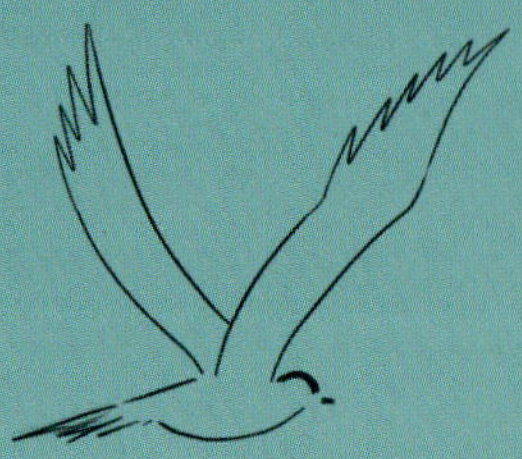
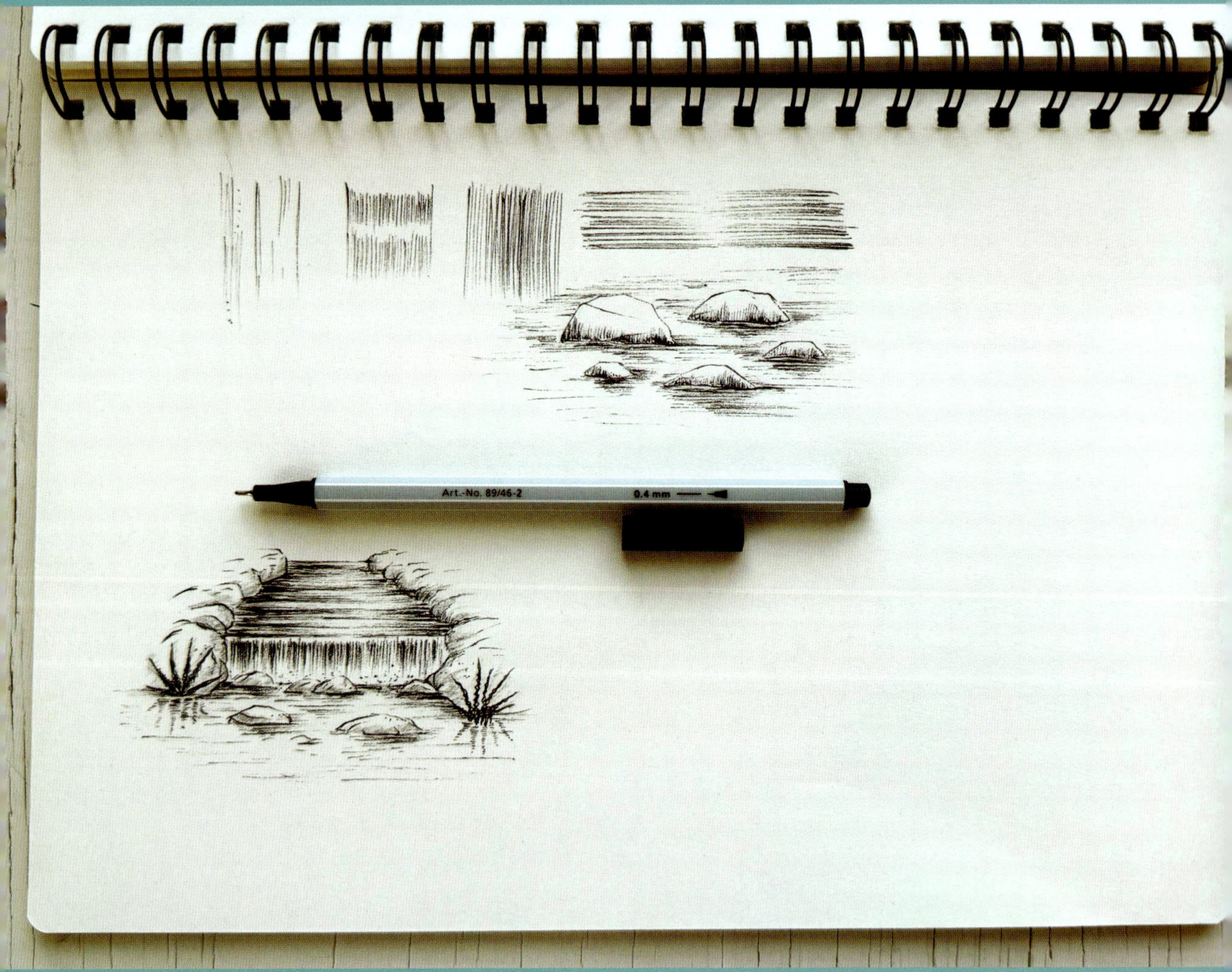
Art.-No. 89/46-2
0.4 mm
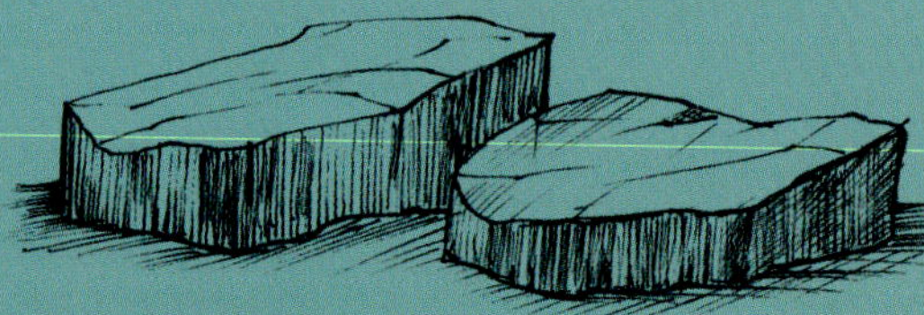
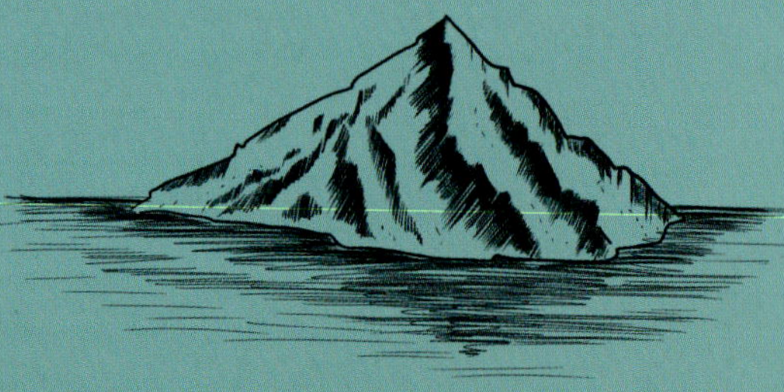

5

DRAWING WATER AND ROCKS

In this chapter, we'll dive into the art of drawing water and rocks, two elements that complement each other beautifully in nature. We'll explore how to use line work to capture the movement of water and the solidity of rocks. You'll also learn how to draw waterfalls and mountains, and we'll talk about composition to make your scene feel balanced. By the end, you'll see how water and rocks create a harmonious, powerful connection in your artwork.

STEP BY STEP:

WATERFALL

In this sketch, you'll practice different types of lines and work on composition. You'll use straight lines to draw water, organic shapes for the rocks, and zigzag lines for the plants and their reflections.

This sketch is interesting because it combines movement, like the flow of water, with the stability of rocks. There's a nice contrast between the vertical and horizontal lines, as well as between dark and light areas. The different sizes of rocks and the mix of thin and thick lines add depth and volume, while the smaller water lines create a sense of perspective. All of this makes it a great exercise, not just for learning how to draw things but also for understanding why and what elements to use.

The step-by-step sequence is just a suggestion. You can skip some steps if they seem easy to you or create your own sequence of steps. Also, feel free to use your imagination to add or change elements as you wish.

Break It Down

Practice the elements of the composition individually before sketching the whole scene. Use this as a warm-up to build confidence and improve your sketching.

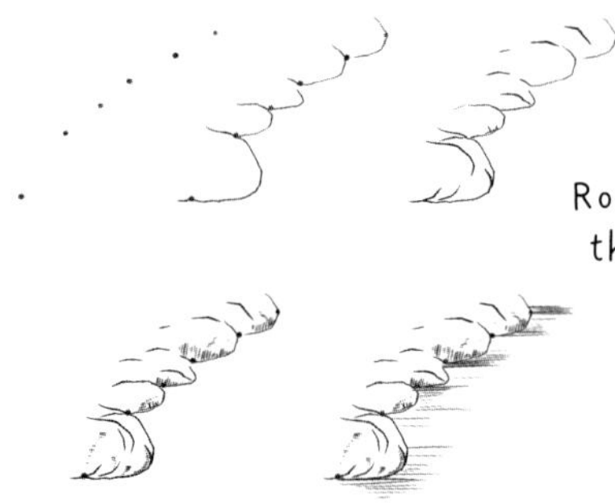

Rocks along the banks

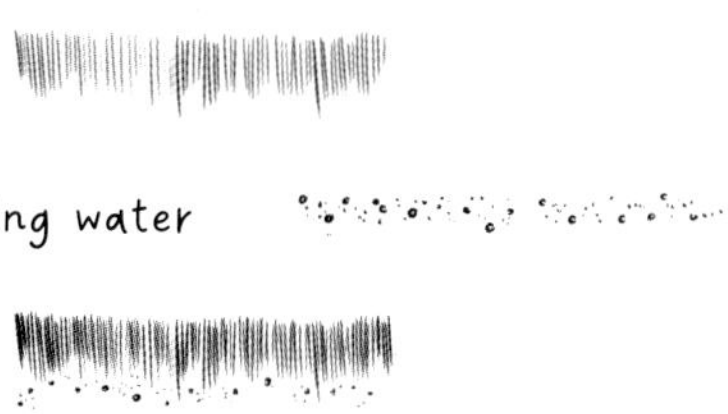

Falling water

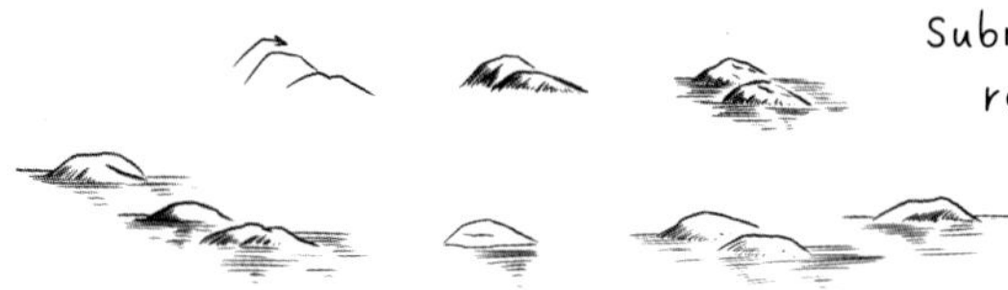

Submerged rocks

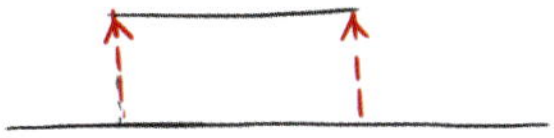

1 Start by marking the spot for the waterfall with two horizontal lines, one shorter and another one longer.

2 Add vertical lines using fast, short strokes. Be careful not to overdo it, leaving some white space for highlights. I prefer to add lines gradually, little by little.

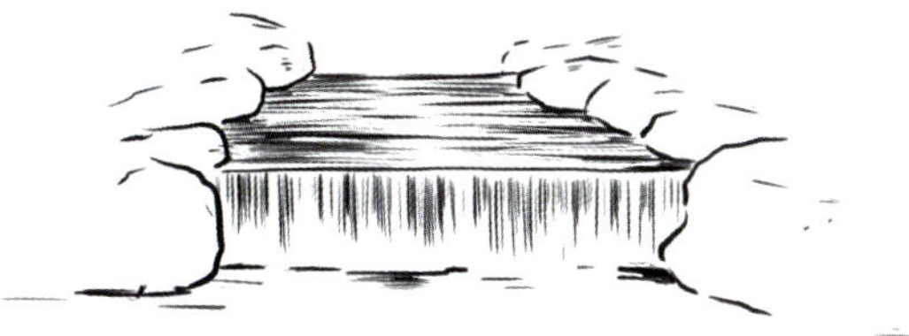

3 Now, draw the rock outlines, making both sides of the waterfall asymmetrical to create a natural look.

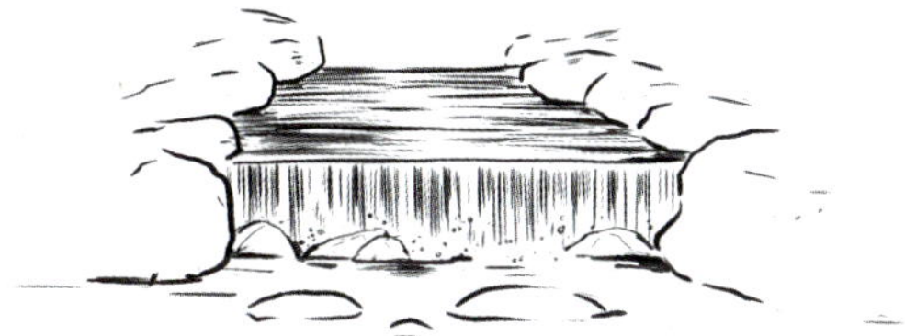

4 In the foreground, draw larger rocks using a mix of thin and bold lines to give them volume.

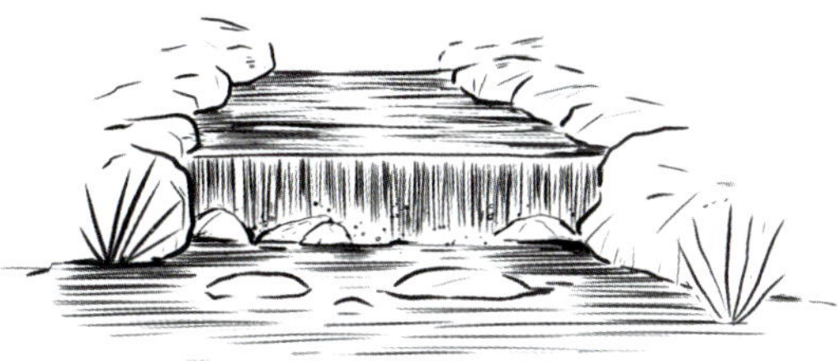

5 Add two plants on either side, placing them unevenly for a natural look. Continue adding horizontal lines for the water.

6 Use zigzag lines to create the plants' leaves and their reflections in the water. If you have a gray pencil or marker, you can add some shading to the plants and rocks. If you wish, add even more contrast by darkening the water.

Scan to watch a tutorial.

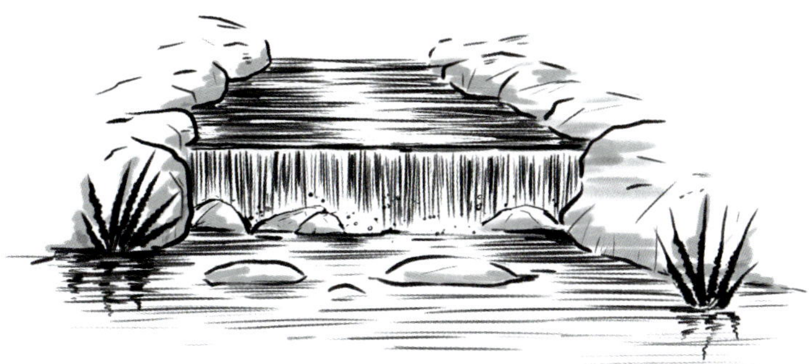

STEP BY STEP:

SMALL POND

In this tutorial, we'll create a small pond scene, practicing composition, line work, and using strong contrast to add depth and interest.

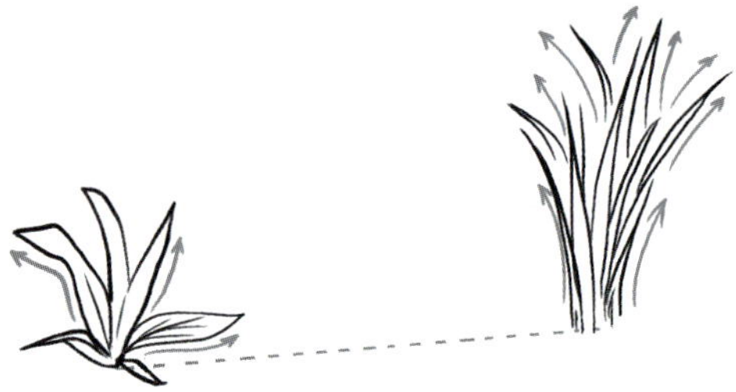

1 Start by drawing the water plants slightly asymmetrically on both sides of the pond (a common feature in Japanese garden design).

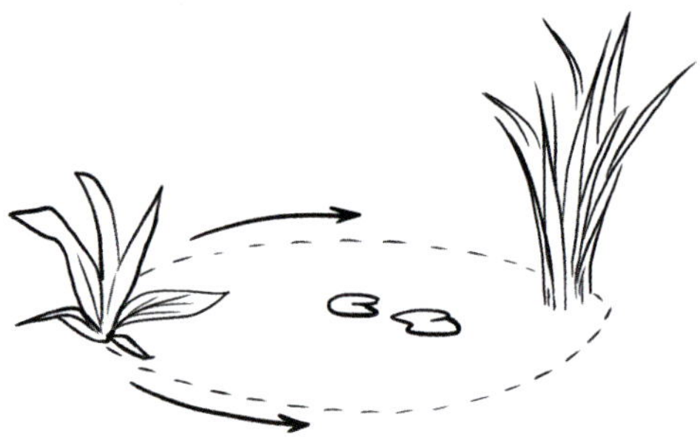

2 Draw two curves to form the pond and use a dotted line as a guide if needed.

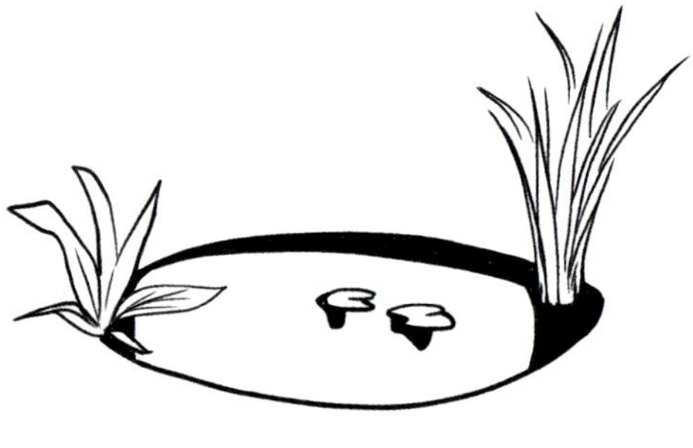

3 Add dark shadows from the plants to create contrast with the light water surface, giving the scene depth.

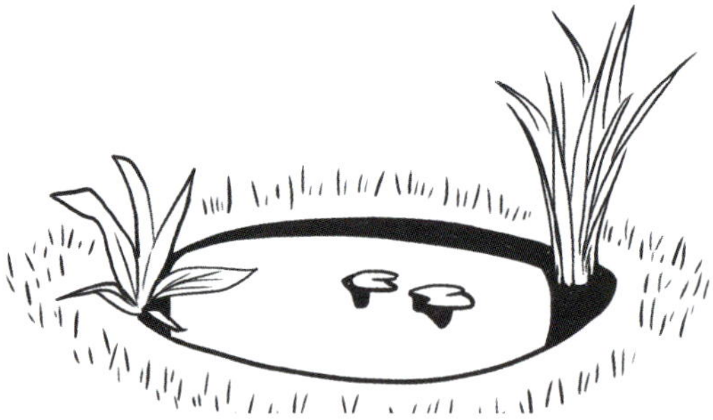

4 Finish by drawing grass around the pond with short, quick strokes, varying the size and spacing for a natural look.

STEP BY STEP:

ROCKS AND STONES

Stones are a great way to add a natural, grounding element to any landscape. They help create interesting compositions when combined with plants, trees, and other elements. Stones are also fun to draw—perfect for practicing texture lines, edges, and volume. Plus, they're simple enough to tackle, making them a great way to experiment and play with details while building your drawing skills.

Single Boulder

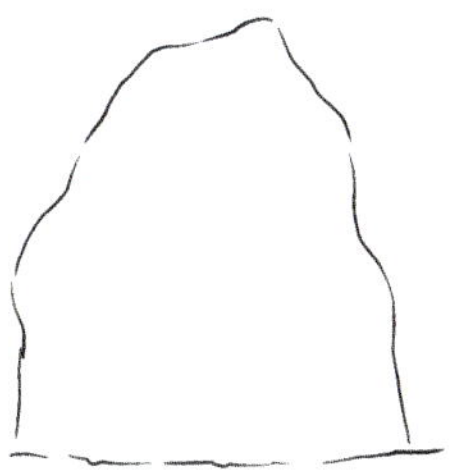

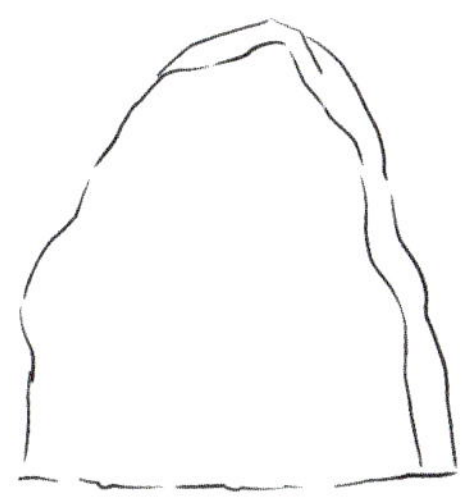

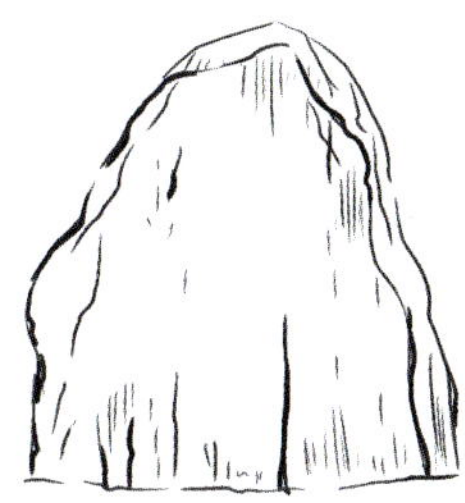

1. Start with a simple outline.
2. Add volume with one more edge.
3. Add texture lines.
4. Sketch in a background and add extra line weight.

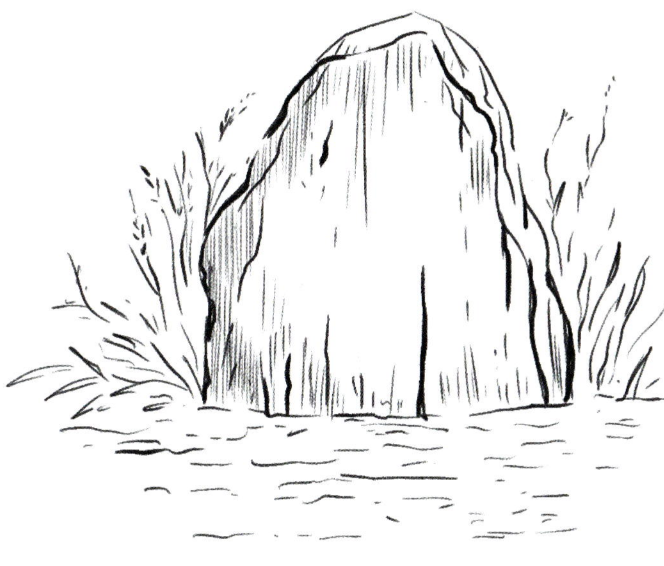

Scan to watch a tutorial.

Stepping Stone

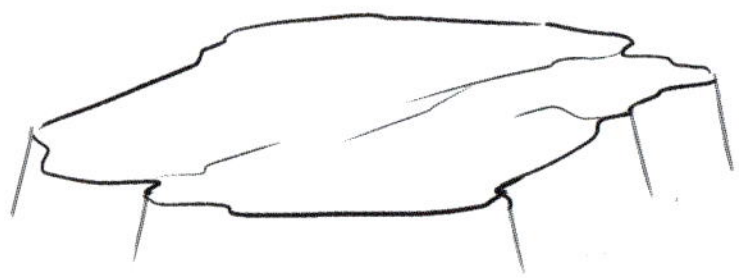

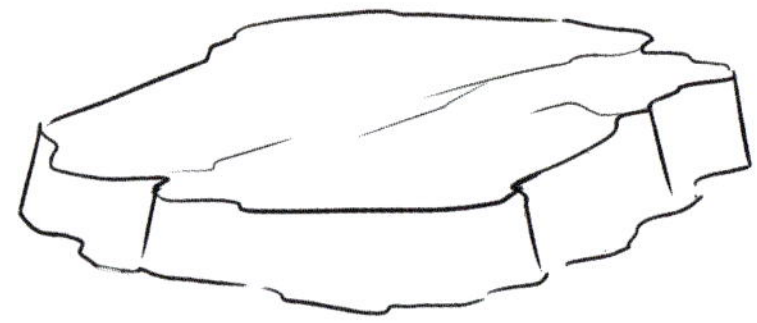

1 Start by drawing the upper surface of the stepping stone, then add the edges to give it shape.

2 Sketch the lower edge.

3 To make it look more realistic, use hatching lines along the edges. Vary the spacing between the lines—some should be close together, others farther apart—to create tonal values. You can also add a second layer of hatching to some areas, making certain edges or parts of the stone appear darker while keeping others lighter.

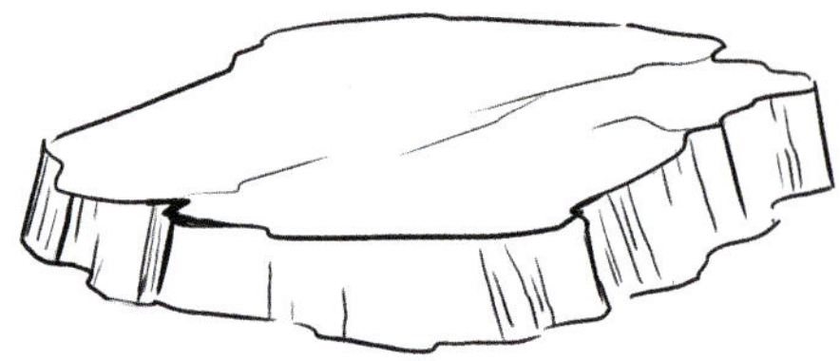

Try drawing multiple stones and add more shading and hatching.

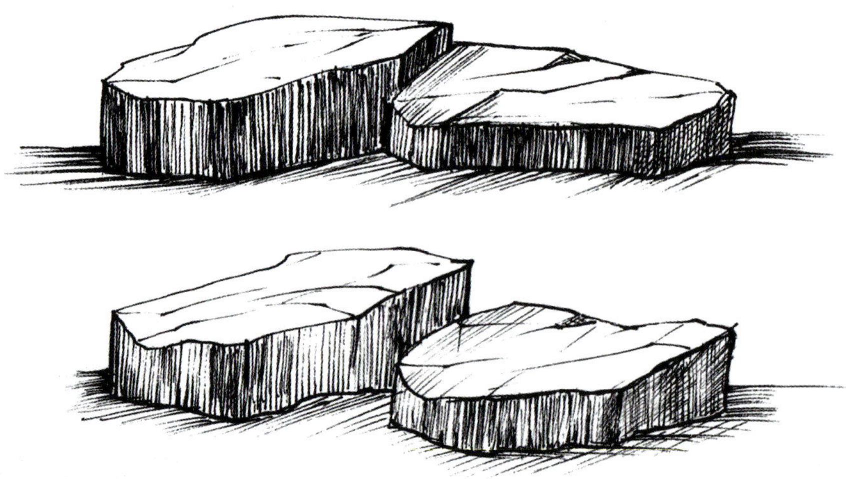

STEP BY STEP:

MOUNTAIN AND WATER

A mountain rising out of the ocean is a dramatic scene.

TIP

Practice your hatching lines before you add them to your mountain.

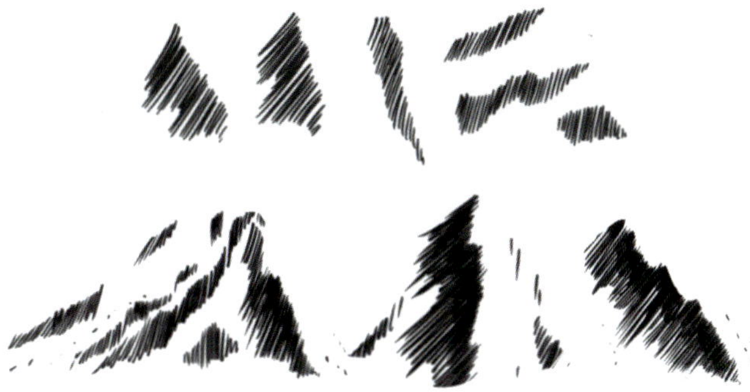

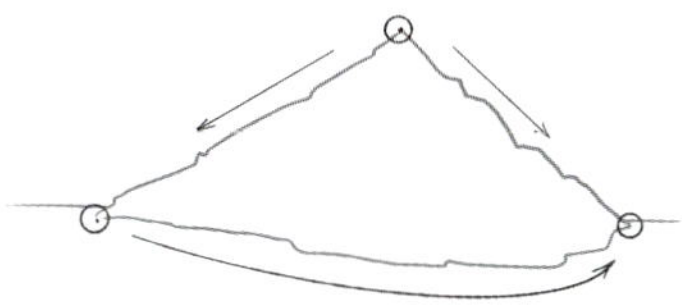

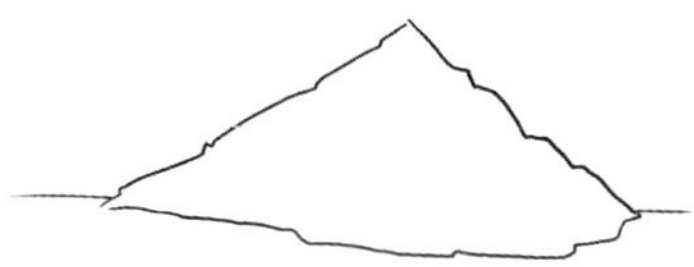

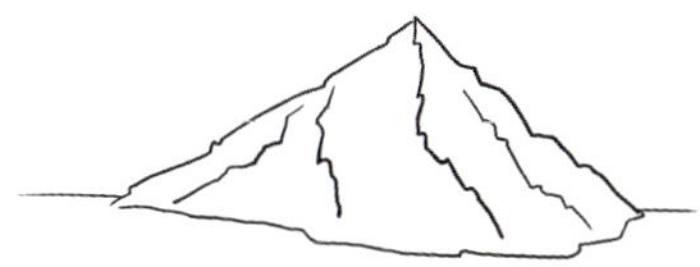

1. To draw a mountain's shape, start by placing dots to mark the outline.
2. Connect the dots.
3. Add some lines to create the edges and cliffs.
4. Use the hatching technique to create some shade and the illusion of dimension. Draw short parallel lines and different angles.

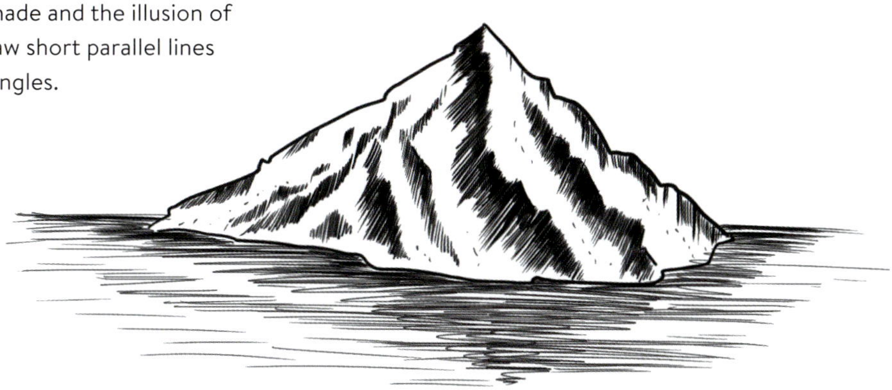

STEP BY STEP:

OCEAN SCENE

Birds are a great element to add to any landscape, especially a sea landscape. They bring a sense of life and movement, making your landscape more engaging and lively.

Seagull

Even though the birds in this seascape are tiny, drawing one step by step is a great exercise.

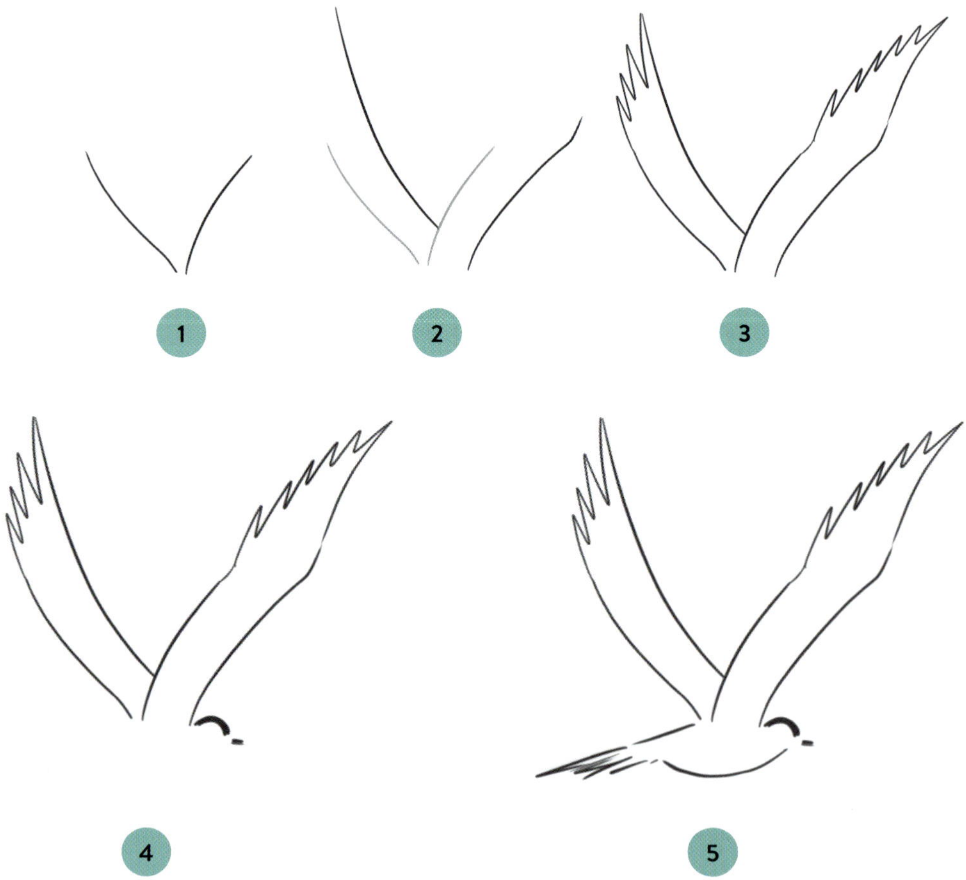

Adding Depth

Notice how changing the size of the birds and the spacing between the waves creates a sense of depth and perspective. The farther away something is, the smaller it appears, and the waves get closer together.

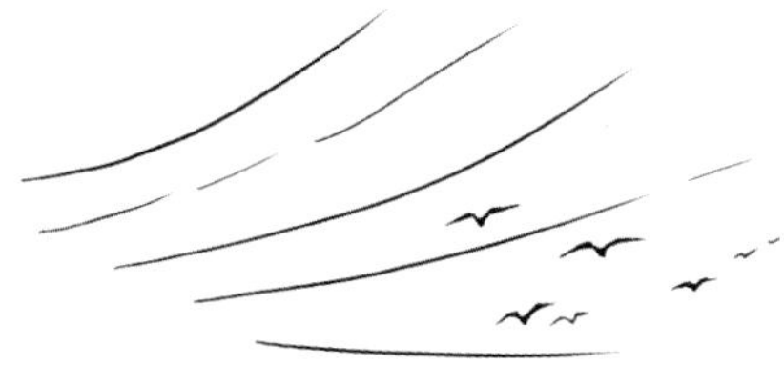

Light on Water

You can create the effect of light or reflections on water by using closely spaced parallel lines. Keep the lines close together to suggest the texture of the water but leave enough white space to create the reflection effect. The contrast between the dark lines and the white space will give the illusion of shimmering water under the moonlight. The key is in the spacing and maintaining that balance between light and dark to evoke a calm, reflective mood.

When creating the water reflection, it's nice to start very lightly. Begin with soft, light lines and gradually add layers, building up the depth little by little.

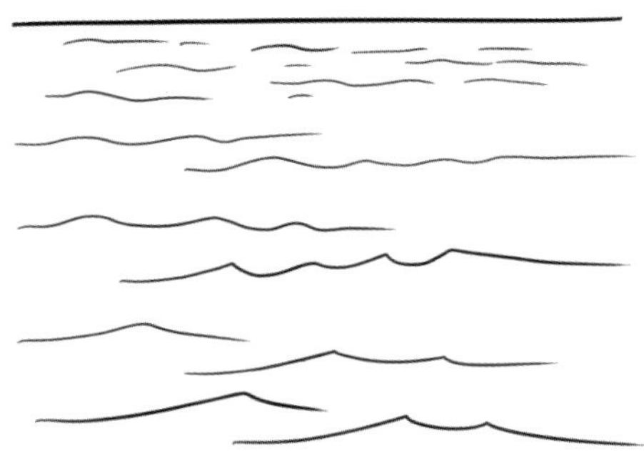

Scan to watch a tutorial.

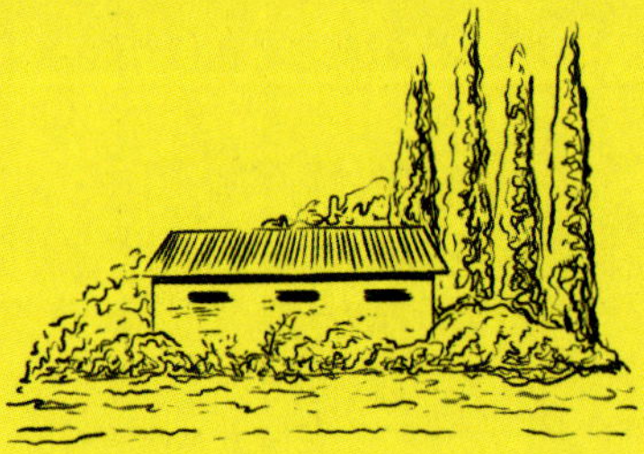
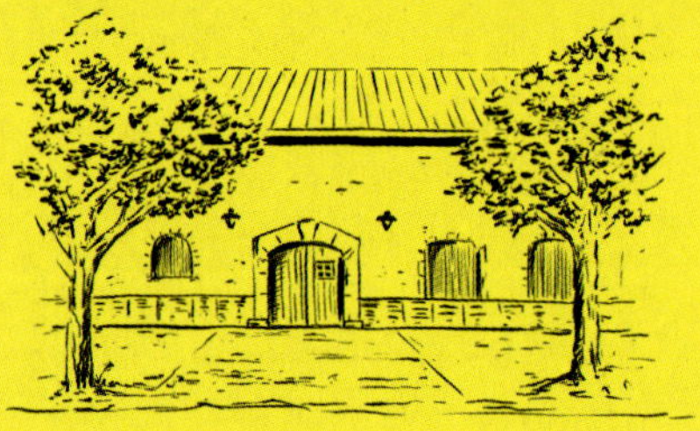
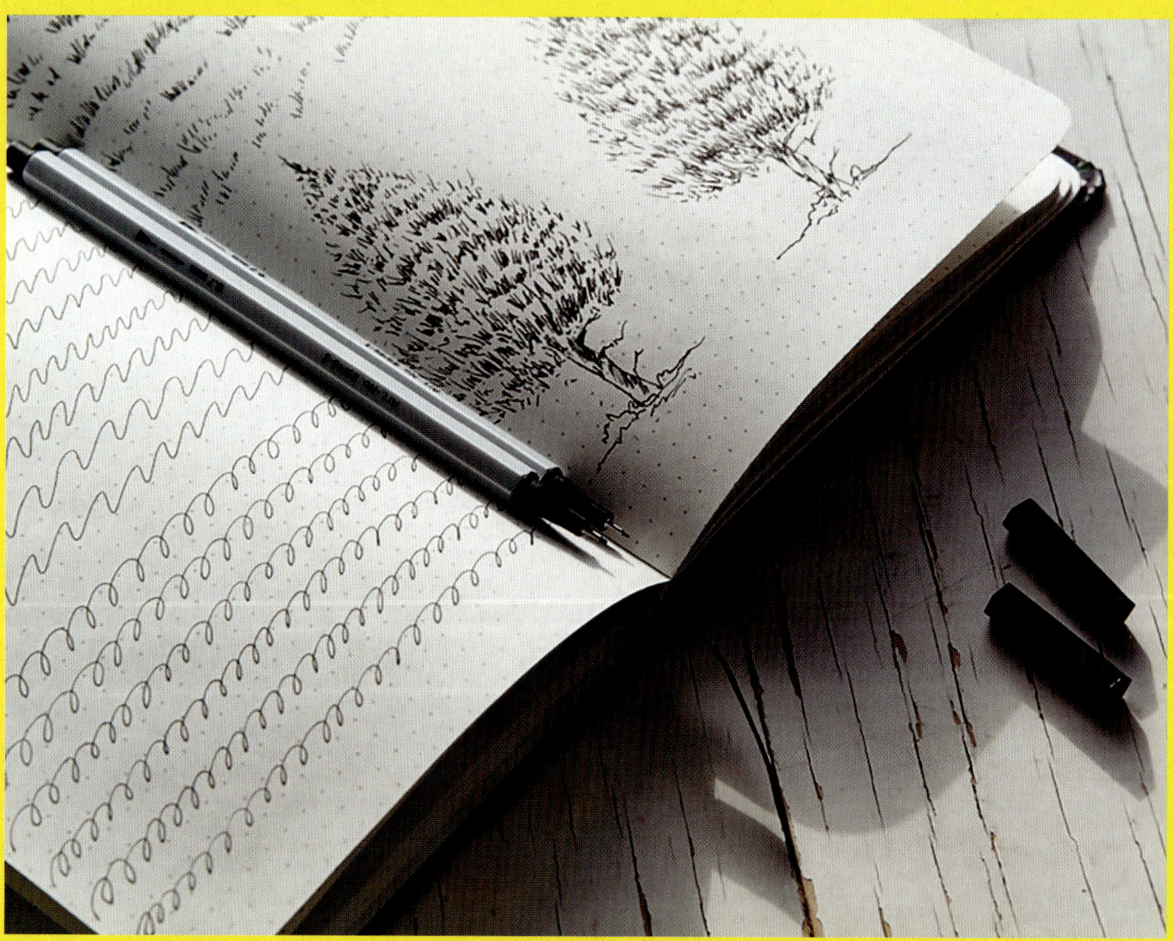
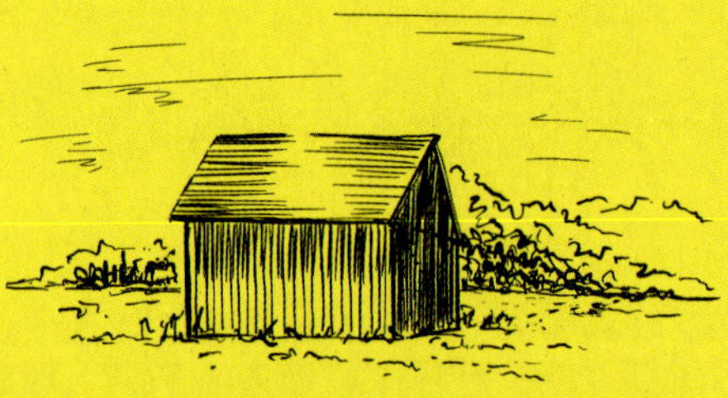
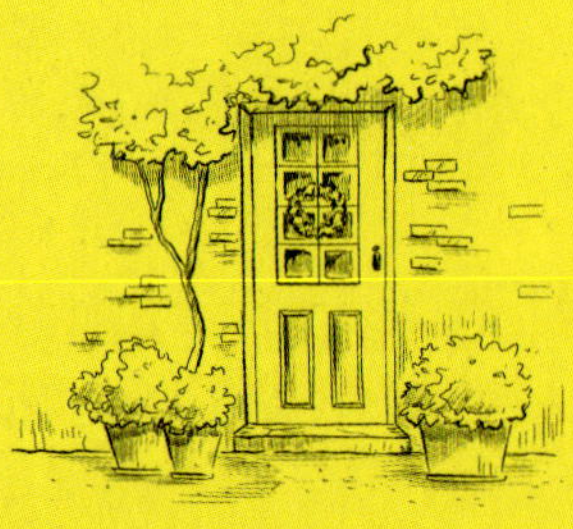

6

DRAWING LANDSCAPE AND ARCHITECTURE

In this chapter, we'll explore the beauty of contrast and symmetry in landscapes and dive into the basics of one-point perspective, a key tool for capturing depth in your scenes. You'll also get hands-on with architectural elements like doors and windows, learning how to incorporate them into your landscape drawings. Along the way, we'll focus on proportions to help you create balanced, realistic compositions that bring both natural and human-made elements to life.

STEP BY STEP:

HOUSE AND TREES

In this exercise, we'll practice contrast in landscape by exploring variations in line work and using different shapes. By contrasting straight and irregular lines, as well as horizontal and vertical objects, we can create a dynamic and visually interesting composition. Each element clearly stands out. We will also focus on repetition to create unity and balance in the sketch.

1 Sketch the central building and ground line lightly in the center of the page. Horizontal lines help you structure the scene.

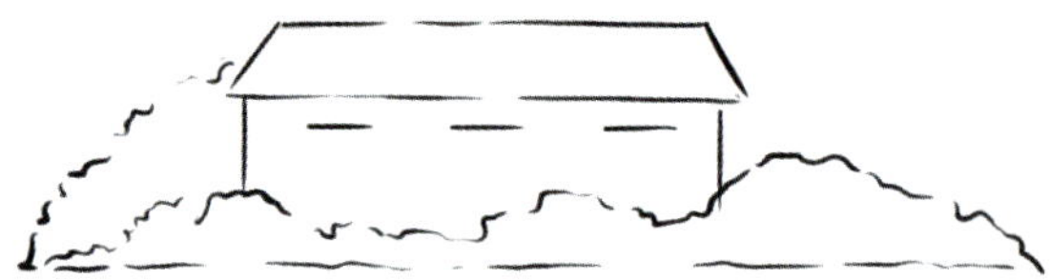

2 Add vegetation around the building using an irregular, wiggly line to represent shrubs and plants.

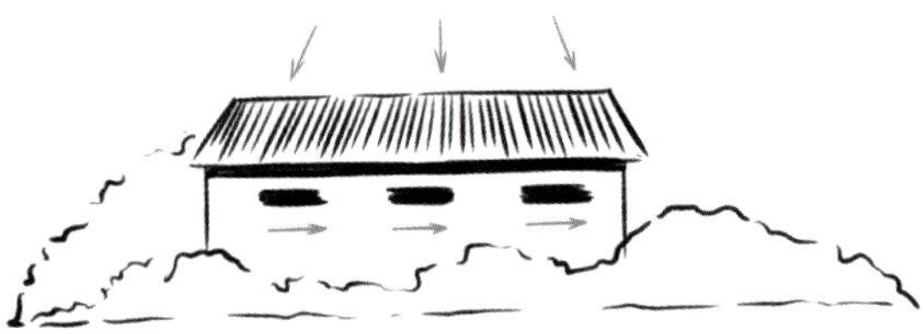

3 Add straight lines to the roof and the windows. Notice the direction of the lines. Add a shadow under the roof to create depth.

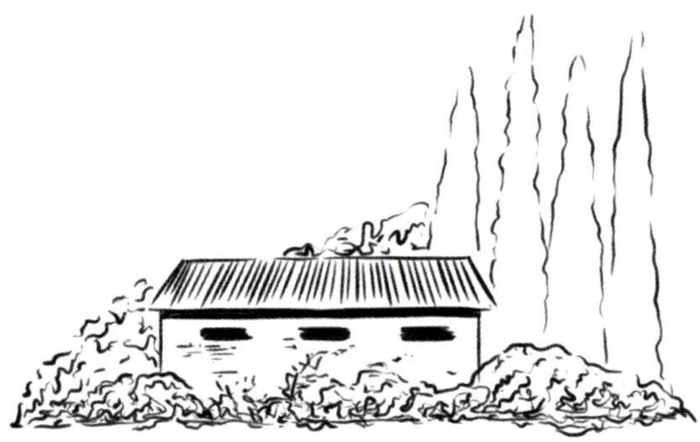

4 Add four columnar trees and a line of vegetation behind the building. Notice the repetitive elements in this sketch—windows and trees.

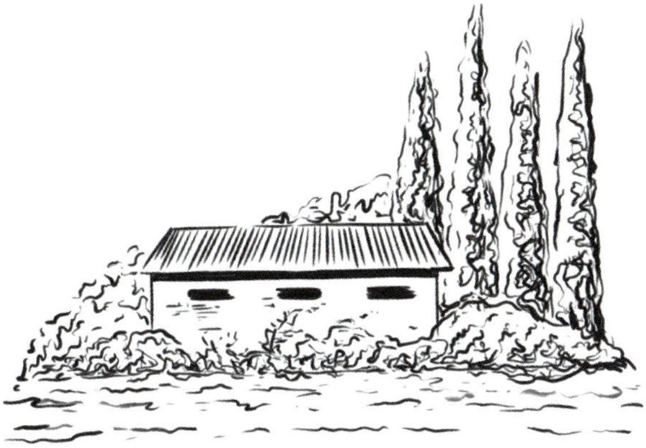

6 Continue with the trees, and don't forget to leave some white space for highlights to create volume and interest. Add the background by sketching the lights in the sky and the field in front of the building. Notice the contrast between these two areas.

5 Add texture to the vegetation by filling it in with wiggly lines. You can repeat the same line for a textured effect.

Scan to watch a tutorial.

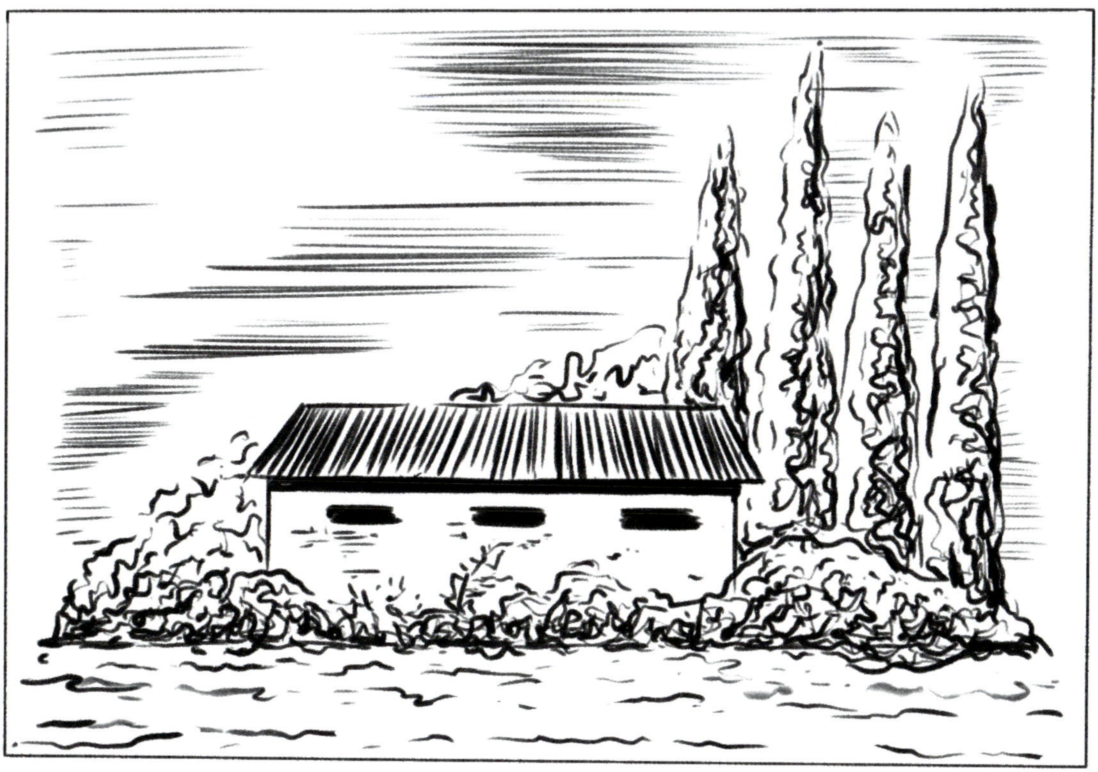

STEP BY STEP:

STONE FARMHOUSE

In this drawing, we'll practice using symmetry. Symmetry in a drawing creates a sense of stability and order. You can achieve unity and balance by placing similar objects on both sides of a central line. However, too much symmetry can sometimes feel repetitive, lacking excitement and appearing too predictable, so we'll also include some elements of asymmetry.

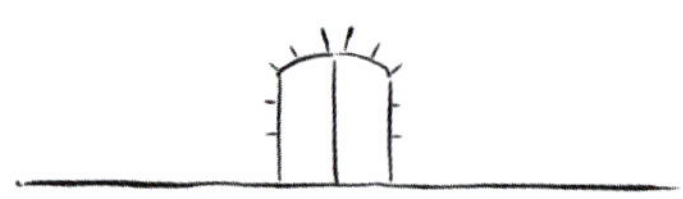

1 Start by sketching the door as the central element of the composition.

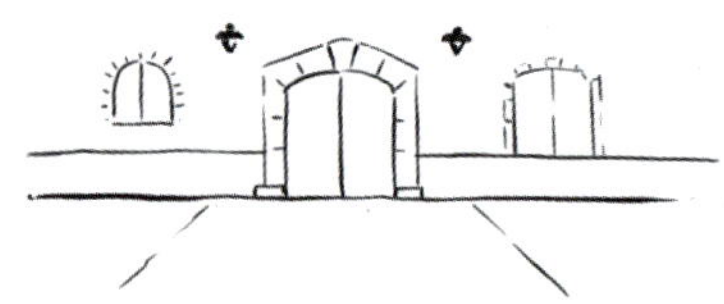

2 Place a lantern on both sides of the door and draw the windows on each side.

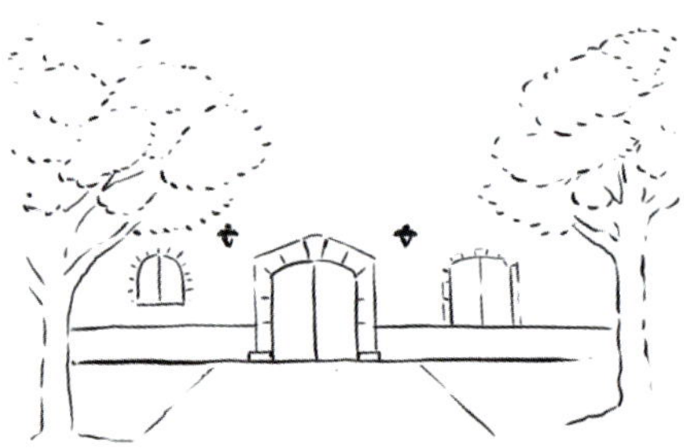

3 Add big trees in the foreground on both sides, lightly sketching their outlines.

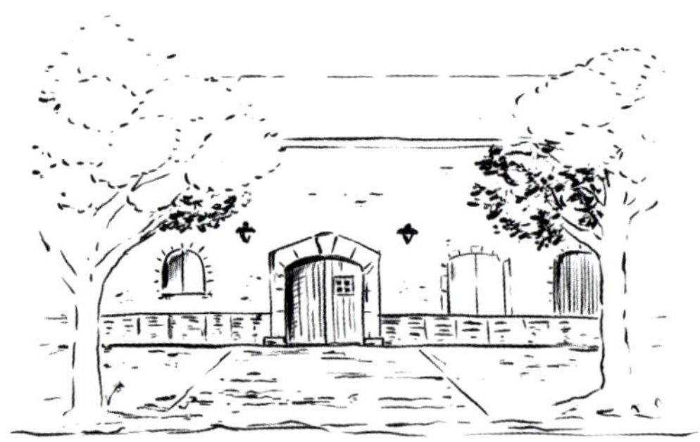

4 Draw the horizontal lines for the roof, add texture to the foreground, and include another window on the right side.

5 Add diagonal lines to the roof and a dark shadow under it to create depth. Add foliage by doodling randomly, focusing on maintaining contrast between black and white for a dynamic effect. Finish the shadows on the windows and the bark of the trees.

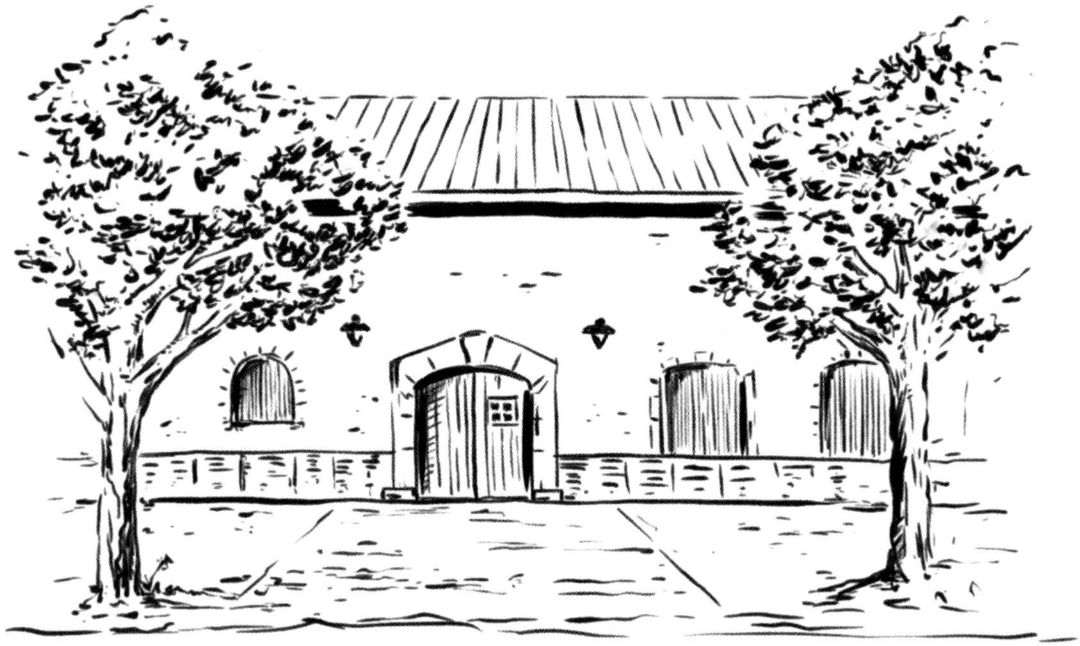

Notice how the symmetrical trees give the scene a sense of order and balance while the off-center elements keep it from being lifeless.

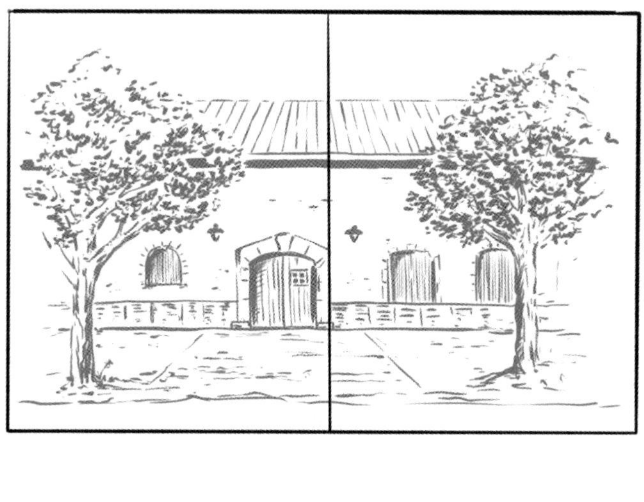

STEP BY STEP:

BARN IN PERSPECTIVE

Perspective creates the illusion of depth in a drawing. In one-point perspective, all lines converge at a single point on the horizon. It's a great tool for drawing objects like buildings, roads, and interiors in a way that feels realistic. In this exercise, we'll create a simple barn using one-point perspective. While the structure is straightforward, we'll make it more interesting by adding contrast, different line work, and texture to bring it to life.

1 Start with a rectangle and a horizon line.

2 Estimate the wall in perspective. (That's how I decided on the placement of the vanishing point.)

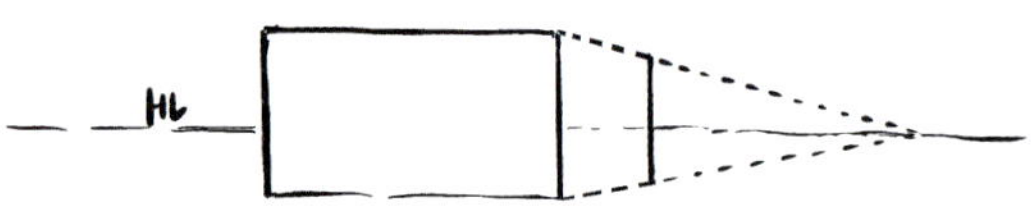

3 Add the converging lines to a vanishing point to draw it in perspective and complete the wall.

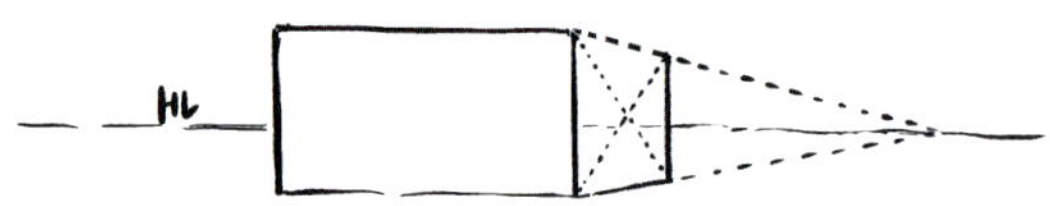

4 With the help of two diagonal lines, find the center of the wall.

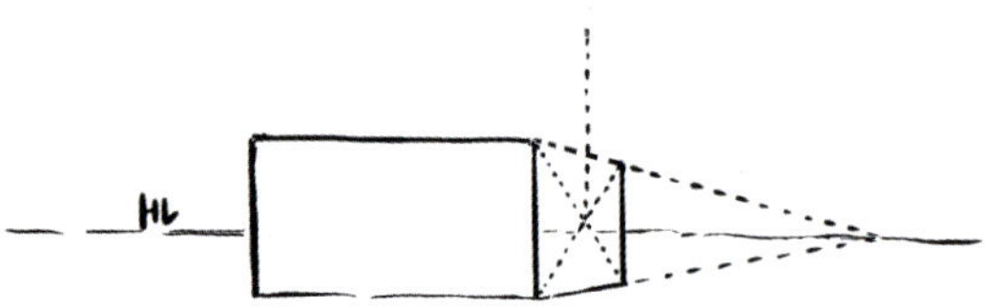

5 From there, draw a straight line up to find the top of the roof.

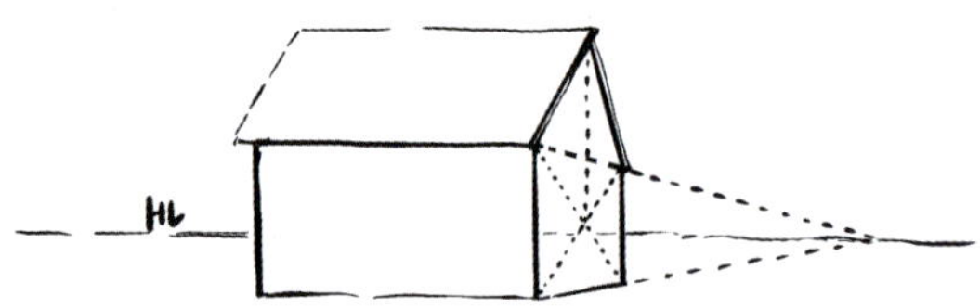

6 Complete the roof. You can make it slightly longer than the walls. Pay attention to which lines are parallel to each other.

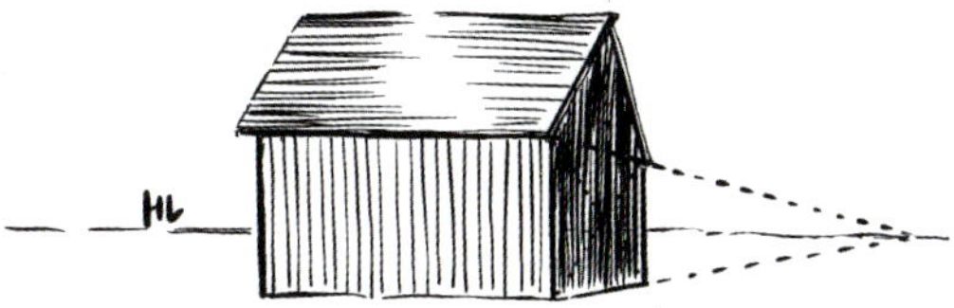

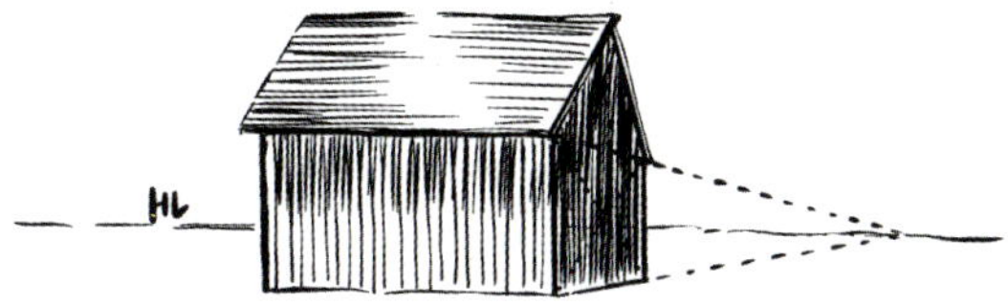

7 Add some shading. Create contrast between highlights and shadows, keeping some white space.

8 Add a cast shadow under the roof.

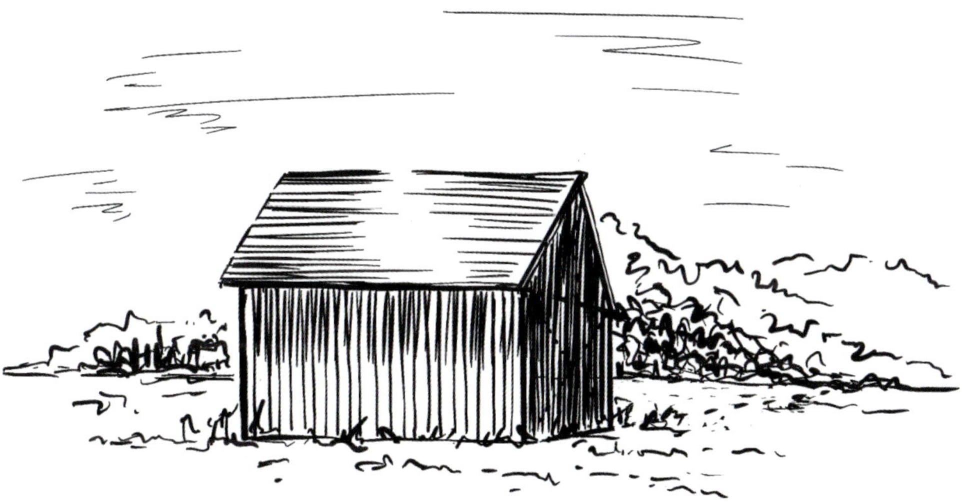

9 Use a “nervous hand” to create trees and grass. Add a few lines to the sky to create depth.

Scan to watch a tutorial.

STEP BY STEP:

FRONT DOOR

At first glance, this is a fairly complex scene with multiple elements and textures and shading that creates depth. But if you break it down, you'll see that it is made up of very simple shapes and marks.

Break It Down

You can practice those individual drawings first if you like before you create your composition. Practice drawing textures.

Brick wall

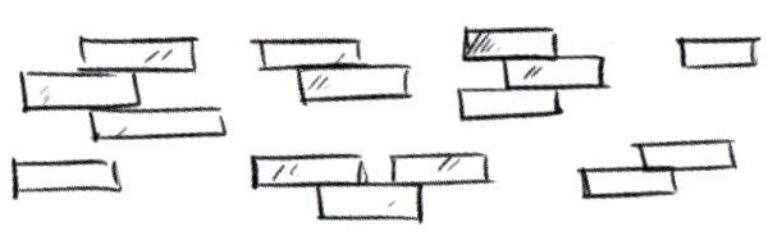

Foliage texture

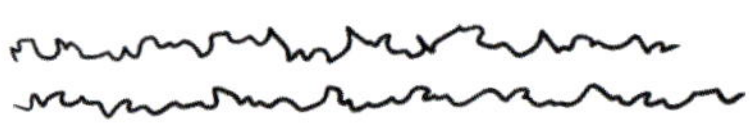

Pots of different sizes

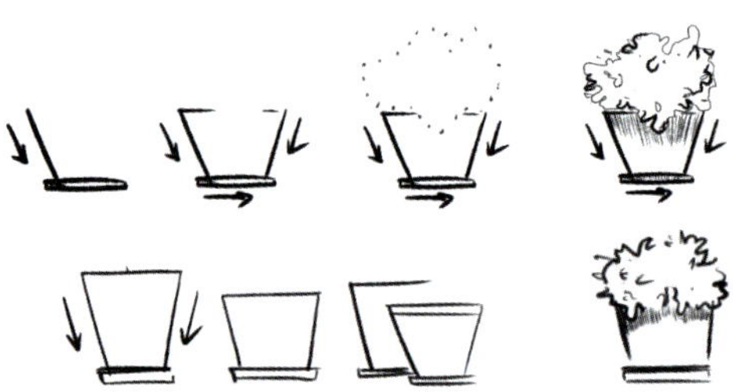

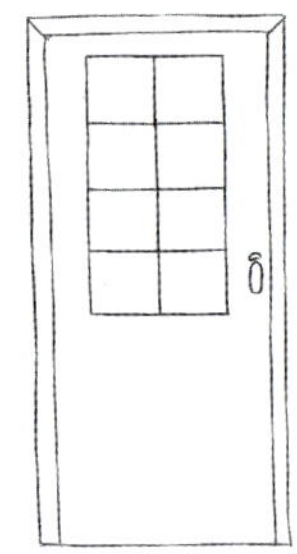

1 Start with the door, which will be the center of the composition. Divide the window into eight equal parts.

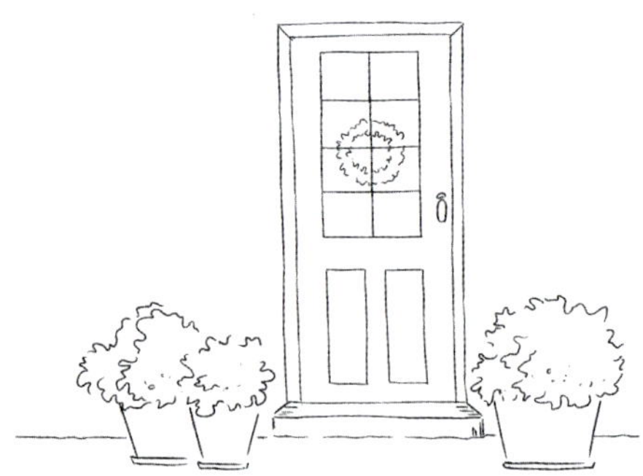

2 Draw the pots on both sides of the door. The wreath on the door adds a nice decorative touch and creates an accent.

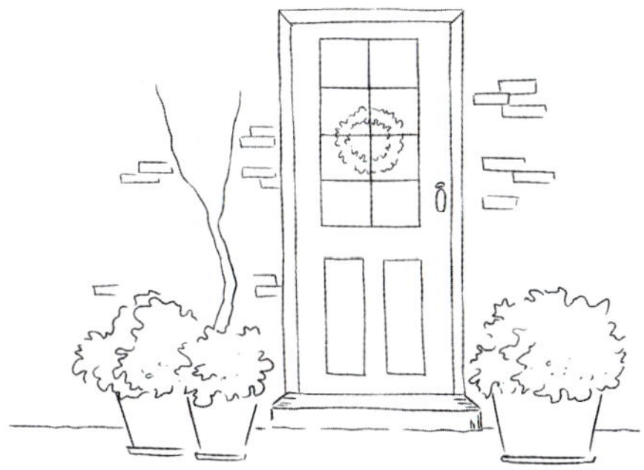

3 Draw the trunk of the climbing plant. Add a brick texture to the wall on both sides.

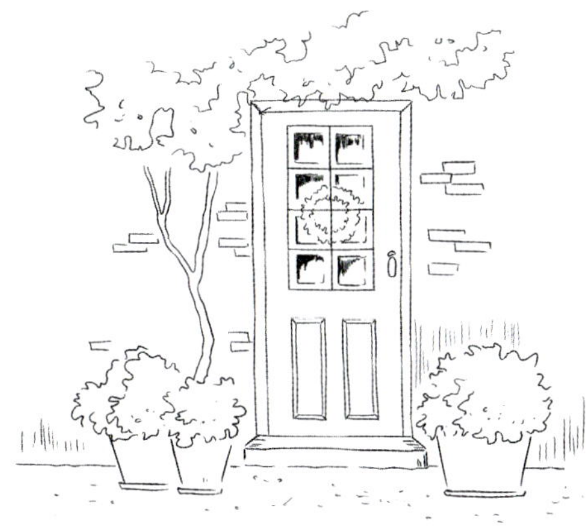

4 Add shadows on the window to create depth. Draw the foliage to complete the climbing plant.

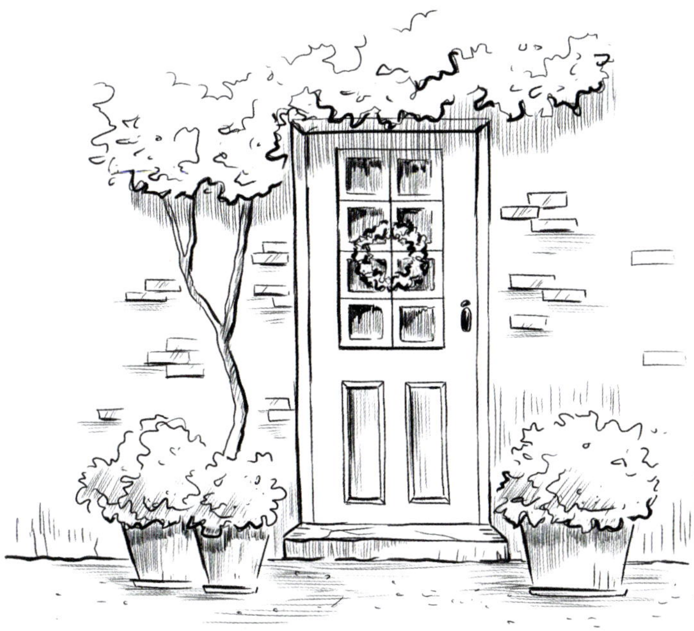

5 Use hatching lines to darken the shadows and add extra line weight and textures for depth and interest. You can use a pen with a bigger nib or draw over the lines a few times to create bolder lines.

TIP

Feel free to change some elements or even add new ones. You can even grab some colored pencils and add color to your sketch.

ARCHITECTURE AND PROPORTIONS

Sharpen your sense of proportions by drawing squares and then rectangles that are two to three times longer on one side than on the other. Draw various types of roofs with sharp, 90-degree angles and blunt angles. Practice drawing a castle and a temple. Focus on symmetry and proportions.

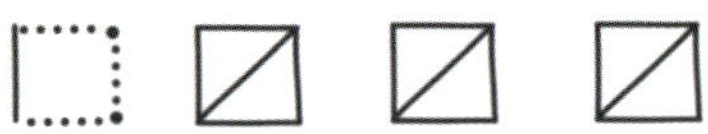

1 Start by drawing a square.

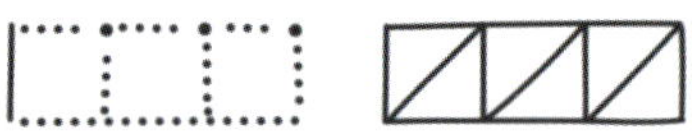

2 To make a proportional rectangle, combine multiple squares. Add additional squares horizontally or vertically to the original square to achieve the desired length ratio.

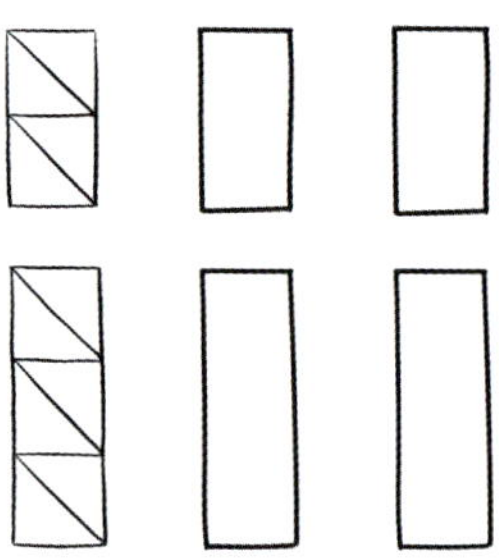

3 Try to draw vertical rectangles. You can color them later or add hatching/crosshatching to them.

Examples of marking proportions of the buildings. I often start with the base and then go up.

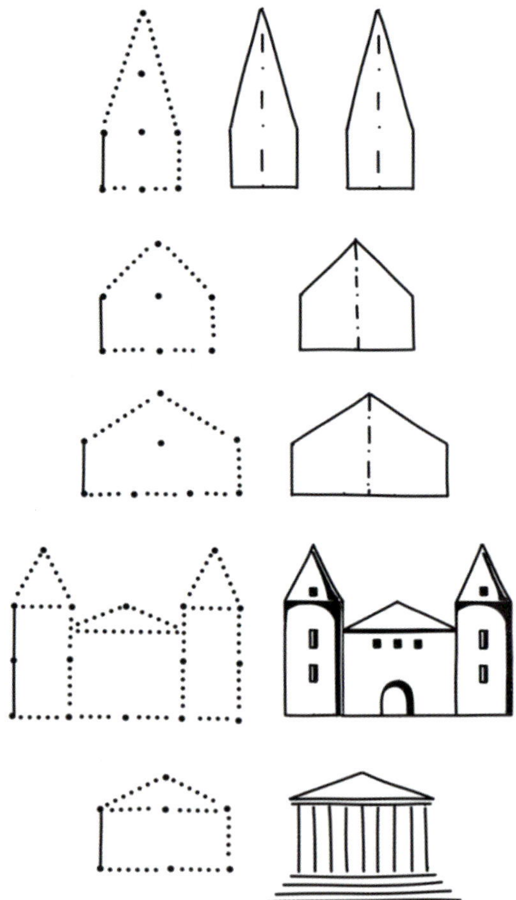

DRAWING WINDOWS

Windows are a great exercise because they allow you to practice proportions and symmetry, which are essential when drawing larger architectural elements. By focusing on windows, you get to understand the relationship between different parts of the building, like the frames, panes, and spacing. This helps develop your eye for detail and the overall structure of the house. Drawing windows first also helps you get comfortable with architectural design elements before jumping into more complex buildings. It's a great way to build up your skills gradually, step by step.

While the main focus is on mastering the basic lines and sections, adding small details—like extra trim around the windows—can be a fun way to spark creativity and make each design your own.

Just remember, keep it simple at first, and then add details as you gain confidence!

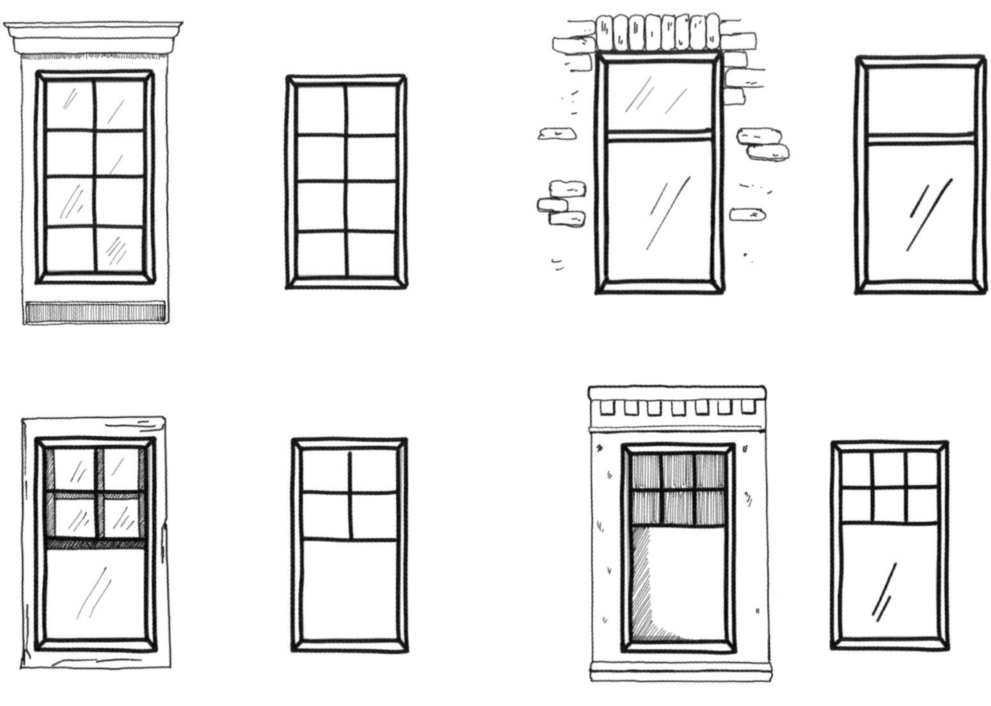

Square Windows

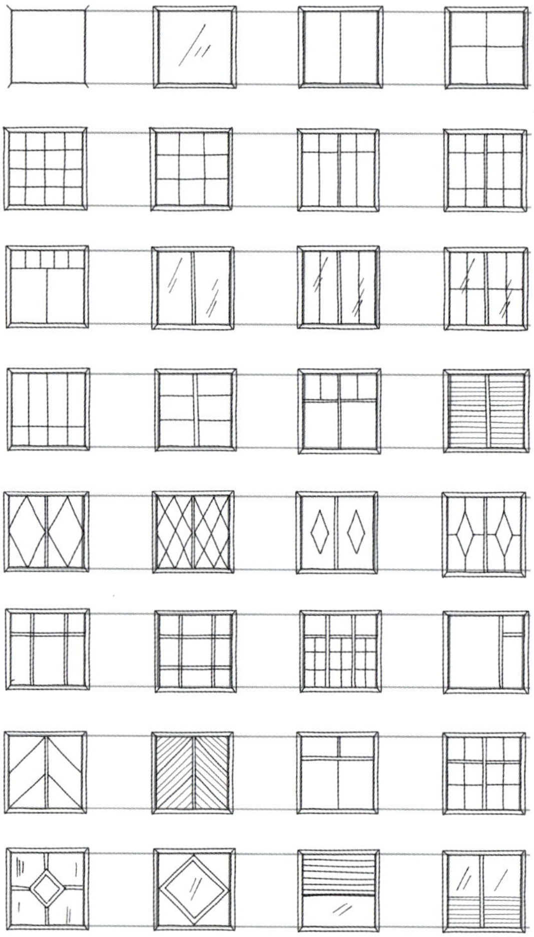

Rectangular Windows

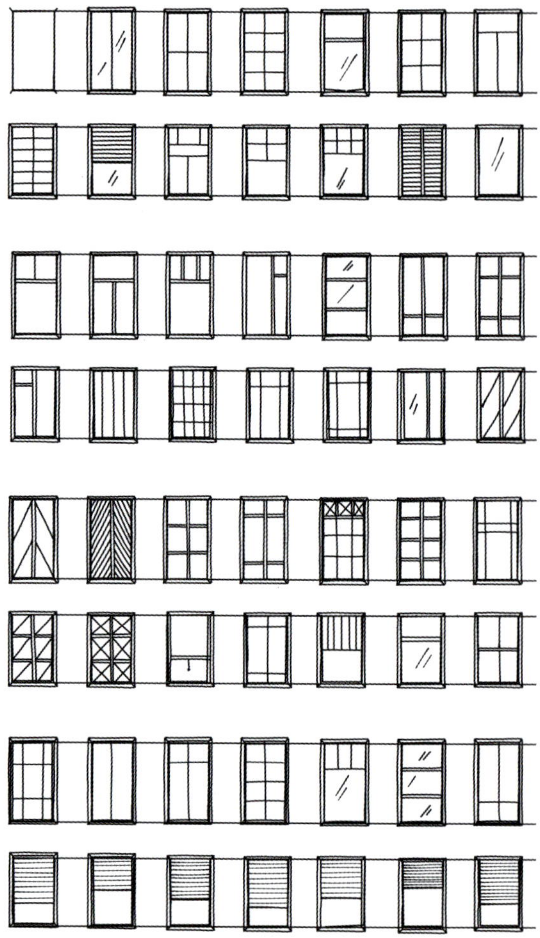

Draw a Building around the Windows

As you get comfortable with your window designs, consider adding buildings around them. Drawing a row of windows and surrounding them with horizontal and vertical lines can create the illusion of a building.

This practice not only reinforces your hand-eye coordination with longer straight lines but also allows you to explore the relationship between windows and architectural structures. You can experiment with adding details to the buildings and practicing parallel lines, which will enhance your overall drawing skills. It's a great way to take your practice a step further.

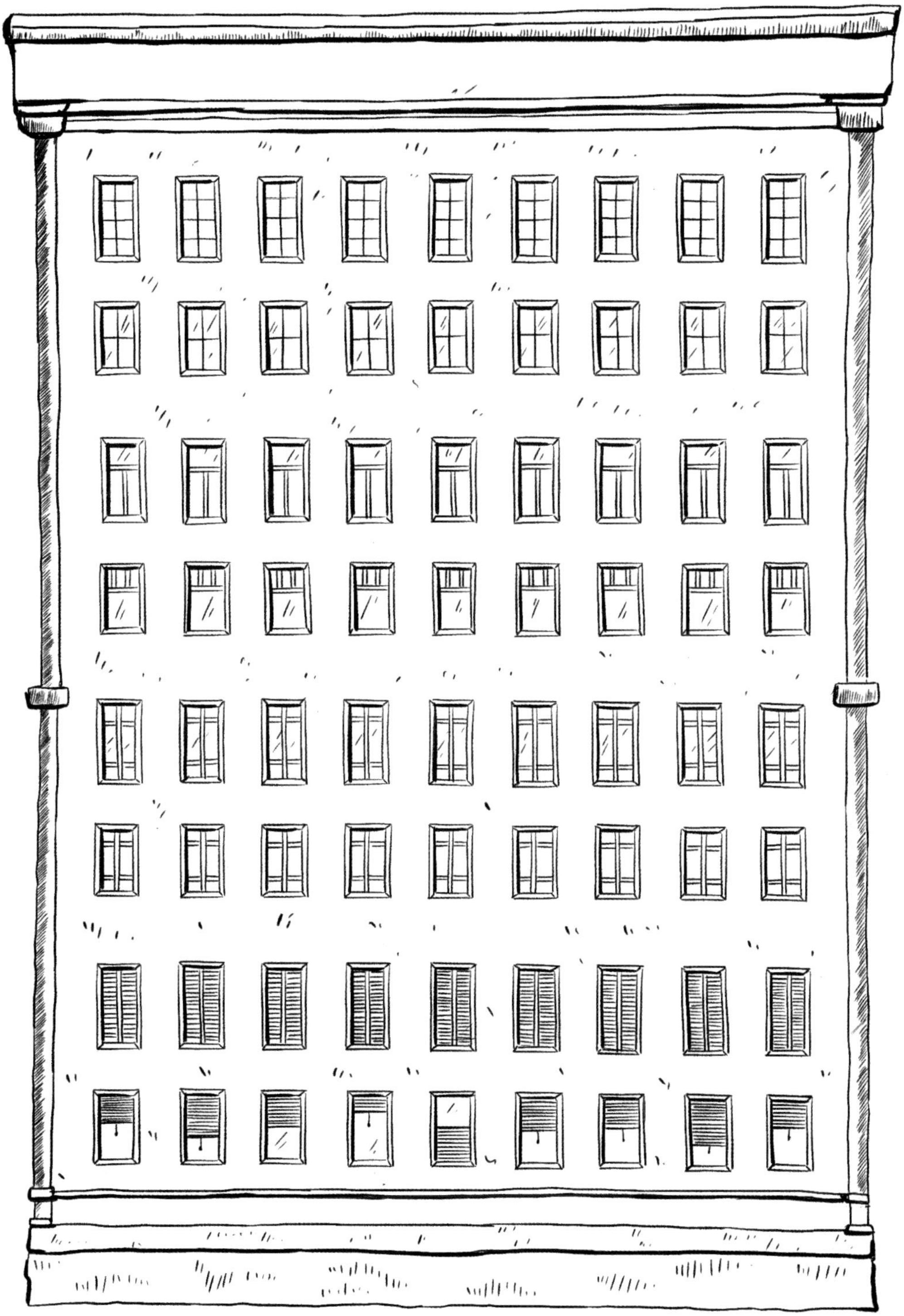

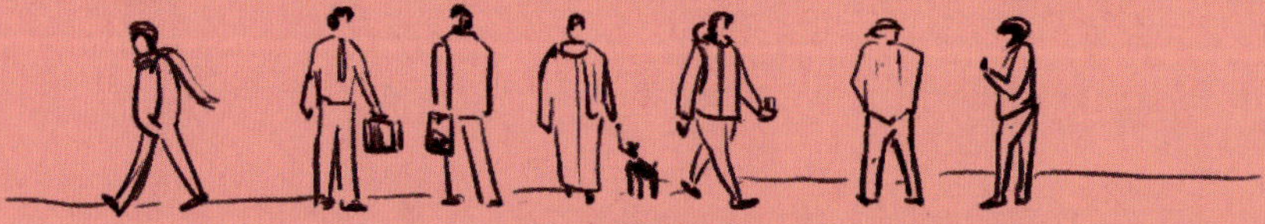

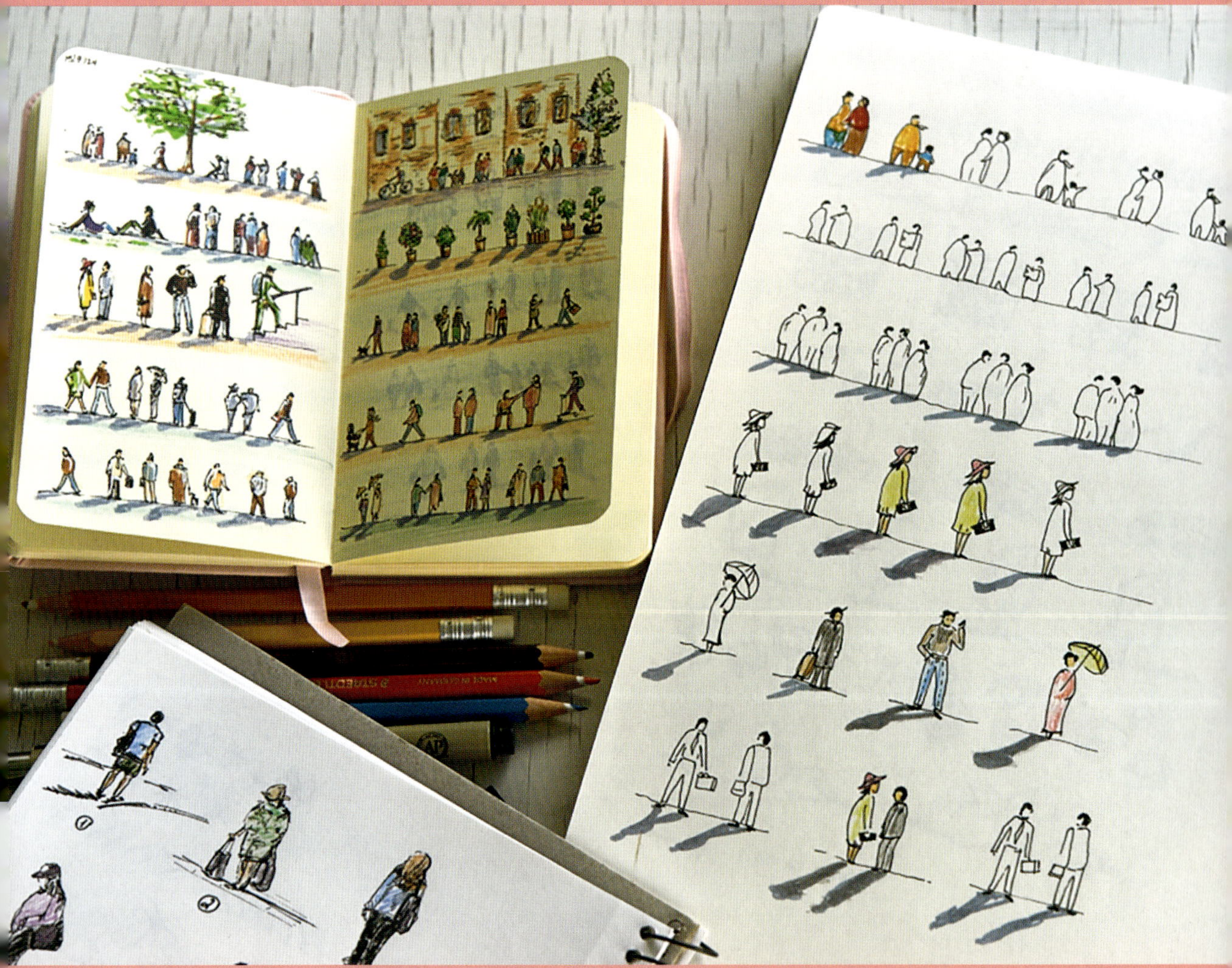

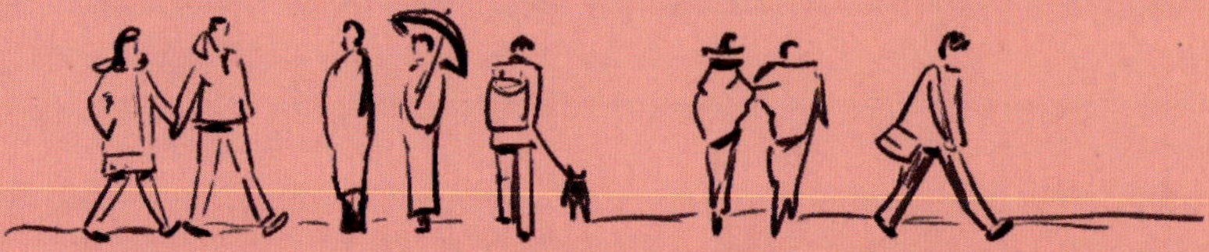

7

DRAWING PEOPLE

In this chapter, we'll take a look at the basics of sketching people, focusing on proportions and key body parts. We'll explore ways to bring your characters to life, from adding shadows to introducing accessories and different poses. You'll learn tips for sketching couples or people interacting, making your scenes more dynamic. Drawing people not only adds energy to your work but also sparks creativity. Simple shapes can lead to incredibly interesting, expressive figures.

COMMON HUMAN PROPORTIONS

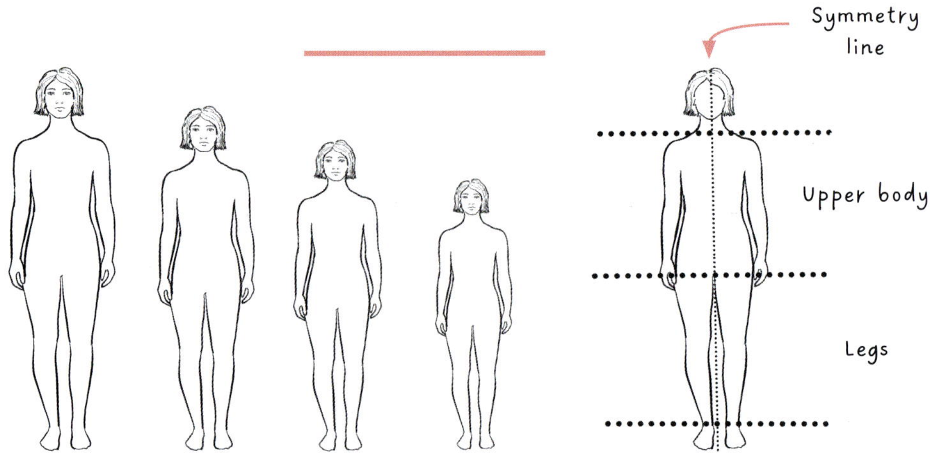

The goal of this practice is to help you learn basic proportions to draw natural-looking figures for your illustrations. We're not worrying about anatomy but focusing on creating believable figures that can fit into landscapes or urban scenes. These figures will be dressed and shaded, so the main focus is on proportions, not hyper realistic details.

A key goal is to develop your intuition for proportions and improve your observational skills. As you practice, you'll notice small details that make the figure look more natural. You'll also build muscle memory for drawing lines that define the figure, which will make it easier to sketch from memory, nature, references, or your imagination. The first step is getting comfortable with the basics by drawing a simple standing figure. Once you're confident with that, you'll be able to draw figures in different poses—whether sitting or moving—or varying in size, all based on understanding core proportions.

As you practice more, feel free to experiment. Try changing things like the height of the waistline, the width of the torso, or the length of the legs. See how these small adjustments affect the overall figure. You can also play with the arms by slightly bending them or adjusting their length. For extra practice, look at yourself in the mirror and experiment with different postures. Notice how your figure changes when you stand tall or slouch a little. These details really matter when you want to draw a believable figure, but it all starts with mastering the basics.

The key proportion to remember is the upper body is roughly equal in length to the legs. You can begin drawing with the biggest sections and then add the neck, head, and feet.

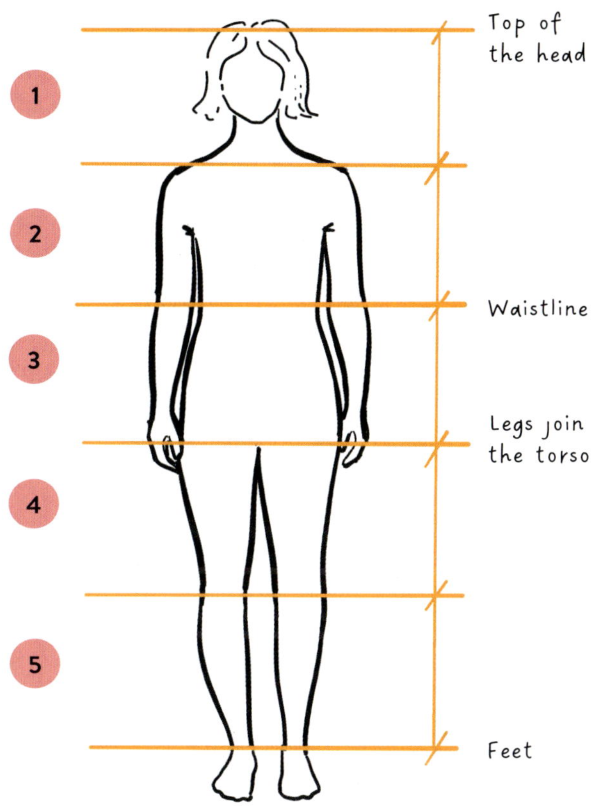

Five Equal Sections

You can divide the figure into five roughly equal sections.

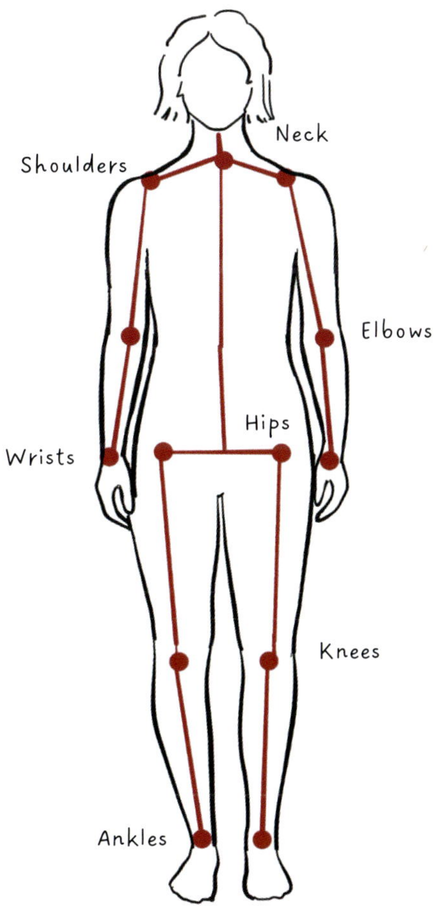

The Joints

Try to remember the main joints. Joints are where two or more bones meet, letting us move and bend. To draw a moving figure, it's important to know where the joints are so it looks natural. Use the marked joints to help with proportions. Look at the picture, study the joints, and try to find them on the body as you draw.

STEP BY STEP:

BASIC FIGURE

Now we'll draw the figure step by step. You can use it as a basis for drawing an infinite number of people.

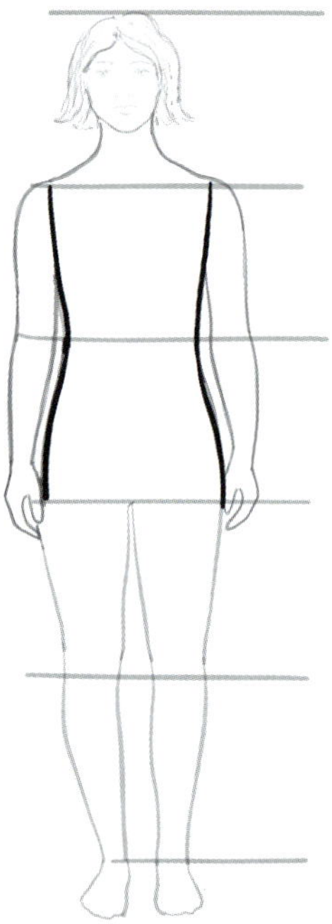

1 Draw the upper body.

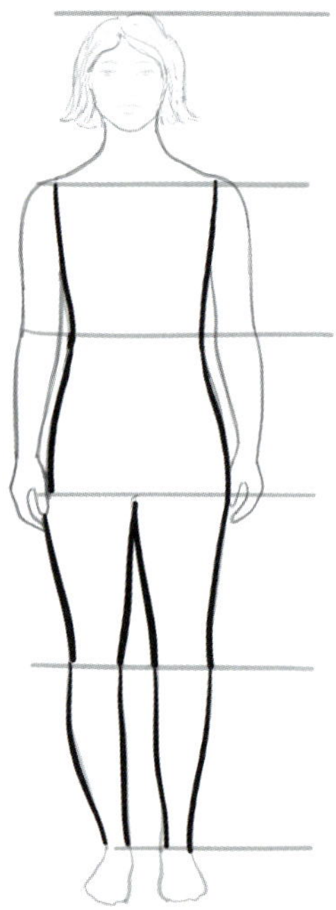

2 Add the legs.

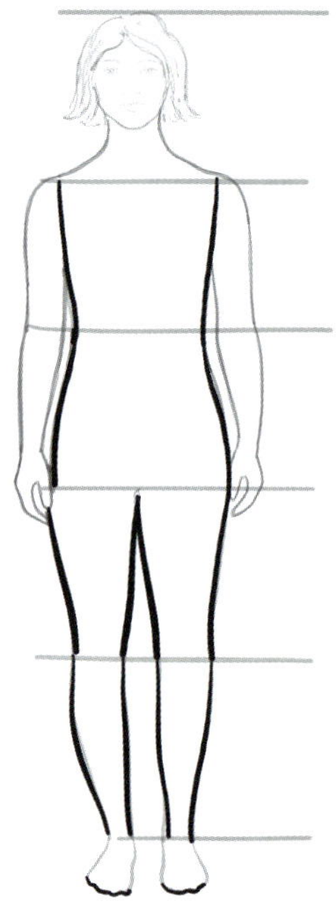

3 Add lines for the feet.

Scan to watch a tutorial.

A KEY GOAL IS TO DEVELOP YOUR INTUITION AND IMPROVE YOUR OBSERVATIONAL SKILLS.

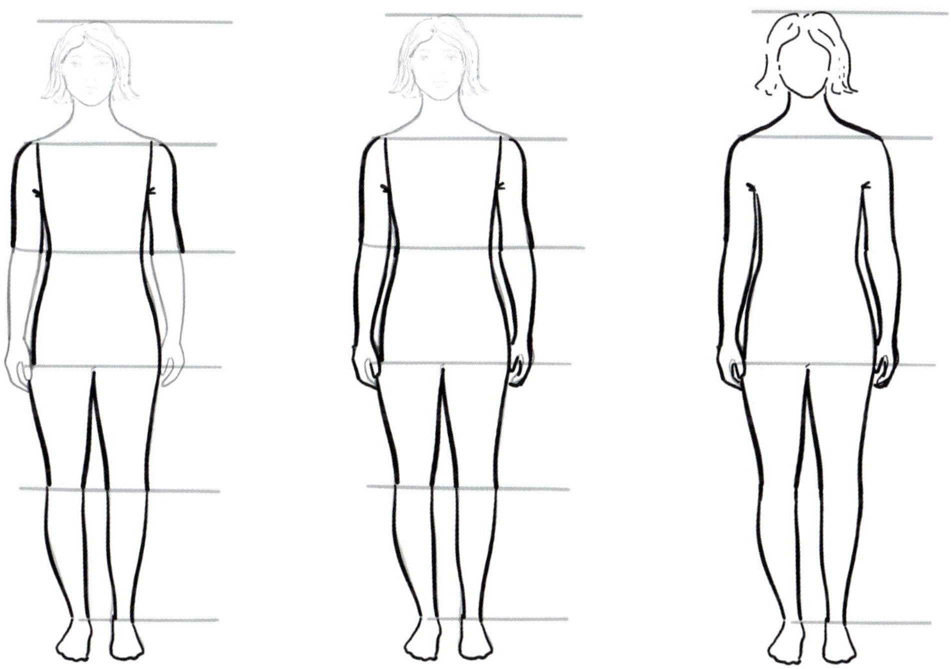

4 Draw the upper part of the arms. Complete the feet.

5 Add the lower part of the arms.

6 Complete the head and neck.

TIP

Try this exercise multiple times, making changes to the length and placement of the different segments of the figure.

STEP BY STEP:

SIMPLIFIED FIGURE

You don't need to include a ton of detail when drawing people. Focus on big shapes and proportions, adding just a few shadows to give depth. The goal is to capture the essence of the character. By changing small elements like scarves, bags, or clothing colors, you can create different characters. It's also interesting to draw people walking away or from behind, as it adds a natural storytelling feel to the scene.

The width of the figure can be about three times its head width. The proportions are approximate because people wear different clothes and hair styles and are shown in various motions or positions. Aspire to develop your instinct for what feels natural when illustrating people.

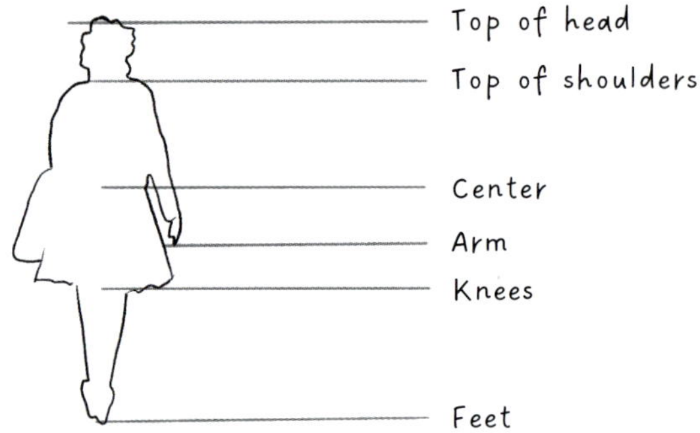

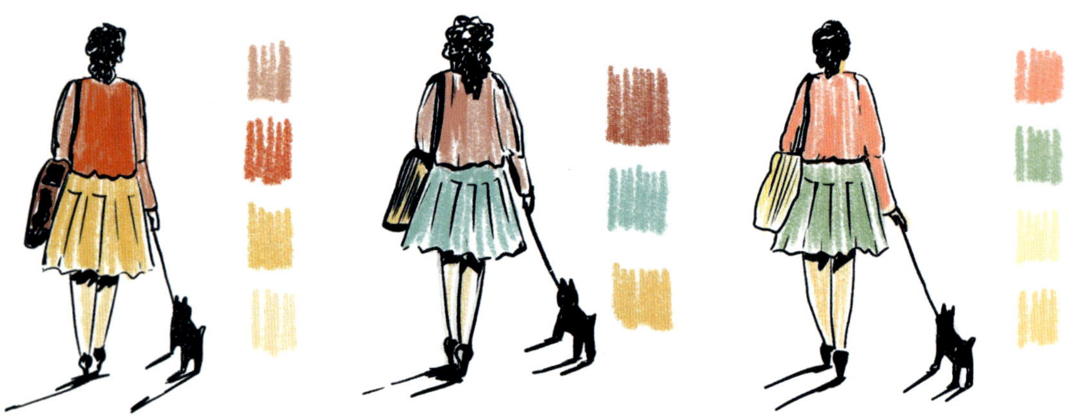

Have fun making slight changes to create different characters.

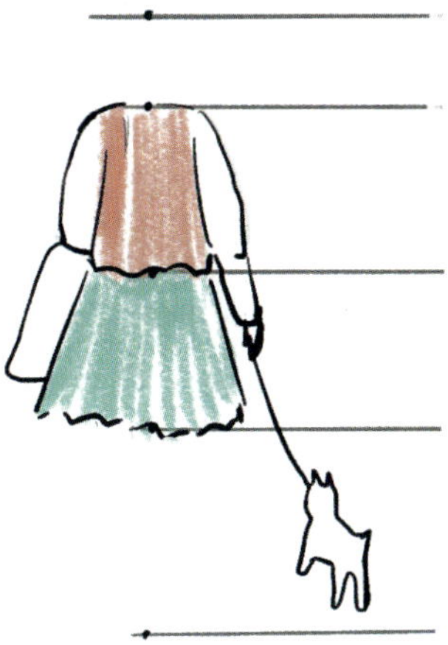

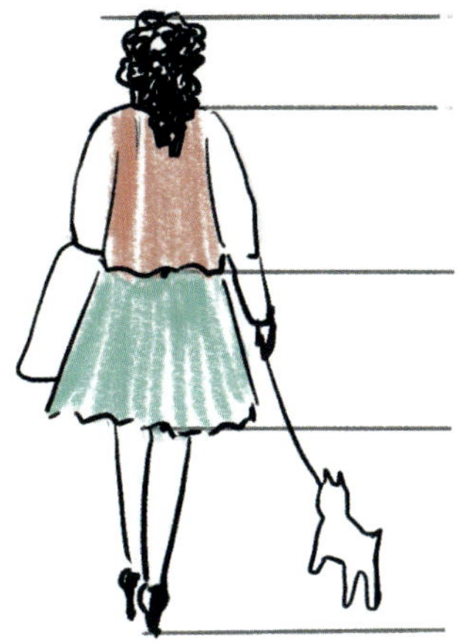

1 Start by marking the figure's height with dots. Divide the figure into three equal parts, and add one extra dot on top for the head. This will help you place the upper body and legs in the right spots. Then, roughly sketch the largest shapes with a colored pencil.

2 Use a fineliner to outline the upper body and the skirt, and add details like the bag and the dog. Then, draw the legs, and finally, the head, ensuring it's in proportion with the figure.

3 Color the figure, and add the shadows. Leave some white space for highlights.

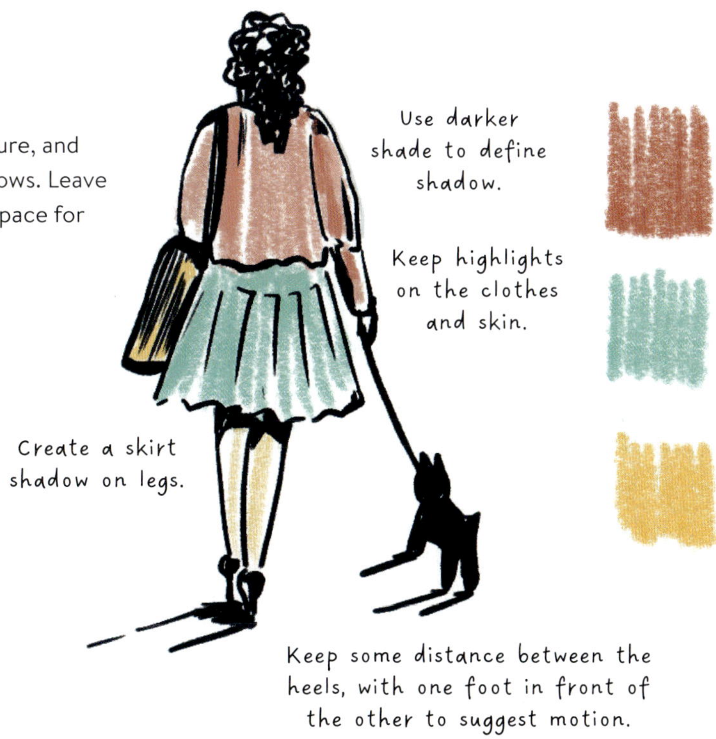

TIPS FOR DRAWING TINY PEOPLE

Adding tiny figures to your scenes give them life and interest. Here are some things to keep in mind when sketching small figures.

- Start by practicing simple, generic figures, focusing on natural proportions.
- Vary the sizes and shapes to represent different types of people, like children or the elderly.
- Focus on simple shapes to outline the body, such as ovals and lines for the arms and legs.
- Once you've mastered the basic outlines, you can begin adding details. A helpful method is to start with the body, as it's the largest shape, then add the head, legs, and accessories.
- Accessories and props can help set the scene, suggest the situation, weather, time of the day, and so on.
- Show interaction between people, like they are having a conversation—this will add life and energy to your drawing.

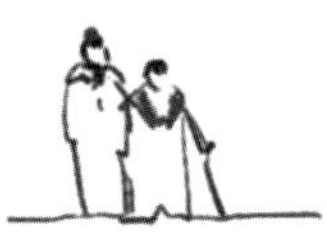
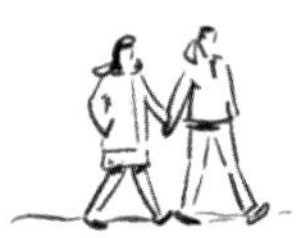
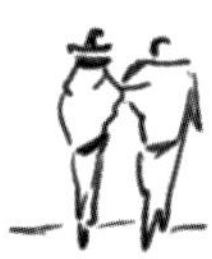
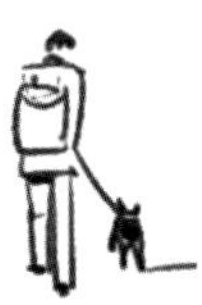
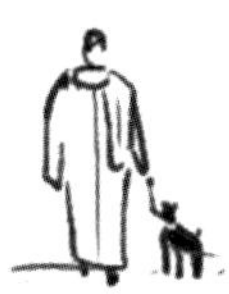
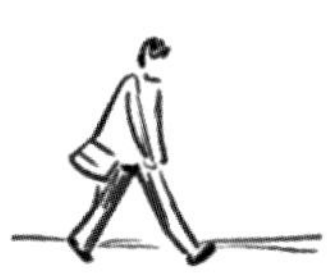
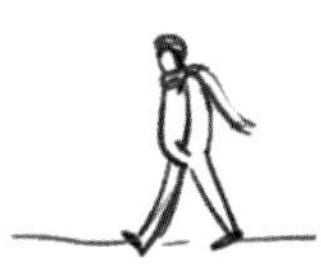
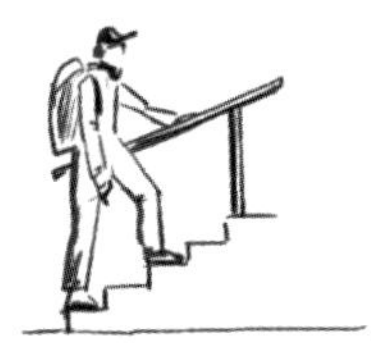
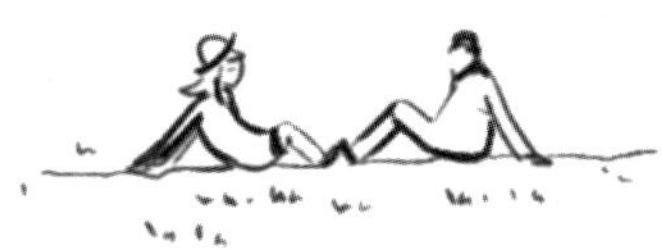
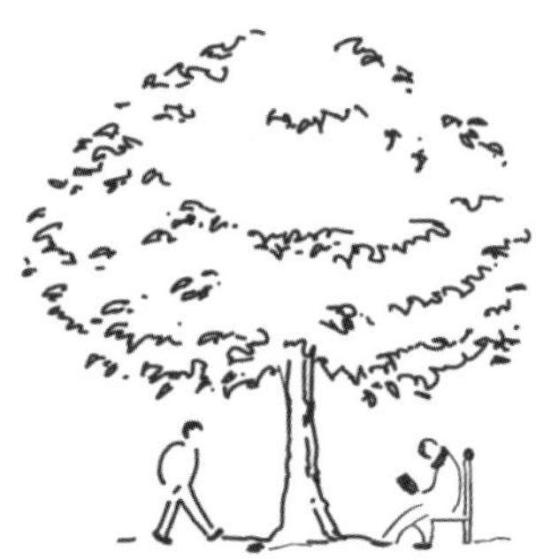

- While drawing couples, you can apply the design principle of similarity and make them have something in common
- To show someone walking, shorten one of their legs to suggest distance and movement.
- For a sense of motion, try drawing details like a bag hanging off the shoulder or a scarf blowing in the wind.
- Show how people interact with their surroundings—like climbing the stairs or sitting in a relaxed posture. These touches will help create a more dynamic and inviting atmosphere in your sketches.
- Use figures for comparative scale to indicate the size of objects, like trees.
- Repeating human figures throughout your drawing can help unify the composition.

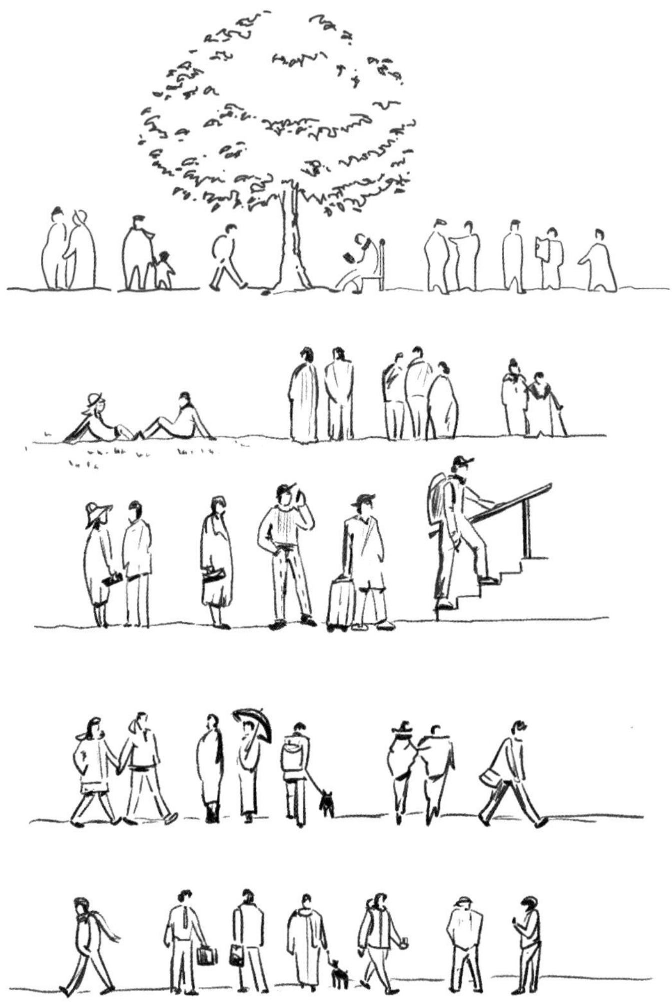

Scan to watch a tutorial.

ADDING COLOR TO YOUR FIGURES

Colors really help bring people to life! To keep the colors harmonious, use shades that are already in your artwork. The easy way is to use colored pencils and sometimes felt-tip pens. For faces, you can use skin tone colors. Try to use a variety of skin tones.

Use neutral colors like gray, brown, black, and blue for items like jeans, trousers, and coats, with occasional accents of color. I like to use lighter and darker shades of the same color to add depth to clothes. Finally, add dark gray shadows to "anchor" the figures.

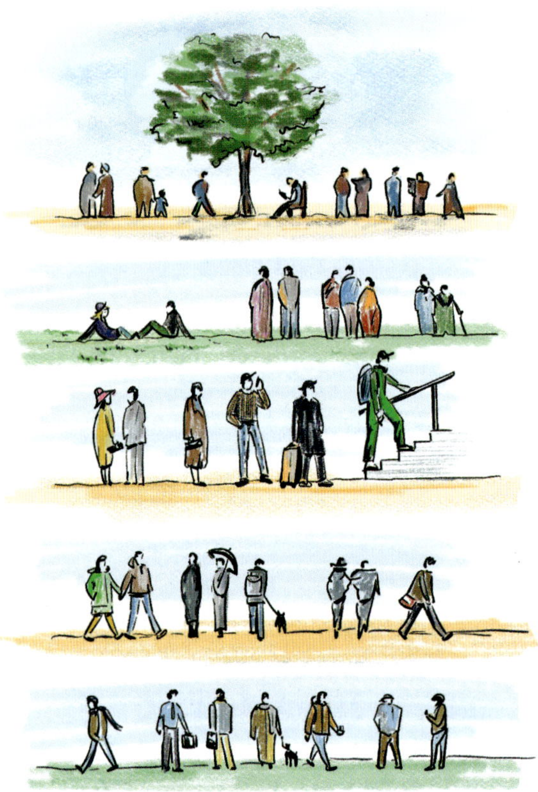

I sketched this image on paper, then colored it digitally in the Procreate app using Derwent brush (Derwent colored pencils).

Palette of colors used

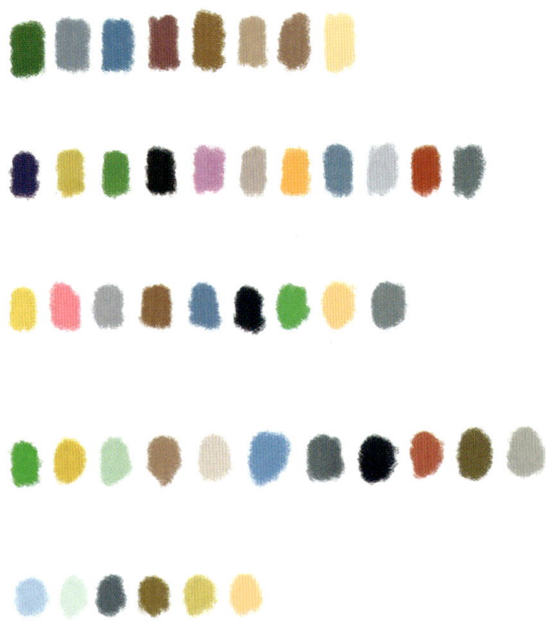

CONCLUSION

Now that you've completed these drawing exercises, I truly hope you'll continue practicing and never stop drawing. Here's a little story to encourage you further.

When you plant a tree, it often needs a lot of attention in the first year. It requires water if the weather is dry, protection from harsh conditions, and consistent care to help it grow strong roots. At first, it may seem like nothing is happening—the tree doesn't look any different after a year. But in reality, it's working hard underground, growing its roots. Once the roots are established, the tree can begin to grow, and you'll start to see visible progress.

Your drawing habit is the same. The first year of developing your drawing practice might feel like you're just planting the roots. It requires consistency, attention, and patience, even if the results aren't immediately visible. But once your drawing habit is established, it becomes a strong foundation, and progress will come. Motivation and inspiration can be fleeting, but a consistent habit, like the roots of a tree, will stay and give you the results you're working toward.

Just like trees, your drawing journey is unique. Some trees grow quickly, while others grow slowly. Some may face challenges, like bad weather, that slow their growth. But no matter the pace or the obstacles, every tree is unique, beautiful, and continues to grow. The key is consistency and trust in the process. Keep going, and your drawing habit will flourish, just like the tree, leading to beautiful results over time.

ONCE YOUR DRAWING HABIT IS ESTABLISHED, IT BECOMES A STRONG FOUNDATION, AND PROGRESS WILL COME.

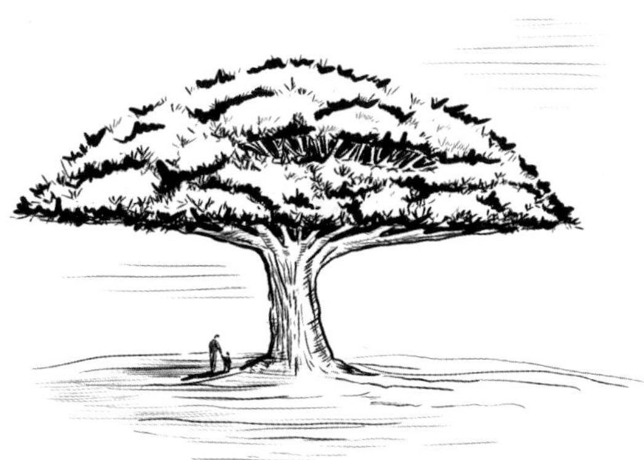

HOW TO USE THE PRACTICE SHEETS

As part of my drawing journey, I developed practice cards I could use to learn certain techniques. When I realized how much they helped me improve my drawings, I began sharing them on my Instagram account and selling them on Gumroad. I have been overwhelmed by the positive response they have received. People all over the world have told me that using the practice cards has made a huge difference in their art journey. For this book, I created twenty practice cards that you can download with the QR code below and use to help develop your drawing habit.

Here are some tips to get started using the practice cards:

- Start with a card that feels easier or more interesting to you.
- Place your sketchbook or drawing paper over the blank area of the card. You can also draw directly on the card, but you won't be able to reuse it, and I encourage you to work with each card many times.
- On the bottom of every page, you will see "Date and time used." This allows you to track your progress. Believe me, it will be eye opening to later compare your older practice sheets to your newer ones.
- To make the most progress, try to draw daily for twenty-five minutes. When I first started doing these exercises, I did exactly twenty-five minutes (with a timer) each day. Now my drawing practice ranges from ten minutes to ninety minutes a day.
- Practice each card until you can draw it from memory. You might notice how much faster you can draw from your memory when you master the subject.
- You can use the cards on your digital device, but I recommend you print them out and practice with a pen, preferably a fineliner. Not only can you achieve a similar look that I did, but you can't erase them, which means you will learn from your mistakes. Get used to the idea that "mistakes" are okay.

Scan the QR code on this page to download the practice sheets that accompany this book.

- Use a fineliner so you can concentrate on the lines. You learn to control them and develop your hand-eye coordination, which is a foundation to draw anything you want.
- Relax! If your hand is hurting after five minutes, it means that you are too tense. Don't hold your pen so tightly.
- For short and quick strokes, keep your wrist on the table and move only the fingers.
- For long strokes, use your whole forearm, rotating at the elbow and letting your fingers simply follow.

It's important to build your visual library to be able to draw well from imagination. I practice every card many times!

Enjoy the process, and the results will appear!

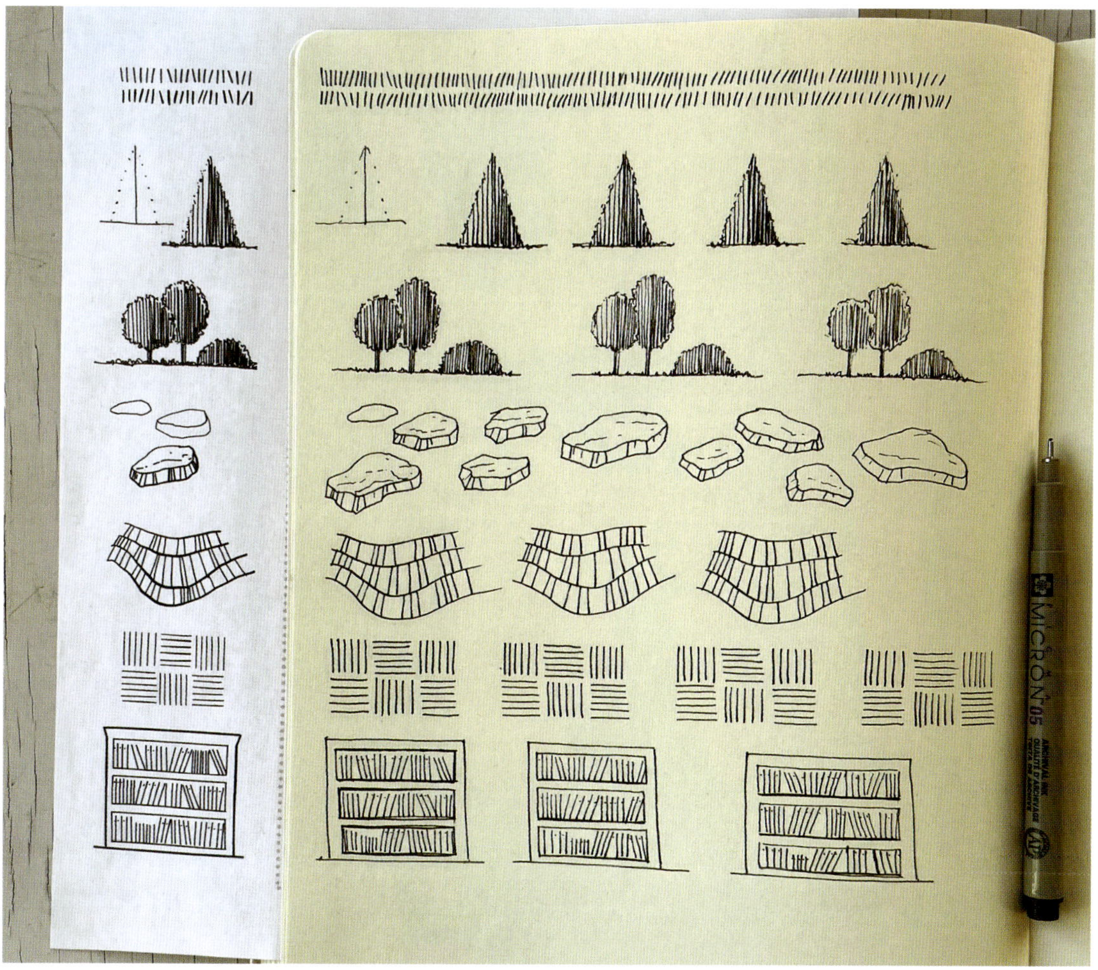

ABOUT THE AUTHOR

Daria is a gardener and landscape designer living in Finland with her husband and son. During her landscape design studies, she realized the importance of hand drawing, even in an era of digital tools. Motivated by this, she decided to teach herself to draw by hand, and it quickly became her passion.

She began documenting her journey on Instagram, where she developed the idea of structured practice. Seeing how overwhelming it could be to find simple, clear advice on learning to draw, she focused on creating an accessible system for independent practice.

Through experimenting with different methods, she built a learning process that encourages steady progress without requiring hours of tutorials. Her followers' encouragement led her to create practice materials and share her techniques more widely.

Daria is also passionate about photography—her photographs have been published in a Finnish landscape design book—and her illustrations have appeared in a textbook for landscape design students.

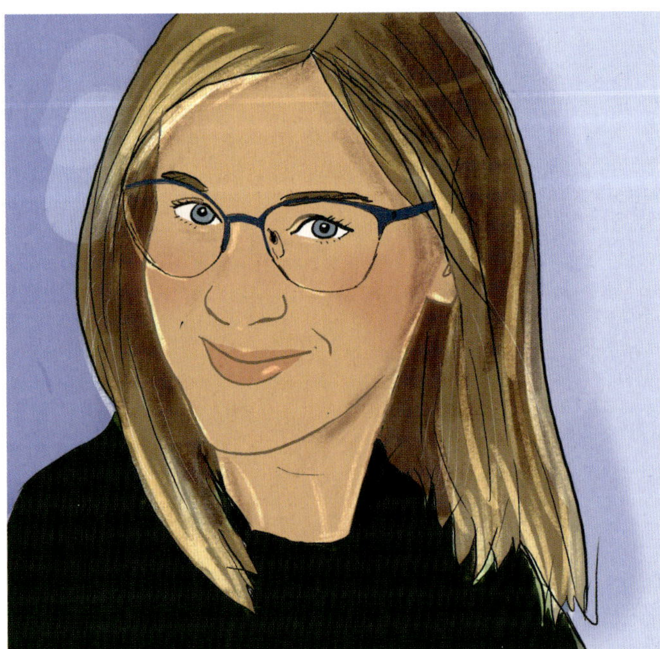

INDEX

Aerial views, of trees, 72–73
African feather grass, 64, 67
Aloe plant, 57
Apple trees, 71
Architecture. *See also* Buildings
- front door, 106–107
- proportions and, 108
- windows and, 109–111

Arm, using your whole, 27, 84
Asymmetry, 48, 82, 86, 103
Australian grass trees, 84

Background, 83, 87
Balance, 22, 66. *See also* Symmetry
Ball of yarn, 42
Barn, 104–105
Baskets, 42
Birch trees, 71
Birds, 96, 97
Blue globe thistle, 65
Boulders, 93
Brick wall, 106
Broken lines, 50
Buildings
- barn, 104–105
- house with trees, 100–101
- marking proportions of, 108
- stone farmhouse, 102–103
- windows drawn around, 110–111

Cactus, 50–51
Calathea plant, 56
Canopy layer, 86
Circular lines, 28, 32
Climbing plant, 107
Color
- adding to houseplant, 51
- adding to human figure, 122

Colored pencils, 19
Columnar trees, 72, 73, 100–101
Composition
- of flowers and grasses, 66–67
- foreground, middle ground, and background in, 83
- with a group of trees, 86–87
- with three grass trees, 84

Cones, 40
Cone-shaped trees, 75
Conical trees, 72, 73
Coniferous trees, 31, 80
Contour lines, 42, 76
Coordination, 39. *See also* Hand-eye coordination
Cubes, 40, 43
Curved lines, 28, 29, 30, 66, 77
Cylinders, 40, 44–45
Cypress trees, 70

Daffodils, 59
Daily practice, 9, 13–14
Daisies, 62
Delphinium, 65, 66, 67
Depth, creating, 49, 97
Design principles, 22
Doors, 102, 106–107
Dotted lines, 28, 32, 92
Drawing habit. *See also* Practice
- benefits of, 8–9
- setting goals for, 14
- as a strong foundation, 123
- tips on starting a, 16–17

Elephant ears plant, 64
Eucalyptus trees, 82–83

Falling water, 90–91
Fan palm plant, 54–55
Feathered lines, 28, 30
Fineliner pens, 18–19
Flowers
- composition of grasses and, 66–67
- perennial, 61–65
- spring, 58–60
- tips for drawing, 48–49

Flow lines, 28, 77
Foreground, 83
Foreground trees, 87
Front door, 106–107

Garden plants, 61–65
Gardner, Paul, 16
Geometric shapes, 40–45
Geraniums, 61
Gift-wrapped box, 43
Goals, setting, 14
Grass(es), 63, 64, 66–67, 80, 84, 92
Guidelines, 49

Habit tracker, 23
Hand-eye coordination, 12, 35
Handwriting, 36
Hatching lines, 39, 40, 76, 78, 94, 95
Heartbeat lines, 28, 77
Houseplants, 50–57
Houses
- stone farmhouse, 102–103
- with trees, 100–101

Hyacinths, 60

Irises, 65, 66, 67

Joints, of the human body, 115

Lady's-mantle, 64
Landscapes
- barn scene, 104–105
- foreground, middle ground, and backgrounds in, 83
- house and trees, 100–101
- sea, 96–97

Leaves. *See also* Flowers
- calathea plant, 56
- fan palm, 54
- Monstera plant, 52–53

symmetry and, 38
tree, 85
Light on water, 97
Lines/linework, 26–33. *See also* specific types of lines
Maple trees, 71
Middle ground/layer, 83, 86
Mindful practice, 13–14
Monet, Claude, 83
Monstera leaves, 52–53
Mountain rising out of the ocean, 95
Muscle memory, 12, 23, 35, 36, 114

"Nervous hand," drawing with a, 27, 105
Nervous lines, 28

Ocean
mountain rising out of, 95
step by step ocean scene, 96–97
One-point perspective, 104–105

Palmer Handwriting Method, 36
Paper, 18
Pencils, colored, 19
Pens, 18–19
People and the human figure
adding color to, 122
drawing a simplified, 118–119
drawing tiny, 120–121
joints in the human body, 115
step by step for drawing the basic, 116–117
Perspective
aerial, 72–73
barn in one-point, 104–105
Pine trees, 70
Plants. *See also* Flowers
climbing, 107
garden, 61–65
houseplants, 50–57
in pots next to a door, 106, 107
Polygons, 28, 31
Ponds, 92
Poplar trees, 70
Practice
feedback on your, 20
finding time for, 13
getting better with, 9
importance of, 8–9
learning and improving with, 9, 12
mindful, 13–14
using the book for your, 21–23
Practice sheets, 23, 124–125
Prisms, 40
Proportions
architecture and, 108
human figure, 114–115, 118
of trees, 70
Pumpkin, 42
Pyramids, 40

Reflections on water, 97
Repetition, 12, 26, 34, 72, 100–101
Rocks and stones
along the banks, 90
in landscape scene, 83
single boulder, 93
stepping stones, 94
submerged, 90, 91
Round trees, 72, 73

Scalloped lines, 28, 31, 57
Seagulls, 96
Sequoia trees, 71
Shading, 51, 58, 76, 105
Short rows, 28, 33
Shrubs, 72, 73
Sketchbooks, 18
Space, 35
Spheres, 40, 42
Spring flowers, 58–60
Stepping stones, 94
Stippling technique, 74, 76
Stone farmhouse, 102–103
Stones, 84
Straight lines, 27, 28, 29
Supplies, 18–19
Swirly lines, 28
Symmetry, 37–38, 48, 50, 51, 108, 192

Texture, 74–75, 80, 87, 93, 101, 106, 107. *See also* Hatching lines
Three-dimensional shapes, 38, 41–45
Timers, 23
Topiary trees, 72, 73
Trail lines, 28
Tree leaves, 38, 85
Trees
aerial views of, 72–73
apple, 71
Australian grass, 84
columnar, 72, 73, 100–101
conical, 72, 73
coniferous, 80
cypress, 70
deciduous, 78–79
eucalyptus, 82–83
with houses, 100–101
maple, 71
pine, 70
poplar, 70
round, 72, 73
sequoia, 71
silhouettes of, 70–71
with stone farmhouse, 102–103
texture and shading in, 74–76
topiary, 72, 73
weeping, 81
willow, 70
Tree trunks, 77
Tulips, 58

Unity, 22, 34, 100

Water
light and reflections on, 97
mountain rising out of, 95
small pond, 92
Waterfalls, 90–91
Wavy lines, 28, 80
Weeping trees, 81
Willow trees, 70
Window(s), 100, 102, 103, 106, 107, 109–111

Zigzag lines, 28, 32, 91